DISCOVERY OF THE YOSEMITE,

AND

THE INDIAN WAR OF 1851,

WHICH LED TO THAT EVENT.

BY

LAFAYETTE HOUGHTON BUNNELL, M.D.,

OF THE MARIPOSA BATTALION, ONE OF THE DISCOVERERS,
LATE SURGEON THIRTY-SIXTH REGIMENT
WISCONSIN VOLUNTEERS.

THIRD EDITION—REVISED AND CORRECTED.

FLEMING H. REVELL COMPANY,

NEW YORK: CHICAGO:
30 UNION SQUARE: EAST.   148 AND 150 MADISON ST

LIST OF ILLUSTRATIONS.

CONTENTS.

CHAPTER I.

CHAPTER II.

CHAPTER III.

CHAPTER IV.

CHAPTER V.

CHAPTER VI.

CHAPTER VII.

CHAPTER VIII.

CHAPTER IX.

CHAPTER X.

CHAPTER XI.

CHAPTER XII.

CHAPTER XIII.

CHAPTER XIV.

CHAPTER XV.

CHAPTER XVI.

CHAPTER XVII.

CHAPTER XVIII.

CHAPTER XIX.

CHAPTER XX.

CHAPTER XXI.

CHAPTER XXII.

INTRODUCTION.

The book here presented is the result of an attempt to correct existing errors relative to the Yosemite Valley. It was originally designed to compress the matter in this volume within the limits of a magazine article, but this was soon found to be impracticable; and, at the suggestion of Gen. C. H. Berry, of Winona, Minnesota, it was decided to "write a book."

This, too, proved more difficult than at first appeared.

Born in Rochester, New York, in 1824, and carried to Western wilds in 1833, the writer's opportunities for culture were limited; and in this, his first attempt at authorship, he has found that the experiences of frontier life are not the best preparations for literary effort. Beside this, he had mainly to rely upon his own resources, for nothing could be obtained in the archives of California that could aid him. It was not deemed just that California should forget the deeds of men who had subdued her savages, and discovered her most sublime scenery. Having been a member of the "Mariposa Battalion," and with it when the Yosemite was discovered, having suggested its name, and named many of the principal objects of interest in and near the valley, it seemed a duty that the writer owed his comrades and himself, to give the full history of these events. Many of the facts incident thereto have already been given to the public by the author at various times since 1851, but these have been so mutilated or blended with fiction, that a renewed and full statement of facts concerning that remarkable locality seems desirable.

While engaged upon this work, the writer was aided by the scientific researches of Prof. J. D. Whitney, and by the "acute and helpful criticism" of Doctor James M. Cole of Winona, Minnesota.

Since the publication of the second edition of this book, and an article from the author's pen in the *Century* Magazine for September, 1890, numerous letters of approval from old comrades have been received, and a few dates obtained from old official correspondence that will now be introduced.

In addition to what may properly belong to this history, there have been introduced a few remarks concerning the habits and character of the Indians. This subject is not *entirely new*, but the opinions expressed are the results of many years acquaintance with various tribes, and may be useful.

The incidental remarks about game will probably interest some. To the author, the study of nature in all its aspects has been interesting.

The author's views regarding the gold deposits and glaciers of the Sierras are given simply as suggestions.

His especial efforts have been directed to the placing on record events connected with the *discovery* of the Yosemite, for description of its scenery he feels to be impossible. In reverent acknowledgment of this, there are submitted as a prologue, some lines written while contemplating the grandeur of his subject.

WONDER LAND.

Hail thee, Yosemite, park of sublimity!
　　Majesty, peerless and old!
Ye mountains and cliffs, ye valleys and rifts,
　　Ye cascades and cataracts bold!
None, none can divine the wonders of thine,
　　When told of the glorious view!

The wild world of light—from "Beatitude's" height,
    Old "Rock Chief,"[1] "El Capitan" true!

Thy head proud and high! white brow to the sky!
    Thy features the thunderbolts dare!
Thou o'erlookest the wall would the boldest appal
    Who enter Yosemite's "Lair."[2]
Fair "Bridal Veil Fall!" the queen over all,
    In beauty and grace intertwined!
Even now from thy height water-rockets of light
    Dart away, and seem floating in wind!

And thou, high "Scho-look!" proud "Ah-wah-ne!" invoke
    To receive from "Kay-o-pha"[3] a boon!
That flowing from pines, in the region of vines,
    May temper the heat of bright noon.
"Nevada" and "Vernal," emblems eternal
    Of winter and loveliest Spring,
No language so bold the truth can unfold—
    No pen can thee offerings bring!

And yet dare I say, of the cool "Vernal Spray,"
    In the flash of the bright sun's power,
I welcome thy "ring,"[4] though a drenching it bring,
    The smile of a god's in the shower!
And thou, "Glacier Fall,"[5] from thy adamant wall,
    And winter-bound lakes at thy head—
Thy nymphs never seen, except by the sheen
    So fitful from "Mirror Lake's" bed.

Ye North and South Domes,[6] "Ten-ie-ya's" lake homes,
    "Cloud's Rest," and high "Tis-sa-ack" lone;
Mute "Sentinel," "Brothers," ye "Starr King," ye others—

---

[1] "Rock Chief," a literal translation of "Tote-ack-ah-noo-la," rendered "El Capitan" in Spanish, from the likeness of a man's head upon the wall.

[2] The Yosemites were known as the "Bear tribe." "Ten-ie-ya" was chief.

[3] "Scho look" is the Indian name for the "High Fall;" "Ah wah-ne," the *old* name of Valley, and "Kay-o pha" (the sky), the name of highest or snow-clad peaks.

[4] At intervals at the Vernal a *round* rainbow is formed, perfect as a finger ring.

[5] "Glacier Fall," in place of "Too loo lo-we ack."

[6] "Sentinel Dome" was known to the discoverers as the "South Dome," and "Tis sa ack," meaning cleft rock, as the "Half Dome."

Oh! what of the past have ye known?
To you has been given the mission from heaven
To watch through the ages of earth!
Your presence sublime is the chronicled time,
From the æon the world had birth!

VIEW OF THE YOSEMITE.

Looking up the valley from a height of about 1,000 feet above the Merced River, and above sea level 5,000 feet, giving some faint idea of the beauty, grandeur and magnitude of this magnificent work of nature.

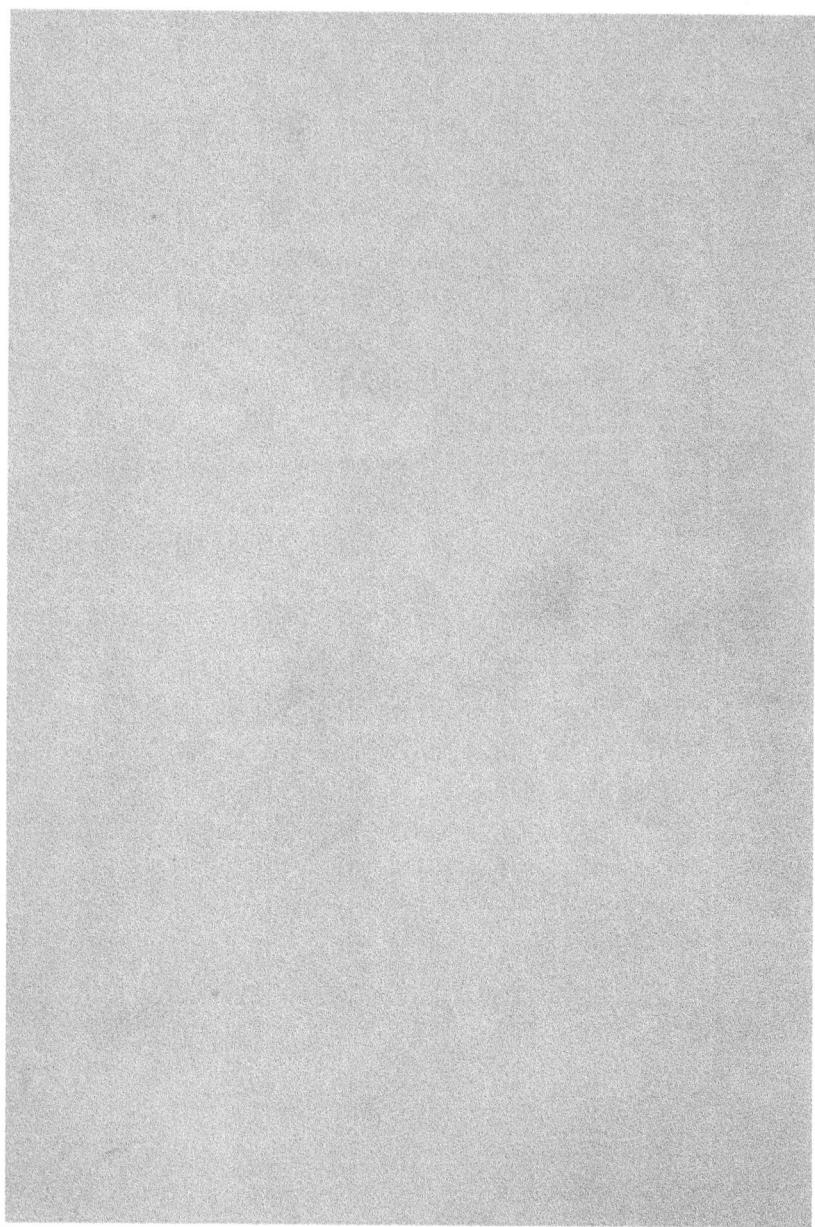

DISCOVERY OF THE YOSEMITE.

CHAPTER I.

Incidents leading to the discovery of the Yosemite Valley—Major Savage and Savages—Whiskey, wrangling and War—Skinned Alive—A brisk Fight—Repulse—Another Fight, and Conflagration.

DURING the winter of 1849–50, while ascending the old Bear Valley trail from Ridley's ferry, on the Merced river, my attention was attracted to the stupendous rocky peaks of the Sierra Nevadas. In the distance an immense cliff loomed, apparently to the summit of the mountains. Although familiar with nature in her wildest moods, I looked upon this awe-inspiring column with wonder and admiration. While vainly endeavoring to realize its peculiar prominence and vast proportions, I turned from it with reluctance to resume the search for coveted gold; but the impressions of that scene were indelibly fixed in my memory. Whenever an opportunity afforded, I made inquiries concerning the scenery of that locality. But few of the miners had noticed any of its special peculiarities. On a second visit to Ridley's, not long after, that towering mountain which had so profoundly interested me was invisible, an intervening haze obscuring it from view. A year or more passed before the mysteries of this wonderful land were satisfactorily solved.

During the winter of 1850–51, I was attached to an expedition that made the first discovery of what is now known as the Yosemite Valley. While entering it, I saw at a glance that the reality of my sublime vision at Ridley's ferry, forty miles away, was before me. The locality of the mysterious cliff was there revealed — its proportions enlarged and perfected.

The discovery of this remarkable region was an event intimately connected with the history of the early settlement of that portion of California. During 1850, the Indians in Mariposa county, which at that date included all the territory south of the divide of the Tuolumne and Merced rivers within the valley proper of the San Joaquin, became very troublesome to the miners and settlers. Their depredations and murderous assaults were continued until the arrival of the United States Indian commissioners, in 1851, when the general government assumed control over them. Through the management of the commissioners, treaties were made, and many of these Indians were transferred to locations reserved for their special occupancy.

It was in the early days of the operations of this commission that the Yosemite Valley was first entered by a command virtually employed to perform the special police duties of capturing and bringing the Indians before these representatives of the government, in order that treaties might be made with them. These wards of the general government were provided with supplies at the expense of the public treasury: provided that they confined themselves to the reservations selected for them.

My recollections of those early days are from personal observations and information derived from the earlier settlers of the San Joaquin valley, with whom I was personally acquainted in the mining camps, and through business connections; and also from comrades in the Indian war of

1850–51. Among these settlers was one James D. Savage. a trader, who in 1849–50 was located in the mountains near the mouth of the South Fork of the Merced river, some fifteen miles below the Yosemite valley.

At this point, engaged in gold mining, he had employed a party of native Indians. Early in the season of 1850 his trading post and mining camp were attacked by a band of the Yosemite Indians. This tribe, or band, claimed the territory in that vicinity, and attempted to drive Savage off. Their real object, however, was plunder. They were considered treacherous and dangerous, and were very troublesome to the miners generally.

Savage and his Indian miners repulsed the attack and drove off the marauders, but from this occurrence he no longer deemed this 1 cation desirable. Being fully aware of the murderous propensities of his assailants, he removed to Mariposa Creek, not far from the junction of the Aqua Fria, and near to the site of the old stone fort. Soon after, he established a branch post on the Fresno, where the mining prospects became most encouraging, as the high water subsided in that stream. This branch station was placed in charge of a man by the name of Greeley.

At these establishments Savage soon built up a prosperous business. He exchanged his goods at enormous profits for the gold obtained from his Indian miners. The white miners and prospecting parties also submitted to his demands rather than lose time by going to Mariposa village. The value of his patrons' time was thus made a source of revenue. As the season advanced, this hardy pioneer of commerce rapidly increased his wealth, but in the midst of renewed prosperity he learned that another cloud was gathering over him. One of his five squaws assured him that a combination was maturing among the mountain Indians, to kill or drive all the white men from the country, and plunder them of their property. To strengthen his influence over the principal tribes, Savage had, according to the custom of many mountain men, taken wives from among them, supposing his personal safety would be somewhat improved by so doing. This is the old story of the prosperous Indian trader. Rumor also came from his Indian miners, that the Yosemites threatened to come down on him again for the purpose of plunder, and that they were urging other tribes to join them.

These reports he affected to disregard, but quietly cautioned the miners to guard against marauders.

He also sent word to the leading men in the settlements that hostilities were threatened, and advised preparations against a surprise.

At his trading posts he treated the rumors with indifference, but instructed the men in his employ to be continually on their guard in his absence. Stating that he was going to "*the Bay*" for a stock of goods, he started for San Francisco, taking with him two Indian wives, and a chief of some note and influence who professed great friendship.

This Indian, Jose Juarez, was in reality one of the leading spirits in arousing hostilities against the whites.

Notwithstanding Juarez appeared to show regard for Savage, the trader had doubts of his sincerity, but, as he had no fears of personal injury, he carefully kept his suspicions to himself. The real object Savage had in making this trip was to place in a safe locality a large amount of gold which he had on hand; and he took the chief to impress him with the futility of any attempted outbreak by his people. He hoped that a visit to Stockton and San Francisco, where Jose could see the numbers and superiority of the whites, would so impress him that on his return to the mountains his report would deter the Indians from their proposed hostilities.

The trip was made without any incidents of importance, but, to Savage's disappointment and regret, Jose developed an instinctive love for whiskey, and having been liberally supplied with gold, he invested heavily in that favorite Indian beverage, and was stupidly drunk nearly all the time he was in the city.

Becoming disgusted with Jose's frequent intoxication, Savage expressed in emphatic terms his disapprobation of such a course. Jose at once became greatly excited, and forgetting his usual reserve, retorted in abusive epithets, and disclosed his secret of the intended war against the whites.

Savage also lost his self-control, and with a blow felled the drunken Indian to the ground. Jose arose apparently sober, and from that time maintained a silent and dignified demeanor. After witnessing the celebration of the admission of the State into the Union—which by appointment occurred on October 29th, 1850, though the act of admission passed Congress on the 9th of September of that year—and making arrangements to have goods forwarded as he should order them, Savage started back with his dusky retainers for Mariposa. On his arrival at Quartzberg, he learned that the Kah-we-ah Indians were exacting tribute from the immigrants passing through their territory, and soon after his return a man by the name of Moore was killed not far from his Mariposa Station. From the information here received, and reported murders of emigrants, he scented danger to himself. Learning that the Indians were too numerous at "Cassady's Bar," on the San-Joaquin, and in the vicinity of his Fresno Station, he at once, with characteristic promptness and courage, took his course direct to that post. He found, on arriving there, that all was quiet, although some Indians were about, as if for trading purposes. Among them were Pon-wat-chee and Vow-ches-ter, two Indian chiefs known to be friendly. The trader had taken two of his wives from their tribes.

Savage greeted all with his customary salutation. Leaving his squaws to confer with their friends and to provide for their own accommodations, he quietly examined the memoranda of his agent, and the supply of goods on hand. With an appearance of great indifference, he listened to the business reports and gossip of Greeley, who informed him that Indians from different tribes had come in but had brought but little gold. To assure himself of the progress made by the Indians in forming a union among themselves. he called those present around him in front of his store, and passed the friendly pipe. After the usual silence and delay. Savage said: "I know that all about me are my friends. and as a friend to all, I wish to have a talk with you before I go back to my home on the Mariposa, from which I have been a long distance away, but where I could not stop until I had warned you.

"I know that some of the Indians do not wish to be friends with the white men, and that they are trying to unite the different tribes for the purpose of a war. It is better for the Indians and white men to be friends. If the Indians make war on the white men, every tribe will be exterminated; not one will be left. I have just been where the white men are more numerous than the wasps and ants; and if war is made and the Americans are aroused to anger, every Indian engaged in the war will be killed before the whites will be satisfied." In a firm and impressive manner Savage laid before them the damaging effects of a war, and the advantages to all of a continued peaceful intercourse. His knowledge of Indian language was sufficient to make his remarks clearly understood, and they were apparently well received.

Not supposing that Jose would attempt there to advocate

any of his schemes, the trader remarked, as he finished his speech: " A chief who has returned with me from the place where the white men are so numerous, can tell that what I have said is true—Jose Juarez—you all know, and will believe him when he tells you the white men are more powerful than the Indians."

The cunning chief with much dignity, deliberately stepped forward, with more assurance than he had shown since the belligerent occurrence at the bay, and spoke with more energy than Savage had anticipated. He commenced by saying: "Our brother has told his Indian relatives much that is truth; we have seen many people; the white men are very numerous; but the white men we saw on our visit are of many tribes; they are not like the tribe that dig gold in the mountains." He then gave an absurd description of what he had seen while below, and said: " Those white tribes will not come to the mountains. They will not help the gold diggers if the Indians make war against them. If the gold diggers go to the white tribes in the big village they give their gold for strong water and games; when they have no more gold the white tribes drive the gold-diggers back to the mountains with clubs. They strike them down (referring to the police), as your white relative struck me while I was with him." (His vindictive glance assured Savage that the blow was not forgotten or forgiven.) " The white tribes will not go to war with the Indians in the mountains. They cannot bring their big ships and big guns to us; we have no cause to fear them. They will not injure us."

To Savage's extreme surprise, he then boldly advocated an immediate war upon the whites, assuring his listeners that, as all the territory belonged to the Indians, if the tribes would unite the whole tribe of gold-diggers could be easily driven from their country ; but, if the gold-diggers should stay longer, their numbers will be too great to make war upon, and the Indians would finally be destroyed. In his speech Jose evinced a keenness of observation inconsistant with his apparent drunken stupidity. Savage had thought this stupidity sometimes assumed. He now felt assured that the chief had expected thereby to learn his plans. To the writer there seems to be nothing inconsistent with Indian craft, keenness of observation and love of revenge in Jose's conduct, though he was frequently drunk while at "the bay." While Jose was speaking other Indians had joined the circle around him. Their expressions of approval indicated the effects of his speech. During this time Savage had been seated on a log in front of the store, a quiet listener. When Jose concluded, the trader arose, and stepping forward, calmly addressed the relatives of his wives and the Indians in whom he still felt confidence. The earnest and positive speech of the cunning chief had greatly surprised him; he was somewhat discouraged at the approval with which it had been received; but with great self-possession, he replied, "I have listened very attentively to what the chief, who went with me as my friend, has been saying to you. I have heard all he has said. He has told you of many things that he saw. He has told you some truth. He has told of many things which he knows nothing about. He has told you of things he saw in his dreams, while "strong water" made him sleep. The white men we saw there are all of the same tribe as the gold-diggers here among the mountains. He has told you he saw white men that were pale, and had tall hats on their heads, with clothing different from the gold-diggers. This was truth, but they are all brothers, all of one tribe. All can wear the clothing of the gold-diggers; all can climb the mountains, and if war is made on the gold-diggers, the white men will come and fight against the Indians. Their numbers will be so great, that every tribe will be destroyed that joins in a war against them."

Jose observing the effects of these statements, excitedly interrupted Savage by entering the circle, exclaiming: "He is telling you words that are not true. His tongue is forked and crooked. He is telling lies to his Indian relatives. This trader is not a friend to the Indians. He is not our brother. He will help the white gold-diggers to drive the Indians from their country. We can now drive them from among us, and if the other white tribes should come to their help, we will go to the mountains; if they follow after us, they cannot find us; none of them will come back; we will kill them with arrows and with rocks." While Jose was thus vociferously haranguing, other Indians came into the grounds, and the crisis was approaching. As Jose Juarez ended his speech, Jose Rey, another influential chief and prominent leader, walked proudly into the now enlarged circle, followed by his suite of treacherous Chow-chillas, among whom were Tom-Kit and Frederico. He keenly glanced about him, and assuming a grandly tragic style, at once commenced a speech by saying: "My people are now ready to begin a war against the white gold-diggers. If all the tribes will be as one tribe, and join with us, we will drive all the white men from our mountains. If all the tribes will go together, the white men will run from us, and leave their property behind them. The tribes who join in with my people will be the first to secure the property of the gold-diggers."

The dignity and eloquent style of Jose Rey controlled the attention of the Indians. This appeal to their cupidity interested them; a common desire for plunder would be the strongest inducement to unite against the whites.

Savage was now fully aware that he had been defeated at this impromptu council he had himself organized, and at once withdrew to prepare for the hostilities he was sure would soon follow. As soon as the Indians dispersed, he started with his squaws for home, and again gave the settlers warning of what was threatened and would soon be attempted.

These occurrences were narrated to me by Savage. The incidents of the council at the Fresno Station were given during the familiar conversations of our intimate acquaintanceship. The Indian speeches here quoted are like all others of their kind, really but poor imitations. The Indian is very figurative in his language. If a literal translation were attempted his speeches would seem so disjointed and inverted in their methods of expression, that their signification could scarcely be understood; hence only the substance is here given.

The reports from Savage were considered by the miners and settlers as absurd. It was generally known that mountain men of Savage's class were inclined to adopt the vagaries and superstitions of the Indians with whom they were associated; and therefore but little attention was given to the trader's warnings. It was believed that he had listened to the blatant palaver of a few vagabond "Digger Indians," and that the threatened hostilities were only a quarrel between Savage and his Indian miners, or with some of his Indian associates. Cassady, a rival trader, especially scoffed at the idea of danger, and took no precautions to guard himself or establishment. The settlers of Indian Gulch and Quartzberg were, however, soon after startled by a report brought by one of Savage's men called "Long-haired Brown," that the traders' store on the Fresno had been robbed, and all connected with it killed except himself. Brown had been warned by an Indian he had favored, known as Polonio-Arosa, but notwithstanding this aid, he had to take the chances of a vigorous pursuit.

Brown was a large man of great strength and activity, and as he said, had dodged their arrows and distanced his pursuers in the race. Close upon the heels of this report, came a rumor from the miners' camp on Mariposa creek, that Savage's establishment at that place had also been plundered and burned, and all connected with it killed. This report was soon after corrected by the appearance of the trader at Quartzberg. Savage was highly offended at the indifference with which his cautions had been received at Mariposa, and by the county authorities, then located at Agua-Fria. He stated that his wives had assured him that a raid was about to be made on his establishment, and warned him of the danger of a surprise. He had at once sought aid from personal friends at Horse Shoe Bend—where he had once traded—to remove or protect his property. While he was absent, Greeley, Stiffner and Kennedy had been killed, his property plundered and burned, and his wives carried off by their own people. These squaws had been importuned to leave the trader, but had been faithful to his interests. The excitement of these occurrences had not subsided before news came of the murder of Cassady and four men near the San Joaquin. Another murderous assault was soon after reported by an immigrant who arrived at Cassady's Bar, on the upper crossing of the San Joaquin. His shattered arm and panting horse excited the sympathies of the settlers, and aroused the whole community. The wounded man was provided for, and a party at once started for the " Four Creeks," where he had left his comrades fighting the Indians.

The arm of the wounded man was amputated by Dr. Lewis Leach, of St. Louis, Mo., an immigrant who had but just come in over the same route. The name of the wounded man was Frank W. Boden. He stated that his party—four men, I believe, besides himself—had halted at the " Four Creeks" to rest and graze their horses, and while there a band of Indians (Ka-we-ahs) came down from their village and demanded tribute for crossing their territory. Looking upon the demand as a new form of Indian beggary, but little attention was paid to them. After considerable bantering talk, some tobacco was given them, and they went off grumbling and threatening. Boden said: "After the Indians left we talked over the matter for a while; none regarded the demand of the 'Indian tax-gathers' but as a trivial affair. I then mounted my horse and rode off in the direction in which we had seen some antelopes as we came on. I had not gone far before I heard firing in the direction of our halting-place.

"Riding back, I saw the house near which I had left my comrades was surrounded by yelling demons. I was discovered by them at the same instant, and some of them dashed toward me. Seeing no possibility of joining my party, I turned and struck my horse with the spurs, but before I could get beyond range of their arrows, I felt a benumbing sensation in my arm, which dropped powerless. Seeing that my arm was shattered or broken, I thought I would give them one shot at least before I fell into their hands. Checking my horse with some difficulty, I turned so as to rest my rifle across my broken arm, and took sight on the nearest of my pursuers, who halted at the same time."

At this point in his story the hardy adventurer remarked with a twinkle of satisfaction in his bright, keen eye: "I never took better aim in my life. That Indian died suddenly. Another dash was made for me. My horse did not now need the spurs, he seemed to be aware that we must leave that locality as soon as possible, and speedily distanced them all. As soon as the first excitement was over I suffered excrutiating pain in my arm. My rifle being useless to me, I broke it against a tree and threw it away. I then took the bridle rein in my teeth and carried the broken arm in my other hand."

The party that went out to the place of attack—Dr. Thomas Payn's, now Visalia, named for Nat. Vice, an acquaintance of the writer—found there the mangled bodies of Boden's four companions. One of these, it was shown by unmistakable evidence, had been skinned by the merciless fiends while yet alive.

These men had doubtless made a stout resistance. Like brave men they had fought for their lives, and caused, no doubt, a heavy loss to their assailants. This, with their refusal to comply with the demand for tribute, was the motive for such wolfish barbarity.

It now became necessary that some prompt action should be taken for general protection. Rumors of other depredations and murders alarmed the inhabitants of Mariposa county. Authentic statements of these events were at once forwarded to Governor John McDougall, by the sheriff and other officials, and citizens, urging the immediate adoption of some measures on the part of the State for the defense of the people. Raids upon the miners' camps and the "Ranch" of the settlers had become so frequent that on its being rumored that the Indians were concentrating for more extensive operations, a party, without waiting for any official authority, collected and started out to check the ravages of the marauders that were found gathering among the foothills. With but limited supplies, and almost without organization, this party made a rapid and toilsome march among the densely wooded mountains in pursuit of the savages, who, upon report of our movements, were now retreating. This party came up with the Indians at a point high up on the Fresno. In the skirmish which followed a Lt. Skeane was killed, William Little was seriously wounded and some others slightly injured.

This engagement, which occurred on January 11th, 1851, was not a very satisfactory one to the whites. The necessity of a more efficient organization was shown.

The Indians had here taken all the advantages of position and successfully repulsed the attack of the whites, who withdrew, and allowed the former to continue their course.

Some of the party returned to the settlements for supplies and reinforcements, taking with them the wounded.

Those who remained, reorganized, and leisurely followed the Indians to near the North Fork of the San Joaquin river, where they had encamped on a round rugged mountain covered with a dense undergrowth—oaks and digger pine. Here, protected by the sheltering rocks and trees, they defiantly taunted the whites with cowardice and their late defeat. They boasted of their robberies and murders, and called upon Savage to come out where he could be killed. In every possible manner they expressed their contempt. Savage—who had joined the expedition—became very much exasperated, and at first favored an immediate assault, but wiser counsels prevailed, and by Captain Boling's prudent advice, Savage kept himself in reserve, knowing that he would be an especial mark, and as Boling had said, his knowledge of the Indians and their territory could not very well be dispensed with. This course did not please all, and, as might have been expected, then and afterwards disparaging remarks were made.

The leaders in exciting hostilities against the whites were Jose Juarez and Jose Rey. The bands collected on this mountain were under the leadership of Jose Rey, who was also known by his English name of "King Joseph." The tribes represented were the Chow-chilla, Chook-chan-cie, Noot-chu, Ho-nah-chee, Po-to-en-cie, Po-ho-no-chee, Kah-we-ah and Yosemite. The number of fighting men or warriors was estimated at about 500, while that of the whites did not exceed 100.

It was late in the day when the Indians were discovered. A general council was held, and it was decided that no attack should be made until their position could be studied, and the probable number to be encountered, ascertained. Captain Kuy-ken-dall, Lieutenants Doss and Chandler, and others, volunteered to make a reconnoissance before night should interfere with their purpose.

The scouting party was not noticed until on its return, when it was followed back to camp by the Indians, where during nearly the whole night their derisive shouts and menaces in broken Spanish and *native American*, made incessant vigilance of the whole camp a necessity. A council was again called to agree on the plan to be adopted. This council of war was general; official position was disregarded except to carry out the decisions of the party or command. The scouts had discovered that this rendezvous was an old Indian village as well as stronghold.

The plan was that an attack should be undertaken at daylight, and that an effort should be made to set fire to the village, preliminary to the general assault. This plan was strongly advocated by the more experienced ones who had seen service in Mexico and in Indian warfare.

Kuy-ken-dall, Doss and Chandler, "as brave men as ever grew," seemed to vie with each other for the leadership, and at starting Kuy-ken-dall seemed to be in command, but when the assault was made, Chandler's *elan* carried him ahead of all, and he thus became the *leader* indeed.

But thirty-six men were detached for the preliminary service. Everything being arranged the attacking party started before daylight. The Indians had but a little while before ceased their annoyances around the camp. The reserve under Savage and Boling were to follow more leisurely. Kuy-ken-dall's command reached the Indian camp without being discovered. Without the least delay the men dashed in and with brands from the camp fires, set the wigwams burning, and at the same time madly attacked the now alarmed camp. The light combustible materials of which the wigwams were composed were soon in a bright blaze. So rapid and so sudden were the charges made, that the panic-stricken warriors at once fled from their stronghold. Jose Rey was among the first shot down. The Indians made a rally to recover their leader; Chandler observing them, shouted "Charge, boys! Charge!!" Discharging another volley, the men rushed forward.

The savages turned and fled down the mountain, answering back the shout of Chandler to charge by replying, "Chargee!" "Chargee!" as they disappeared.

The whole camp was routed, and sought safety among the rocks and brush, and by flight.

This was an unexpected result. The whole transaction had been so quickly and recklessly done that the reserve under Boling and Savage had no opportunity to participate in the assault, and but imperfectly witnessed the scattering of the terrified warriors. Kuy-ken-dall, especially, displayed a coolness and valor entitling him to command, though outrun by Chandler in the assault. The fire from the burning village spread so rapidly down the mountain side toward our camp as to endanger its safety. While the whites were saving their camp supplies, the Indians under cover of the smoke escaped. No prisoners were taken; twenty-three were killed; the number wounded was never known. Of the settlers, but one was really wounded, though several were scorched and bruised in the fight. None were killed. The scattering flight of the Indians made a further pursuit uncertain. The supplies were too limited for an extended chase; and as none had reached the little army from those who had returned, and time would be lost in waiting, it was decided to return to the settlements before taking any other active measures. The return was accomplished without interruption.

CHAPTER II.

THE State authorities had in the meantime become aroused. The reports of Indian depredations multiplied, and a general uprising was for a time threatened.

Proclamations were therefore issued by Gov. McDougal, calling for volunteers, to prevent further outrages and to punish the marauders. Our impromptu organization formed the nucleus of the volunteer force in Mariposa county, as a large majority of the men at once enlisted. Another battalion was organized for the region of Los Angelos. Our new organization, when full, numbered two hundred mounted men. This was accomplished in time, by Major Savage riding over to the San Joaquin, and bringing back men from Cassady's Bar.

The date from which we were regularly mustered into the service was January 24th, 1851. The volunteers provided their own horses and equipments. The camp supplies and baggage trains were furnished by the State. This military force was called into existence by the State authorities, but by act of Congress its maintenance was at the expense of the general government, under direction of Indian commissioners. Major Ben McCullough was offered the command of this battalion, but he declined it. This position was urged upon him with the supposition that if he accepted it the men who had once served under him would be induced to enlist—many of the "Texan Rangers" being residents of Mariposa county.

Major McCullough was at that time employed as Collector of "Foreign Miners' Tax," a very lucrative office. As a personal acquaintance, he stated to me that the position was not one that would bring him honor or pecuniary advantages. That he had no desire to leave a good position, except for one more profitable.

The officers, chosen by the men, recommended to and commissioned by Governor McDougall, were James D. Savage, as Major; John J. Kuy-ken-dall, John Boling, and William Dill, as Captains; M. B. Lewis, as Adjutant; John I. Scott, Reuben T. Chandler, and Hugh W. Farrell, as First Lieutentants; Robert E. Russell, as Sergeant Major; Dr. A. Bronson, as Surgeon, and Drs. Pfifer and Black as Assistant Surgeons. A few changes of Lieutenants and subordinate officers were afterward made.

Upon the resignation of Surgeon Bronson, Dr. Lewis Leach, was appointed to fill the vacancy.

While writing up these recollections, in order to verify my dates, which I knew were not always chronologically exact, I addressed letters to the State departments of California making inquiries relative to the "Mariposa Battalion," organized in 1851. In answer to my inquiry concerning these known facts, the following was received from Adj. General L. H. Foot. He says: "The records of this office, both written and printed, are so incomplete, that I am not aware from consulting them that the organization to which you allude had existence." It is a matter of regret that the history of the early settlement of California is, to so great an extent, traditionary, without public records of many important events. It is not deemed just that the faithful services of the "Mariposa Battalion," should be forgotten with the fading memory of the pioneers of that period. There is in the State, an almost entire absence of any public record of the "Indian war," of which the discovery of the Yosemite valley was an important episode.

Until the publication of Mr. J. M. Hutching's book, "In The Heart of The Sierras, Yo-Semite, Big Trees, etc.," which contains valuable public documents, the author of "Discovery of The Yosemite" was, as stated on page 30, unable to obtain any official records concerning the operations of the Mariposa battalion, or of the events which preceded and caused the Indian War of 1851. Now that Mr. Hutching's persistent industry has brought light from darkness, I interrupt my narrative to make clear the origin of the war, and to justify the early Pioneers engaged in it. As a sample, also, of many obstructions encountered, I insert a few extracts from letters relating to the "Date of Discovery," furnished the *Century* Magazine.

The attack made upon Savage on the Merced river in 1850, had for its object plunder and intimidation, and as an invasion of Ten-ie-ya's territory was no longer threatened after the removal of Mr. Savage to the Mariposa, the Yo Semites contented themselves with the theft of horses and clothing, but a general war was still impending, as may be seen by reference to page 31 of "In The Heart of The Sierras," where appears: Report of Col. Adam Johnston, a special agent, to Gov. Peter H. Burnett, upon his return from Mariposa county to San Jose, then the Capital of California, and which I here present: San Jose, January 2, 1851. Sir: I have the honor to submit to you, as the executive of the State of California, some facts connected with the recent depredations committed by the Indians, within the bounds of the State, upon the persons and property of her citizens. The immediate scene of their hostile movements are at and in the vicinity of the Mariposa and Fresno. The Indians in that portion of your

State have, for some time past, exhibited disaffection and a restless feeling toward the whites. Thefts were continually being perpetrated by them, but no act of hostility had been committed by them on the person of any individual, which indicated general emnity on the part of the Indians, until the night of the 17th December last. I was then at the camp of Mr. James D. Savage, on the Mariposa, where I had gone for the purpose of reconciling any difficulty that might exist between the Indians and the whites in that vicinity. From various conversations which I had held with different chiefs, I concluded there was no immediate danger to be apprehended. On the evening of the 17th of December, we were, however, surprised by the sudden disappearance of the Indians. They left in a body, but no one knew why, or where they had gone. From the fact that Mr. Savage's domestic Indians had forsaken him and gone with those of the rancheria, or village, he immediately suspected that something of a serious nature was in contemplation, or had already been committed by them.

The manner of their leaving, in the night, and by stealth, induced Mr. Savage to believe that whatever act they had committed or intended to commit, might be connected with himself. Believing that he could overhaul his Indians before others could join them, and defeat any contemplated depredations on their part, he, with sixteen men, started in pursuit. He continued upon their traces for about thirty miles, when he came upon their encampment. The Indians had discovered his approach, and fled to an adjacent mountain, leaving behind them two small boys asleep, and the remains of an aged female, who had died, no doubt from fatigue. Near to the encampment Mr. Savage ascended a mountain in pursuit of the Indians, from which he discovered them upon another mountain at a distance.

From these two mountain tops, conversation was commenced and kept up for some time between Mr. Savage and the chief, who told him that they had murdered the men on the Fresno, and robbed the camp. The chief had formerly been on the most friendly terms with Savage, but would not now permit him to approach him. Savage said to them it would be better for them to return to their village—that with very little labor daily, they could procure sufficient gold to purchase them clothing and food. To this the chief replied it was a hard way to get a living, and that they could more easily supply their wants by stealing from the whites. He also said to Savage he must not deceive the whites by telling them lies, he must not tell them that the Indians were friendly; they were not, but on the contrary were their deadly enemies, and that they intended killing and plundering them so long as a white face was seen in the country. Finding all efforts to induce them to return, or to otherwise reach them, had failed, Mr. Savage and his company concluded to return. When about leaving, they discovered a body of Indians, numbering about two hundred, on a distant mountain, who seemed to be approaching those with whom he had been talking.

Mr. Savage and company arrived at his camp in the night of Thursday in safety. In the mean time, as news had reached us of murders committed on the Fresno, we had determined to proceed to the Fresno, where the men had been murdered. Accordingly on the day following, Friday, the 20th, I left the Mariposa camp with thirty-five men, for the camp on the Fresno, to see the situation of things there, and to bury the dead. I also dispatched couriers to Agua Fria, Mariposa, and several other mining sections, hoping to concentrate a sufficient force on the Fresno to pursue the Indians into the mountains. Several small companies of men left their respective places of residence to join us, but being unacquainted with the country they were unable to meet us. We reached the camp on the Fresno a short time after daylight. It presented a horrid scene of savage cruelty. The Indians had destroyed everything they could not use or carry with them. The store was stripped of blankets, clothing, flour, and everything of value; the safe was broken open and rifled of its contents; the cattle, horses and mules had been run into the mountains; the murdered men had been stripped of their clothing, and lay before us filled with arrows; one of them had yet twenty perfect arrows sticking in him. A grave was prepared, and the unfortunate persons interred. Our force being small, we thought it not prudent to pursue the Indians farther into the mountains, and determined to return. The Indians in that part of the country are quite numerous, and have been uniting other tribes with them for some time. On reaching our camp on the Mariposa, we learned that most of the Indians in the valley had left their villages and taken their women and children to the mountains. This is generally looked upon as a sure indication of their hostile intentions. It is feared that many of the miners in the more remote regions have already been cut off, and Agua Fria and Mariposa are hourly threatened.

Under this state of things, I come here at the earnest solicitations of the people of that region, to ask such aid from the state government as will enable them to protect their persons and property. I submit these facts for your consideration, and have the honor to remain,

Yours very respectfully,
ADAM JOHNSTON.

To his excellency Peter H. Burnett.

The report of Col. Johnston to Gov. Burnett had the desired result, for immediately after inauguration, his successor, Gov. McDougal, on January 13, 1851, issued a proclamation calling for one hundred volunteers, and this number by a subsequent order dated January 24th, 1851, after receipt of Sheriff James Burney's report, bearing the same date of the governor's first call for one hundred men, was increased to "two hundred able bodied men, under officers of their own selection."

To insure a prompt suppression of hostilities, or a vigorous prosecution of the war, on January 25th, 1851, Gov. McDougal appointed Col. J. Neely Johnson of his staff a special envoy to visit Mariposa county, and in an emergency, to call out additional forces if required, and do whatever seemed best for the interests and safety of the people endangered.

Col. Adam Johnston, before leaving for San Jose, had, as he reported, "dispatched couriers to Agua Fria, Mariposa, and several other mining sections, hoping to concentrate a sufficient force on the Fresno to pursue the Indians into the mountains. Several small companies of men left their respective places of residence to join us, but being unacquainted with the country they were unable to meet us."

The same apparent difficulties beset Sheriff Burney, as he was able to collect but seventy-four men, but want of knowledge of the country was not the sole cause of delay. The Indians of the mountains at that time having been accustomed to the occupation for many years of despoiling the Californians, were the most expert bare back riders and horse thieves in the world, and when many of us who had horses and mules herding in the valley ranches of the foot-hills and Merced bottoms, sent for them to carry us into the distant mountains of the Fresno, where we had heard the Indians were concentrating, our messengers in many instances found the animals stolen or stampeded, and hence the delay in most instances, though some of the mining population who had arrived in California by water, never seemed able to guide themselves without a compass, and would get lost if they left a beaten trail. As for myself, I could scarcely become lost, except in a heavy fog or snow storm, and upon two occasions in the mountains was compelled to leave my comrades, who were utterly and wilfully lost, but who, finding me the most persistent, finally called to me and followed out to well known land marks.

It will appear by the letter of Major Burney that "The different squads from the various places rendezvoused not far from this place (Agua Fria), on Monday, 6th, and numbered but seventy-four men." 1 was at Shirlock's Creek on the night before, Jan. 5th, 1851, and had promised to join the Major in the morning; but when the morning came, my animals were gone, stolen by Indians from my Mexican herdman.

Mr. C. H. Spencer had sent his servant "Jimmy," to Snelling's ranche, on the Merced River, for his animals, and after a delay of perhaps two or three days, they were brought up for use. Mr. Spencer kindly loaned me a mule for temporary use, but upon his having his saddle mule stolen a few nights after, I gave back his mule and bought a fine one of Thos. J. Whitlock, for whom Whitlock's Creek was named. I had previously been able to start with a small squad on the trail of Major Burney and his brave men, but met some of them returning after the fight, among whom I remember, were Wm. Little, shot through the lungs, but who finally recovered, a Mr. Smith, known as "Yankee Smith," sick, as he said, "from a bare-footed fool exposure in the snow," and Dr. Phifer, who had been given the care of the wounded and sick men. There were several others unknown to me, or whose names I have now forgotten.

The different accounts I received from the men engaged in the fight, were so conflicting, that in referring to it in previous editions, on page 25, I could only say that it "was not a very satisfactory one to the whites." I could only state the general impression received from Mr. Little's account, which was that the men had been unnecessarily exposed to cold and danger, and that only by the dash and bravery of the officers and men engaged in the affair were they able to withdraw into a place of temporary safety, until joined by re-inforcements.

Indian fighting was new to most of the men engaged, and, like the soldiers on both sides at the outbreak of the Rebellion, they had been led to expect a too easy victory.

But we have now the report of Major Burney to Gov. McDougal, and also a letter from Mr. Theodore G. Palmer, of Newark, New Jersey, to his father, written five days after the battle, and which has been kindly placed at my disposal. Military men will readily perceive and enjoy the entire artlessness and intended truthfulness of Mr. Palmer's letter, as well as his modest bravery. The two letters read in connection with that of Col. Adam Johnston, are most valuable in fixing dates and locations for any one with a knowledge of the topography of the country, and of the events they narrate. They set at rest forever the absurd claim that the first battle of the Indian War of 1851 was fought in the Yosemite valley, for the battle was fought on a mountain. Mr. Hutchings, to whose industry so much is due, has strangely overlooked the fact, that the reference to "Monday 6th," in Major Burney's letter, could only have reference to Monday, January 6th, 1851, the month in which the letter was written, and not to December, 1850, as given by Mr. Hutchings, in brackets. The 6th of December, 1850, occurred on a Friday; on Tuesday, December 17, 1850, the three men were killed on the Fresno river station of James D. Savage; on Friday, December 20th, 1850, they were buried; on Monday, January 6th, 1851, Major Burney, sheriff of Mariposa County, assembled a strong *posse* to go in pursuit of the Indian murderers, and coming up with them on a mountain stronghold on Jan. 11th, 1851, destroyed their villages, and then retreated *down* the mountain some four miles to *a plain* in the Fresno valley, where he erected a log breastwork for temporary defense. Nothing but the most vivid imagination, coupled with an entire ignorance of the region of the Yosemite, could liken the two localities to each other. The Hetch Hetchy valley of the Tuolumne river and some of the cliffs of the Tuolumne and of the King's river, bear a general resemblance to some of the scenery of the Yosemite, but when the Yosemite valley itself has been seen, it will never be forgotten by the visitor.

MAJOR BURNEY'S LETTER TO GOV. McDOUGAL.

AGUA FRIA, January 13, 1851.

SIR: Your Excellency has doubtlessly been informed by Mr. Johnston and others, of repeated and aggravated depredations of the Indians in this part of the State. Their more recent outrages you are probably not aware of. Since the departure of Mr. Johnston, the Indian agent, they have killed a portion of the citizens on the head of the San Joaquin river, driven the balance off, taken away all movable property, and destroyed all they could not take away. They have invariably murdered and robbed all the small parties they fell in with between here and the San Joaquin. News came here last night that seventy-two men were killed on Rattlesnake Creek; several men have been killed in Bear Valley. The Fine Gold Gulch has been deserted, and the men came in here yesterday. Nearly all the mules and horses in this part of the State have been stolen, both from the mines and the ranches. And I now, in the name of the people of this part of the State, and for the good of our country, appeal to your Excellency for assistance.

In order to show your Excellency that the people have done all that they can do to suppress these things, to secure quiet and safety in the possession of our property and lives, I will make a brief statement of what has been done here.

After the massacres on the Fresno, San Joaquin, etc., we endeavored to raise a volunteer company to drive the Indians back, if not to take them or force them into measures. The different squads from the various places rendezvoused not far from this place on Monday, 6th, and numbered but seventy-four men. A company was formed, and I was elected captain; J. W. Riley, first lieutenant; E. Skeane, second lieutenant. We had but eight day's provisions, and not enough animals to pack our provisions and blankets, as it should have been done. We, however, marched, and on the following day struck a large trail of horses that had been stolen by the Indians. I sent forward James D. Savage with a small spy force, and I followed the trail with my company. About two o'clock in the morning, Savage came in and reported the village near, as he had heard the Indians singing. Here I halted, left a small guard with my animals, and went forward with the balance of my men. We reached the village just before day, and at dawn, but before there was light enough to see how to fire our rifles with accuracy, we were discovered by their sentinel. When I saw that he had seen us, I ordered a charge on the village (this had been reconnoitered by Savage and myself). The Indian sentinel and my company got to the village at the same time, he yelling to give the alarm. I ordered them to surrender, some of them ran off, some seemed disposed to surrender, but others fired on us; we fired and charged into the village. Their ground had been selected on account of the advantages it possessed in their mode of warfare. They numbered about four hundred, and fought us three hours and a half.

We killed from forty to fifty, but cannot exactly tell how many, as they took off all they could get to. Twenty-six were killed in and around the village, and a number of others in the chaparrel. We burned the village and provisions, and took four horses. Our loss was six wounded, two mortally; one of the latter was Lieutenant Skeane, the other a Mr. Little, whose bravery and conduct through the battle cannot be spoken of too highly. We made litters, on which we conveyed our wounded, and had to march four miles down the mountain, to a suitable place to camp, the Indians firing at us all the way, from peaks on either side, but so far off as to do little damage. My men had been marching or fighting from the morning of the day before, without sleep, and with but little to eat. On the plain, at the foot of the mountain, we made a rude, but substantial fortification; and at a late hour those who were not on guard, were permitted to sleep. Our sentinels were (as I anticipated they would be) firing at the Indians occasionally all night, but I had ordered them not to come in until they were driven in.

I left my wounded men there, with enough of my company to defend the little fort, and returned to this place for provisions and recruits. I send them to-day re-inforcements and provisions, and in two days more I march by another route, with another re-inforcement, and intend to attack another village before going to the fort. The Indians are watching the movements at the fort, and I can come up in the rear of them unsuspectedly, and we can keep them back until I can hear from Your Excellency.

If Your Excellency thinks proper to authorize me or any other person to keep this company together, we can force them into measures in a short time. But if not authorized and commissioned to do so, and furnished with some arms and provisions, or the means to buy them, and pay for the services of the men, my company must be disbanded, as they are not able to lose so much time without any compensation.

Very respectfully, your obedient servant,

JAMES BURNEY.

In a subsequent letter of Major Burney, addressed to Hon. W. J. Howard, occurs the following passage:

"The first night out you came into my camp and reported that the Indians had stolen all your horses and mules—a very large number; that you had followed their trail into the hill country, but, deeming it imprudent to go there alone, had turned northward, hoping to strike my trail, having heard that I had gone out after Indians. I immediately, at sunset, sent ten men (yourself among the number) under Lieutenant Skeane—who was killed in the fight next day—to look out for the trail, and report, which was very promptly carried out."

Page 35, "In Heart of S. and Legislative Journal" for 1851, page 600.

It is only required of me to say here that re-inforced by such leaders of men as Kuykendall, Boling, Chandler and Doss, there was no delay, and the campaign was completed at "Battle Mountain," a water shed of the San Joaquin.

I now introduce a letter of great value, to me. as it fixes the date of the first battle, and disproves assertions made in the *Century* Magazine:

HART'S RANCH, CALIFORNIA, JANUARY 16th, 1851.

MY DEAR FATHER: When I wrote my last letter to you I had fully determined to take a Ranch near Pacheco's Pass, as I informed you, but before three days had passed the report of Jim Kennedy's murder on the Fresno was confirmed, and I started for the mountains in pursuit of the Indians who were committing depredations all through the country and had sworn to kill every white man in it. Four hundred men had promised to go, but at the appointed time only seventy-seven made their appearance. With these we started under the command of Major Burney, Sheriff of Mariposa County, guided by Mr. Jas. D. Savage, who is without doubt the best man in the world for hunting them out.

From his long acquaintance with the Indians, Mr. Savage has learned their ways so thoroughly that they cannot deceive him. He has been one of their greatest chiefs, and speaks their language as well as they can themselves. No dog can follow a trail like he can. No horse endure half so much. He sleeps but little, can go days without food, and can run a hundred miles in a day and night over the mountains and then sit and laugh for hours over a camp-fire as fresh and lively as if he had just been taking a little walk for exercise.

With him for a guide we felt little fear of not being able to find them.

On Friday morning about ten o'clock, our camp again moved forward and kept traveling until one that night, when "halt! we are on the Indians," passed in a whisper down the line. Every heart beat quicker as we silently unsaddled our animals and tied them to the bushes around us. Commands were given in whispers and we were formed in a line. Sixty were chosen for the expedition, the balance remaining behind in charge of camp.

Savage said the Indians were about six miles off; that they were engaged in a feast. He pointed out their fires, could hear them sing and could smell them, but his eyes were the only ones that could see; his ears alone could hear, and his nose smell anything unusual. Still, there was such confidence placed in him that not one doubted for an instant that everything was as he said.

About two o'clock we started in Indian file, as still as it was possible for sixty men to move in the dark, for the moon had set. For three long hours did we walk slowly and cautiously over the rocks and bushes, through the deepest ravines and up steep and ragged mountain, until within a half mile of the enemy.

Here every one took off his boots, when we again pushed forward to about two hundred yards from the camp. Another halt was called to wait for daylight, while Savage went forward to reconnoitre. He succeeded in getting within ten paces of the Rancharia, and listened to a conversation among them in which his name was frequently mentioned. He found that it was a town of the Kee-chees, but that there were about one hundred and fifty of the Chow-chil la warriors with them and several of the Chuc-chan-ces. Had he found only the Kee-chees as he expected, we were to surround the Rancharia and take all prisoners, but the presence of so many Chow-chil-las, the most warlike tribe in California, made a change of plan necessary.

Daylight by this time began to appear. We had been lying in our stocking-feet on the ground on the top of a mountain within a few paces of the snow for more than an hour, almost frozen by the intense cold, not daring to move or speak a word.

It was not yet light enough to see the sight of our rifles, when an Indian's head was seen rising on the hill before us. For a moment his eyes wandered, then rested on us, and with a yell like a Coyote he turned for the Rancharia. Never did I hear before such an infernal howling, whooping and yelling, as saluted us then from the throats of about six hundred savages, as they rushed down the hill into the gim-o-sell bushes below.

Our huzzahs could, however, hardly have sounded more

pleasant to them, as when finding we were discovered, we charged on their town. Fifty rifles cracked almost instantaneously; a dozen Indians lay groaning before their huts, and many supposed we had undisturbed possession. Our firing had ceased and we were looking around for plunder, when a rifle fired from the bushes below, struck a young Texan, Charley Huston, standing by my side. He fell with a single groan, and we all supposed him dead. My first impression was that I was shot, for I plainly heard the ball strike and almost felt it. This was a surprise that almost whipped us, for not knowing that the Indians had fire-arms, we were only expecting arrows. Before that shot was fired, I had always entertained the idea that I could run about as fast as common men (and I was one of the first in the charge), but by the time I had collected my wandering senses, I was nearly alone; the majority of the party some thirty paces ahead, and running as if they never intended to stop.

Captain Burney and Mr. Savage were on top of the hill using every exertion to make the company halt and form. He had partly succeeded, when a pistol ball struck a man in the face, he fell, but raising himself up said, "if we stay here we will be all shot" and a break was made for the trees.

Still some few remained in rank and others slowly answered to the orders to form, when our Second Lieutenant fell mortally wounded. He was carried off, and every man took his tree.

The Indians had again possession of their Rancharia, and of a slight eminence to the left, and were sending showers of bullets and arrows upon us from three sides. These two points had to be gained even if it cost half our men. Leaving then, enough to guard our present position, the rest of us charged on the hill, took it, stormed the Rancharia, took and burnt it, and returned to our former position with only one man wounded, Wm. Little, shot through the lungs.

The close fighting was now over, for we could not give chase and were forced to lie behind trees and rocks and pick out such as exposed themselves. It was about half past ten when, finding it useless to remain longer, litters were made for the wounded and we started for camp. Then again we had warm work, for all down the pass, the Indians had stationed themselves to fire on us, forcing us to charge on them several times, for while we were in plain sight, they were completely hid behind the gim-o-sell brush.

In our march back, the rear guard was kept at work about as hard as at any time during the morning, but not a single man was hurt, and only one mule was killed.

We moved our camp that night, six miles lower down, where we laid the foundations of a fort and left thirty men to guard it and take care of the wounded.

The rest of us started below the next morning, after burying Lieutenant Skeane, who died in the night.

The Indians acknowledged to eleven men killed, though fifty killed and wounded would be a moderate estimate. Our loss was seven wounded—two mortally (as we then supposed, but Mr. Little finally recovered.—Author.)

The force of the Savages consisted of, as near as could be ascertained, four hundred warriors. We burned a hundred wigwams, several tons of dried horse and mule meat, a great number of bows and arrows, and took six mules.

Several amusing incidents occurred during the fight and others of the most heroic bravery on the part of the Indians. One old squaw was wounded accidentally at the first charge, and was unable to get off. One of our men was going to finish her with his knife, but seeing it was a woman he left her. No sooner had he gone than she picked up a bow and lodged three arrows in another man. I believe she was not touched after that.

The whole body of Indians seemed bent on killing Mr. Savage, partly because he would not be their chief and lead them against the whites, and partly because he was, they knew, our greatest dependence as guide, and their particular dread. To kill him, many of them sacrificed their own lives. They would come one at a time and, standing in open ground, send arrows at him until shot down; and one old chief who used to cook for Savage, would ask him after every shot where he had hit him. They would talk to him to find out where he was, and as soon as he would answer, the balls and arrows would fly thick around his head: but he escaped unhurt; but as he said, worse frightened than he ever was before. He did not fancy such partiality.

A large party has started on a second expedition, but I believe I am perfectly satisfied with Indian fighting.

T. G. PALMER.

NOTE.—It will have been observed that especial reference has twice been made to Gim-o-sell brush, a shrub that grows only on warm slatey soil, on Southern exposures, sought by Indians for winter quarters, and not on the granite cliffs and mountains of the Yosemite. I had not thought it necessary to draw upon nature for testimony, but a new generation has sprung into existence, and the eternal hills may speak to them.

The mining camp or village of Agua Fria, at the date of the organization of the battalion, was the county seat of Mariposa County, and the residence of the Sheriff, Major James Burney. Whittier's Hotel was the headquarters for enlistment. Finding the number called for incomplete, while yet in daily expectation of the arrival of the mustering officer, James D. Savage made a rapid ride to the San Joaquin diggings, and returned with men enough to complete the organization.

We were formally reported for duty, and went into camp about two miles below Agua Fria, on about the 10th of Feb., 1851, but when mustered in, the rolls were dated to include service from Jan. 24th, 1851, the date of the last order of enlistment. An informal ballot was taken to show the preference of the men for officers to command us, Major Burney having previously declined, and when that had been demonstrated, other aspirants were withdrawn by their friends, a formal ballot was taken and a regular organization of three companies completed. The Governor was duly notified of our proceedings, and in a few days the commissions were received by our respective officers.

After a few days in camp on Agua Fria Creek, we moved down to a camp in the foot hills, known afterwards as

Lewis Ranch, were we had abundant grass and good water, and there was established our head-quarters, while waiting for Col. J. Neely Johnson and the U. S. Indian Commission, as stated in this chapter.

After instructions were given us by Col. Johnson, and the Commission had exhausted its eloquence upon the "Children of the Great Father at Washington," and had started for the Fresno, we were allowed to go in pursuit of some very sly marauders who had stolen into our camp in the night, loosened and run off some of our animals, and taken some others herded in the foot hills, but no extended operations were allowed, as Major Savage ordered us to be in readiness for a campaign against the Yosemities, when the first big storm should come, that would prevent their escape across the Sierra Nevada. After a few days' delay the storm did come with continued violence, as recorded.

In view of the facts and dates here given how absurd the statement that we did not go to the Yosemite "until about the 5th or 6th of May, 1851." Our idleness in camp from Feb. 10th and the patient indulgence of the Commissioners, while waiting for the results of our first operations, surpass belief.

And now I reluctantly notice an error of statement by Mr. Julius N. Pratt in the *Century* Magazine for December, 1890.

Had the usual courtesy been extended of allowing me to see and answer Mr. Pratt's erroneous impressions in the same number, I am convinced that he would have kindly withdrawn his article. I am led to this belief, not alone from letters received, but from the *internal evidence* of an upright character conveyed by Mr. Pratt's graphic account of "A Trip to California by way of Panama in 1849," in the *Century* for April 1891.

The *Century* Magazine is a most powerful disseminator of truth, or error, and though I cannot hope for a complete vindication through this volume, its readers shall have the facts of "The Date of Discovery" set before them, "for a truthful regard for history" and my own self-respect require it.

In the *Century* Magazine for September, 1890, page 795, is an article from my pen which gives the date of discovery of the Yosemite as March, 1851. Mr. Pratt, in the December number following, assumes, with "a truthful regard for history," that I was in error, and gives about "January 10th, 1851, as the approximate, if not exact date of discovery." Many of the men whom Mr. Pratt supposed to have been the discoverers, were, or became, my own comrades. When Mr. Pratt's article appeared, I at once sent a reply, but it received no recognition.

Knowing that Mr. Theodore G. Palmer, of Newark, New Jersey, was in the only engagement occurring with Indians in Mariposa county at the time given by Mr. Pratt as the date of his supposed discovery of the Yosemite, I wrote, requesting Mr. Palmer to call on the editor of the *Century* in my behalf.

In a letter of January 9th, 1891, Mr. Palmer wrote: "It is the unexpected which always happens, and your communication to the *Century* in response to Pratt's 'California,' was never received. Mr. Johnson, the associate editor, received me very pleasantly. He assured me that although he sent you an advance copy of Pratt's article, nothing had been received in the office from you since in reply, and he presumed you had given up the case in default.

"I so completely satisfied him that Mr. Pratt is in error, that he requested me to express my reasons in the *Century*, and to assure you that any communication from you will always have respectful attention."

On January 24th, 1891, Mr. R. W. Johnson, associate editor, wrote me, saying: "Since telling your friend, Mr. Palmer, that we had not received an article from you in reply to Mr. Pratt, we have discovered the manuscript. We have in type a short note from Mr. Palmer which will be acceptable to you."

A few days after Mr. Johnson kindly sent me the proof. On March 12th, 1891, Mr. Johnson wrote me: "Mr. Pratt, after examination of the subject, has written us a short letter, withdrawing his contention of your claim to the discovery of the Yosemite, the publication of which we trust will be satisfactory to you and also to Mr. Palmer. Will you now tell us whether there is anything in this new claim that Walker was the discoverer of the Valley?"

I at once saw that if Mr. Pratt's retraction was published there would be no need of the publication of Mr. Palmer's communication. About this time a letter of earlier date, January 28, 1891, was sent me by Mr. Palmer, received from Mr. Pratt, in which the latter gentleman says: "I enclose a letter which seems to prove that the party about which I wrote to the *Century* was not your party. One went to the North fork, the other (yours) to the South." That statement left no base whatever for Mr. Pratt's imaginary "fight at the Yosemite, and thus of the discovery," for the North Fork affair was not a battle at all, but "a scare" on a fork which enters the Merced river thirty-five miles below the Yosemite, and as for the battle fought on the 11th of January, 1851, by Major Burney's company, in which Mr. Palmer was engaged, it was not fought on the South fork or in any valley, but upon a high mountain of the Fresno river.

Mr. Palmer now felt that his note to *The Century* was too long delayed, and wrote asking for its withdrawal or its publication. Mr. R. U. Johnson replied: "*The Century* is made up two months in advance," but that he intended inserting it in the April number, &c. Mr. Palmer added in his letter to me, "I think he will."

The matter had now become not only interesting, but amusing to me; for very soon Mr. Palmer wrote, "whether my answer to Pratt will be published or not, is doubtful. I infer (from a letter) that Pratt will not rest quiescent under my contradiction." Again Mr. Palmer wrote, enclosing copy of letter to Mr. Johnson of March 14th, 1891, answering Mr. Johnson's Statement, "that Mr. Pratt, while being convinced of his injustice to Dr. Bunnell and being ready himself to withdraw his former statement, takes issue with you as to the identity of the two parties," and then Mr. Johnson asks, "would it not be just as well and more effective if we were simply to print from Mr. Pratt that he is 'pleased to withdraw all contention of the claim made by Dr. Bunnell that he was the original discoverer?'" Let me here say, in passing, that I never made such a claim.

Mr. Palmer very properly objects to becoming the "scapegoat" for me or any one else, and replying to Mr. Johnson, says: "Whether my letter is printed or not, is a matter of entire indifference to me, (personally) * * it was only at your desire, and to please Dr. Bunnell, that I wrote the little I did. I left you under the impression that you desired to get at the exact facts and would be glad to rectify the injustice done to the doctor by the publication of Mr. Pratt's communication. * * * I believe that the publication of my letter would not only gratify him, but also place the *Century* right upon the record, where it surely desires to stand."

Mr. Palmer could say no more, but to his great chagrin, but not surprise, on March 17th, he received a letter of *thanks* from the associate editor of the *Century*, in which

Mr. Johnson says: "Please accept our thanks for your letter of the 14th, and for your obliging attitude in the matter." Whether any retraction from Mr. Pratt will ever appear in the *Century* is now, in view of the long delay, a a matter of great indifference to me.*

Now a few facts in regard to the Discovery of the Yosemite Valley by Capt. Joseph Reddeford Walker, for whom Walker's river, Lake and Pass were named. It is not a new claim, as supposed by Mr. R. U. Johnson, but appears in the *Peoples Encyclopædia* and was set up in the *San Jose Pioneer* soon after Capt. Walker's death, and answered by me in the same paper in 1880.

I cheerfully concede the fact set forth in the *Pioneer* article that, "*His were the first white man's eyes that ever looked upon the Yosemite*" *above* the valley, and in that sense, he was certainly the original white discoverer.

The topography of the country over which the Mono trail ran, and which was followed by Capt. Walker, did not admit of his seeing the valley proper. The depression indicating the valley, and its magnificent surroundings, could alone have been discovered, and in Capt. Walker's conversations with me at various times while encamped between Coultersville and the Yosemite, he was manly enough to say so. Upon one occaision I told Capt. Walker that Ten-ie-ya had said that, "A small party of white men once crossed the mountains on the north side, but were so guided as not to see the valley proper." With a smile the Captain said: "That was my party, but I was not deceived, for the lay of the land showed there was a valley below; but we had become nearly bare-footed, our animals poor, and ourselves on the verge of starvation, so we followed down the ridge to Bull Creek, where, killing a deer, we went into camp."

*Mr. Pratt's retraction has finally appeared in the June number for 1891.

The captain remained at his camp near Coultersville for some weeks, and disappeared as suddenly as he came. He once expressed a desire to re-visit the region of the Yosemite in company with me, but could fix no date, as he told me he was in daily expectation of a government appointment as guide, which I learned was finally given him.

Captain Walker was a very eccentric man, well versed in the vocal and sign languages of the Indians, and went at his will among them. He may have visited the Yosemite from his camp before leaving. I was strongly impressed by the simple and upright character of Captain Walker, and his mountain comrades spoke in the highest praise of his ability. Fremont, Kit Carson, Bill Williams, Alex Gody, Vincenthaler (not Vincent Haler, as erroneously appeared in the March number of the *Century*), Ferguson and others, all agreed in saying that as a mountain man, Captain Walker had no superior.

Rev. D. D. Chapin, of Maysville, Kentucky, formerly rector of Trinity Church, San Jose, and of St. Peter's Church, San Francisco, as well as editor of *Pacific Churchman*, kindly called my attention to a seeming neglect of the claim for Captain Walker as the discoverer of the Yosemite. All that I have ever claimed for myself is, that I was *one* of the party of white men who first *entered* the Yosemite valley, as far as known to the Indians.

The fact of my naming the valley cannot be disputed. The existence of some terribly yawning abyss in the mountains, guarded at its entrance by a frightful "Rock Chief," from whose head rocks would be hurled down upon us if we attempted to enter that resort of demons, was frequently described to us by crafty or superstitious Indians. Hence the greater our surprise upon first beholding a fit abode for angels of light. As for myself, I freely confess that my feelings of hostility against the Indians were overcome by a sense of exaltation; and although I had suffered losses of property and friends, the natural right of the Indians to their inheritance forced itself upon my mind.

The Mariposa Battalion, was assigned by Governor Mc-Dougall to the duty of keeping in subjection the Indian tribes on the east side of the San Joaquin and Tulare valleys, from the Tuolumne river to the Te-hon Pass. As soon as the battalion was organized, Major Savage began his preparations for an expedition. There was but little delay in fitting out. Scouting parties were sent out, but with no other effect than to cause a general retreat of the Indians to the mountains, and a cessation of hostilities, except the annoyances from the small bands of thieving maranders. No Indians were overtaken by those detachments, though they were often seen provokingly near. When about to start on a more extended expedition to the mountains, Major Savage received an order from the Governor to suspend hostile operations until he should receive further instructions. We learned at about the same time through the newspapers, as well as from the Governor's messenger, that the United States Commissioners had arrived in San Francisco. Their arrival had for some time been expected.

Up to this period the Indian affairs of California had not been officially administered upon. Public officers had not before been appointed to look after the vast landed estates of the aboriginal proprietors of this territory, and to provide for their heirs. After some delay, the commissioners arrived at our camp, which was located about fifteen miles below Mariposa village. Here the grazing was most excellent, and for that reason they temporarily established their head-quarters. These officials were Colonels Barbour and McKee, and Dr. Woozencroft. They were accompanied by Col. Neely Johnson, the Governor's aid, and by a small detachment of regulars. The commissioners at once proceeded to make a thorough investigation into the cause of the war, and of the condition of affairs generally. Having secured the services of some of the Mission Indians, these were sent out with instructions to notify all the tribes that the commissioners had been directed by the President to make peace between them and the white settlers; and that if they would come in, they should be assured protection.

The so-called Mission Indians were members of different tribes who had been instructed in the belief of the Catholic Church, at the old Spanish Missions. These Indians had not generally taken part in the war against the white settlers, although some of them, with the hostiles, were the most treacherous of their race, having acquired the vices and none of the virtues of their white instructors.

During this period of preliminaries a few Indians ventured in to have a talk with the commissioners. They were very shy and suspicious, for all had been more or less implicated in the depredations that had been committed. Presents were lavishly distributed, and assurances were given that all who came in should be supplied with food and clothing and other useful things. This policy soon became generally known to the Indians.

Among the delegations that visited the commissioners were Vow-ches-ter,* chief of one of the more peaceful bands, and Russio, a Mission Indian from the Tuolumne, but who in former years had belonged to some of the San Joaquin tribes. These chiefs had always appeared friendly, and had not joined in the hostile attitude assumed by the others. At the outbreak on the Fresno, Vow-ches-ter had been temporarily forced into hostilities by the powerful influence of Jose Rey, and by his desire to secure protection to his relative, one of Savage's squaws. But with the fall of Jose Rey, his influence over Vow-ches-ter declined, and he was once more left free to show his friendship for the whites.

---

*An Indian corruption of Bautista.

As for Russio, his intelligent services were secured as peace-maker and general Indian interpreter by the commissioners, while a much less competent Mission Indian, Sandino, served in the capacity of interpreter during expeditions into the mountains.

Having been assured of safety, these two chiefs promised to bring in their people and make peace with the whites. All that came in promised a cessation, on the part of their tribes, of the hostilties begun, for which they were rewarded with presents.

Vow-chester, when questioned, stated " that the mountain tribes would not listen to any terms of peace involving the abandonment of their territory; that in the fight near the North Fork of the San Joaquin, Jose Rey had been badly wounded and probably would die; that his tribe were very angry, and would not make peace." We had up to this time supposed Jose Rey had been killed at " Battle Mountain." Russio said: " The Indians in the deep rocky valley on the Merced river do not wish for peace, and will not come in to see the chiefs sent by the great father to make treaties. They think the white men cannot find their hiding places, and that therefore they cannot be driven out." The other Indians of the party confirmed Russio's statements. Vow-chester was the principal spokesman, and he said: " In this deep valley spoken of by Russio, one Indian is more than ten white men. The hiding places are many. They will throw rocks down on the white men, if any should come near them. The other tribes dare not make war upon them, for they are lawless like the grizzlies, and as strong. We are afraid to go to this valley, for there are many witches there."

Some of us did not consider Vow-chester's promise of friendship as reliable. We regarded him as one of the hostile mountain Indians. He, however, was never again engaged in hostilities against the whites. I afterwards learned that Vow-chester and Savage had once professed a strong friendship for each other. The trader at that time had taken a bride who was closely allied to the chief. After the destruction of Savage's trading posts, in which Vow-chester had taken an active part in procuring a forcible divorce and division of property (though the murders were ascribed to the Chow-chillas), all forms of friendship or relationship had ceased. At this interview no sign of recognition passed. After listening to this parley between the Commissioners and the Indians, I asked Major Savage, who had been acting as interpreter, if he had ever been into the deep valley the Indians had been speaking of. He at first replied that he had, but on a subsequent conversation he corrected this statement by saying, "Last year while I was located at the mouth of the South Fork of the Merced, I was attacked by the Yosemites, but with the Indian miners I had in my employ, drove them off, and followed some of them up the Merced river into a cañon, which I supposed led to their stronghold, as the Indians then with me said it was not a safe place to go into. From the appearance of this rocky gorge I had no difficulty in believing them. Fearing an ambush, I did not follow them. It was on this account that I changed my location to Mariposa creek. I would like to get into the den of the thieving murderers. If ever I have a chance I will smoke out the Grizzly Bears (the Yosemites) from their holes, where they are thought to be so secure."

No peace messengers came in from the mountain Indians, who continued to annoy the settlers with their depredations, thieving from the miner's camps, and stealing horses and mules from the ranches. While we were awaiting the action of the commissioners, we lost some horses and mules, which were stolen from the vicinity of our camp. After the commissioners had decided upon the measures to be adopted, our battalion was ordered into line and we were then officially informed by Col. Johnson, that our operations as a military organization, would henceforth be under the direction of the United States Commissioners. That by their order we were now assigned to the duty of subduing such Indian tribes as could not otherwise be induced to make treaties with them, and at once c.ase hostilities and depredations. "Your officers will make all reports to the commissioners. Your orders and instructions will hereafter be issued by them." The colonel then complimented the soldierly appearance of the battalion (very customary in later years) and then said: "While I do not hesitate to denounce the Indians for the murders and robberies committed by them, we should not forget that there may perhaps be circumstances which, if taken into consideration, might to some extent excuse their hostility to the whites. They probably feel that they themselves are the aggrieved party, looking upon us as trespassers upon their territory, invaders of their country, and seeking to dispossess them of their homes. It may be, they class us with the Spanish invaders of Mexico and California, whose cruelties in civilizing and christianizing them are still traditionally fresh in their memories," etc. In conclusion the colonel said: "As I am about to leave, I will now bid you 'good bye,' with the hope that your actions will be in harmony with the wishes of the commissioners, and that in the performance of your duties, you will in all cases observe mercy where severity is not justly demanded."

Colonel Johnson gave us a very excellent little speech; but at that time we were not fully impressed with the justness of the remarks which had been made from kindness of heart and sincerely humane feelings. Many of us had lost—some heavily—by the depredations of the Indians.

Friends and relatives had been victims of their atrocities. Murders and robberies had been committed without provocations then discernible to us. Many of us would then have been willing to adopt the methods of the old Spanish missionaries, who, it was said, sometimes brought in their converts with the lasso. However, these orders and the speech from Col. Johnson were received with cheers by the more impatient and impulsive of the volunteers, who preferred active service to the comparative quiet of the camp.

The commissioners selected a reservation on the Fresno, near the foot-hills, about eighteen or twenty miles from our camp, to which the Indian tribes with whom treaties had been made were to be removed, and at this locality the commissioners also established a camp, as head-quarters.

The deliberative action on the part of the commissioners, who were very desirous of having the Indians voluntarily come in to make treaties with them, delayed any active co-operation on the part of our battalion until the winter rains had fully set in. Our first extended expedition to the mountains was made during the prevailing storms of the vernal equinox, although detachments had previously made excursions into the country bordering upon the Sierras. This region, like parts of Virginia, proved impassable to a mounted force during the wet season, and our operations were confined to a limited area.

It was at last decided that more extended operations were necessary to bring in the mountain tribes. Although there was no longer unity of action among them, they refused to leave their retreats, and had become even suspicious of each other. The defeat of Jose Rey, and the desertion of the tribes who had made, or had promised to make, treaties with the commissioners, and had ceased from all hostile demonstrations, had   jealousies and discontent to divide even the most turbulent bands. For the extended operations of the battalion among the mountains, it was decided that Major Savage, with the companies of Captains Boling and Dill, should make expeditions which would require him to traverse the regions of the San Joaquin and Merced rivers. Captain Kuy-ken-dall with his company were to be detached to operate for the same purpose in the regions of the Kings and Kah-we-ah rivers. The Indians captured were to be escorted to the commissioners' camp on the Fresno. Notwithstanding a storm was gathering, our preparations were cheerfully made, and when the order to "form into line" was given, it was obeyed with alacrity. No "bugle call" announced orders to us; the "details" were made quietly, and we as quietly assembled. Promptly as the word of command "mount," was given, every saddle was filled. With "forward march," we naturally filed off into the order of march so readily assumed by mounted frontiersmen while traveling on a trail.

We left our camp as quietly and as orderly as such an undisciplined body could be expected to move, but Major Savage said that we must all learn to be as still as Indians, or we would never find them.

This battalion was a body of hardy, resolute pioneers. Many of them had seen service, and had fought their way against the Indians across the plains; some had served in the war with Mexico and been under military discipline.

Although ununiformed, they were well armed, and their similarities of dress and accoutrements, gave them a general military appearance.

The temperature was mild and agreeable at our camp near the plain, but we began to encounter storms of cold rain as we reached the more elevated localities.

Major Savage being aware that rain on the foot-hills and plain at that season of the year indicated snow higher up, sent forward scouts to intercept such parties as might attempt to escape, but the storm continued to rage with such violence as to render this order useless, and we found the scouts awaiting us at the foot of a mountain known as the Black Ridge. This ridge is a spur of the Sierra Nevada. It separates the Mariposa, Chow-chilla, Fresno and San Joaquin rivers on the south from the Merced on the north. While halting for a rest, and sipping his coffee, Savage expressed an earnest desire to capture the village he had ascertained to be located over the ridge on the south fork of the Merced. He was of the opinion that if it could be reached without their discovery of us, we should have no fighting to do there, as that band would surrender at once rather than endanger their women and children, who would be unable to escape through the snow. Toward this village we therefore marched as rapidly as the nature of the steep and snow-obstructed trail would permit us to travel. An Indian that answered to the name of "Bob," an *attaché* of the Major, serving as guide. Climbing up this steep black mountain, we soon reached the region of snow, which at the summit, was fully four feet deep, though the cold was not intense. By this time, night was upon us. The trail led over the ridge at a point where its tabled summit was wooded with a forest of pines, cedars and firs, so dense as almost to exclude the light of the stars that now and then appeared struggling through the gloom.

We laboriously followed our guide and file leader, but this trail was so indistinctly seen in the darkness, that at intervals deep mutterings would be heard from some drowsy rider who missed the beaten path. As we commenced the descent of the ridge, the expressions became more forcible than polite when some unlucky ones found themselves floundering in the snow below the uncertain trail. If left to their own sagacity, a horse or mule will follow its leader; but if a self-willed rider insists upon his own judgment, the poor animal has not only to suffer the extra fatigue incurred by a mistep, but also the punishment of the spur, and hear the explosive maledictions of the master. The irritating responses of his comrades that " another fool has been discovered," was not then calculated to sooth the wrath that was then let loose.

With short halts and repeated burrowings in the deep, damp snow, the South Fork of the Merced was at length reached about a mile below what is now known as Clark's, or Wah-wo-na, from Wah-ha wo-na, a Big Tree. We here made a halt, and our weary animals were provided with some barley, for the snow was here over a foot deep. The major announced that it was but a short distance below to the Indian village, and called for volunteers to accompany him—it might be for a fight or perhaps only a foot-race—circumstances would determine which. The major's call was promptly and fully answered, although all were much fatigued with the tedious night march. The animals were left, and a sufficient number was selected to remain as a reserve force and camp guard. At daylight we filed away on foot to our destination, following the major who was guided by " Bob."

CHAPTER III.

THERE was a very passable trail for horses leading down
the right bank of the river, but it was overlooked on the
left bank by the Indian village, which was situated on a
high point at a curve in the river that commanded an extensive view up and down. To avoid being seen, the Major led
us along down the left bank, where we were compelled, at
times, to wade into the rushing torrent to avoid the precipitous and slippery rocks, which, in places, dipped into the
stream. Occasionally, from a stumble, or from the deceptive depths of the clear mountain stream, an unfortunate
one was immersed in the icy fluid, which seemed colder
than the snow-baths of the mountain. With every precaution, some became victims to these mischances, and gave
vent to their emotions, when suddenly immersed, by hoarse
curses, which could be heard above the splash and roar of
the noisy water. These men (headed by Surgeon Bronson)
chilled and benumbed, were sent back to the camp to " dry
their ammunition." (?) After passing this locality—our
march thus far having alternated in snow and water—we arrived, without being discovered, in sight of the smoke of
their camp-fires, where we halted for a short rest.

Major Savage gave some orders to Captain Boling which were not then understood by me. On again resuming our march, the Major, with "Bob," started at a rapid step, while the others maintained a slow gait.

I followed the Major as I had been accustomed during the march. I soon heard an *audible smile*, evidently at my expense. I comprehended that I had somehow "sold" myself, but as the Major said nothing, I continued my march. I observed a pleased expression in the Major's countenance, and a twinkle of his eyes when he glanced back at me as if he enjoyed the fun of the "boys" behind us, while he increased his speed to an Indian jog-trot. I determined to appear as unconscious, as innocent of my blunder, and accommodate my gait to his movements. My pride or vanity was touched, and I kept at his heels as he left the trot for a more rapid motion. After a run of a mile or more, we reached the top of a narrow ridge which overlooked the village. The Major here cast a side glace at me as he threw himself on the ground, saying: "I always prided myself on my endurance, but somehow this morning my bottom fails me." As quietly as I could I remarked that he had probably been traveling faster than he was aware of, as "Bob" must be some way behind us. After a short scrutiny of my unconcerned innocence, he burst into a low laugh and said: "Bunnell, you play it well, and you have beaten me at a game of my own choosing. I have tested your endurance, however; such qualifications are really valuable in our present business." He then told me as I seated myself near him, that he saw I had not understood the order, and had increased his speed, thinking I would drop back and wait for the others to come up, as he did not wish to order me back, although he had preferred to make this scout alone with "Bob," as they were both acquainted with the band and the region they occupy. While we were resting "Bob" came up. The Major gave him some direction in an Indian dialect I did not understand, and he moved on to an adjoining thicket, while the Major and myself crawled to the shelter of a bunch of blue brush (California lilac), just above where we had halted.

After obtaining the desired information without being seen, Bob was sent back to Captain Boling to "hurry him up." While awaiting the arrival of our command, I, in answer to his inquiries, informed the Major that I had come to Detroit, Michigan, in 1833, when it was but little more than a frontier village; that the Indians annually assembled there and at Malden, Canada, to receive their annuities. At that time, being but nine years of age, and related to Indian traders, I was brought in contact with their customers, and soon learned their language, habits and character, which all subsequent attempts to civilize me had failed entirely to eradicate. This statement evidently pleased the Major, and finding me familiar with frontier life, he continued his conversation, and I soon learned that I was acquainted with some of his friends in the Northwest. I have related this incident because it was the beginning of an intimate friendship which ever afterward existed between us.

On the arrival of Captains Boling and Dill with their respective companies, we were deployed into skirmish line, and advanced toward the encampment without any effort at concealment. On discovering us the Indians hurriedly ran to and fro, as if uncertain what course to pursue. Seeing an unknown force approaching, they threw up their hands in token of submission, crying out at the same time in Spanish, "*Pace! pace!*" (peace! peace!) We were at once ordered to halt while Major Savage went forward to arrange for the surrender. The Major was at once recognized and cordially received by such of the band as he desired to confer with officially. We found the village to be that of Pon-wat-chee, a chief of the Noot-chü tribe, whose people had formerly worked for Savage under direction of Cow-chit-ty, his brother, and from whose tribe Savage had taken Ee-e-ke-no, one of his former wives. The chief professed still to entertain feelings of friendship for Savage, saying that he was now willing to obey his counsels. Savage, in response, lost no time in preliminary affairs.

He at once told the chief the object of the expedition, and his requirements. His terms were promptly agreed to, and before we had time to examine the captives or their wig-wams, they had commenced packing their supplies and re-moving their property from their bark huts. This done, the torch was applied by the Indians themselves, in token of their sincerity in removing to the Reservations on the Fresno.

By the Major's orders they had at once commenced their preparations for removal to a rendezvous, which he had se-lected nearly opposite this encampment, which was accessi-ble to horses. This plateau was also the location designated for our camp. This camp was afterwards used by an employé at the agency, whose name was Bishop, and was known as Bishop's Camp. It is situated on an elevated table, on the right side of the valley of the South Fork.

While the Indians were preparing for their transfer to the place selected, our tired and hungry men began to feel the need of rest and refreshments. We had traveled a much longer distance since the morning before than had been estimated in expectation of a halt, and many of the men had not tasted food since the day before.

John Hankin told Major Savage that if a roast dog could be procured, he would esteem it an especial favor. Bob McKee thought this a capital time to learn to eat acorn bread, but after trying some set before him by "a young and accomplished squaw," as the Major cynically termed her, concluded he was not yet hungry enough for its enjoy ment.

A call was made for volunteers to go back to bring up the reserve and supplies, but the service was not very promptly accepted. McKee, myself and two others, however, offered to go with the order to move down to the selected rendezvous. Three Indians volunteerd to go with us as guides; one will seldom serve alone. We found the trail on the right bank less laborious to travel than was expected, for the snow had mostly disappeared from the loose, sandy soil, which upon this side of the river has a southwesterly exposure. On our arrival in camp preparations were begun to obey the order of the Major. While coffee was being prepared Doctor Bronson wisely prescribed and most skillfully administered to us a refreshing draught of "*Aqua Ardente.*"

After a hasty *breakfast*, we took to our saddles, and taking a supply of biscuits and cold meat, left the train and arrived at the new camp ground just as our hungry comrades came up from the Indian village. The scanty supplies, carried on our saddles, were thankfully received and speedily disposed of. The Indians had not yet crossed the river. We found that we had traveled about twelve miles, while our comrades and the captives had accomplished only three.

From this camp, established as our headquarters, or as a base of operations while in this vicinity, Major Savage sent Indian runners to the bands who were supposed to be hiding in the mountains. These messengers were instructed to assure all the Indians that if they would go and make treaties with the commissioners. they would there be furnished with food and clothing, and receive protection, but if they did not come in, he should make war upon them until he destroyed them all.

Pon-wat-chee had told the Major when his own village was captured, that a small band of Po-ho-no-chees were encamped on the sunny slope of the divide of the Merced, and he having at once dispatched a runner to them, they began to come into camp. This circumstance afforded encouragement to the Major, but Pon-wat-chee was not entirely sanguine of success with the Yosemites, though he told the Major that if the snow continued deep they could not escape.

At first but few Indians came in, and these were very cautious—dodging behind rocks and trees, as if fearful we would not recognize their friendly signals.

Being fully assured by those who had already come in, of friendly treatment, all soon came in who were in our immediate vicinity. None of the Yosemites had responded to the general message sent. Upon a special envoy being sent to the chief, he appeared the next day in person. He came alone, and stood in dignified silence before one of the guard, until motioned to enter camp. He was immediately recognized by Pon-wat-chee as Ten-ie-ya, the old chief of the Yosemites, and was kindly cared for—being well supplied with food—after which, with the aid of the other Indians, the Major informed him of the wishes of the commissioners. The old sachem was very suspicious of Savage, and feared he was taking this method of getting the Yosemites into his power for the purpose of revenging his personal wrongs. Savage told him that if he would go to the commissioners and make a treaty of peace with them, as the other Indians were going to do, there would be no more war. Ten-ie-ya cautiously inquired as to the object of taking all the Indians to the plains of the San Joaquin valley, and said: "My people do not want anything from the 'Great Father' you tell me about. The Great Spirit is our father, and he has always supplied us with all we need. We do not want anything from white men. Our women are able to do our work. Go, then; let us remain in the mountains where we were born; where the ashes of our fathers have been given to the winds. I have said enough!"

This was abruptly answered by Savage, in Indian dialect and gestures: "If you and your people have all you desire, why do you steal our horses and mules? Why do you rob the miners' camps? Why do you murder the white men, and plunder and burn their houses?"

Ten-ie-ya sat silent for some time; it was evident he understood what Savage had said, for he replied: "My young men have sometimes taken horses and mules from the whites. It was wrong for them to do so. It is not wrong to take the property of enemies, who have wronged my people. My young men believed the white gold-diggers were our enemies; we now know they are not, and we will be glad to live in peace with them. We will stay here and be friends. My people do not want to go to the plains. The tribes who go there are some of them very bad. They will make war on my people. We cannot live on the plains with them. Here we can defend ourselves against them."

In reply to this Savage very deliberately and firmly said: "Your people must go to the Commissioners and make terms with them. If they do not, your young men will again steal our horses, your people will again kill and plunder the whites. It was your people who robbed my stores, burned my houses, and murdered my men. If they do not make a treaty, your whole tribe will be destroyed, not one of them will be left alive." At this vigorous ending of the Major's speech, the old chief replied: "It is useless to talk to you about who destroyed your property and killed your people. If the Chow-chillas do not boast of it, they are cowards, for they led us on. I am old and you can kill me if you will, but what use to lie to you who know more than all the Indians, and can beat them in their big hunts of deer and bear. Therefore I will not lie to you, but promise that if allowed to return to my people I will bring them in." He was allowed to go. The next day he came back, and said his people would soon come to our camp; that when he had told them they could come with safety they were willing to go and make a treaty with the men sent by the "Great Father," who was so good and rich. Another day passed, but no Indians made their appearance from the " deep valley," spoken of so frequently by those at our camp. The old chief said the snow was so deep that they could not travel fast, that his village was so far down (gesticulating, by way of illustration, with his hands) that when the snow was deep on the mountains they would be a long time climbing out of it. As we were at the time having another storm Ten-ie-ya's explanation was accepted, but was closely watched.

The next day passed without their coming, although the snow storm had ceased during the night before. It was then decided that it would be necessary to go to the village of the Yosemites, and bring them in; and in case they could not be found there, to follow to their hiding-places in the deep cañon, so often represented as such a dangerous locality. Ten-ie-ya was questioned as to the route and the time it would take his people to come in; and when he learned we were going to his village, he represented that the snow was so deep that the horses could not go through it. He also stated that the rocks were so steep that our horses could not climb out of the valley if they should go into it. Captain Boling caused Ten-ie-ya's statements to be made known to his men. It was customary in all of our expeditions where the force was divided, to call for volunteers. The men were accordingly drawn up into line, and the call made that all who wished to go to the village of the Yosemites were to step three paces to the front. When the order to advance was given, to the surprise of Captains Boling and Dill, each company moved in line as if on parade. The entire body had volunteered. As a camp-guard was necessary, a call was then made for volunteers for this duty. When the word "march" was again repeated, but a limited number stepped to the front. Captain Boling, with a smile on his good-natured face, said: "A camp-guard will have to be provided in some way. I honor the sentiment that prompted you all to volunteer for the exploration, and I also appreciate the sacrifice made by those who are willing to stay; but these are too few. Our baggage, supplies and Indian captives must be well guarded. I endeavored to make the choice of duty voluntary, by representing the difficulties that might reasonably be expected, and thus secure those best suited for the respective duty of field and camp. I am baffled, but not defeated, for I have another test of your fitness; it is a foot-race. You know it has been represented to us by Ten-ie-ya that the route to his village is an extremely difficult one, and impassable for our horses. It may not be true, but it will be prudent to select men for the expedition who have proved their endurance and fleetness. I now propose that you decide what I have found so difficult."

This proposition was received with shouts of laughter, and the arrangements for the contest were at once commenced, as it afforded a source of frolicsome amusement. A hundred yards were paced off, and the goal conspicuously marked. A distance line was to determine who should constitute the camp-guard. I doubt if such boisterous hilarity and almost boyish merriment was ever before seen while making a detail from any military organization.

The Indians were at first somewhat alarmed at the noisy preparations, and began to be fearful of their safety, but on learning the cause of the excitement, they, too, became interested in the proceedings, and expressed a desire to participate in the race. Two or three were allowed to join in as proxies for the "*heavy ones*" who concluded not to run, though willing to pay the young Indians to represent them in the race, provided they came out ahead. One young Indian did beat every man, except Bob McKee, for whom he manifested great admiration. Many anxious ones ran barefooted in the snow. The Indian's motions were not impeded by any civilized garments; a modest waist cloth was all they had on. In subsequent races, after a long rest, several of our men demonstrated that their racing powers were superior to the fastest of the Indian runners. Captain Boling's racing scheme brought out the strong points of the runners. Enough were distanced in both companies to secure an ample camp-guard. The envious guard raised the point that this method of detail was simply a proof of legs, not brains. It was reported in camp that Captain Boling had kept a record of the speedy ones which he had filed away for future use in cases where fleetness of foot would be required for extra duties.

Preparations were made for an early start the next morning. The officer to be left in charge of the camp was instructed to allow the Indians all liberty consistent with *safety*, and to exercise no personal restraint over them unless there should be an evident attempt to leave in a body; when, of course, any movement of the kind was to be defeated. The Major said: "I deem the presence of the women and children a sufficient hostage for the peaceful conduct of the men, but do not allow *any of them* to enter our tents, or we may lose possession."

This last injunction was to guard against annoyance from vermin. The *pediculi* of the Indian race have an especial affinity for them. White people have but little to fear from

Indian vermin except the temporary annoyance that is experienced from some species that infest animals and birds. They do not find the transfer congenial, and soon disappear. This fact may not be generally known, but I believe it to be a normal arrangement for the exclusive *comfort* of the Indian.

To me this is quite suggestive, when considered as evidence of a diversity of origin of the races. I have been very particular in my observations in this matter, and have compared my own with the experiences of others, and have been led to the conclusion that each separate race has parasites indigenous to that race, although the genus may be common to each.

This reluctant adaptability of these "entomological inconveniences" saved us from one of the curses of the ancient Egyptians, when contact was unavoidable.

As no information had been received from the camp of the Yosemites, after an early breakfast, the order was passed to "fall in," and when the order "march" was given, we moved off in single file, Savage leading, with Ten-ie-ya as guide.

From the length of time taken by the chief to go and return from his encampment, it was supposed that with horses, and an early start, we should be able to go and return the same day, if for any cause it should be deemed desirable, although sufficient supplies were taken, in case of a longer delay.

While ascending to the divide between the South Fork and the main Merced we found but little snow, but at the divide, and beyond, it was from three to five feet in depth, and in places much deeper. The sight of this somewhat cooled our ardor, but none asked for a "*furlough.*"

To somewhat equalize the laborious duties of making a trail, each man was required to take his turn in front.

The leader of the column was frequently changed; no horse or mule could long endure the fatigue without relief. To effect this, the tired leader dropped out of line, resigning his position to his followers, taking a place in the rear, on the beaten trail, exemplifying, that "the first shall be last, and the last shall be first." The snow packed readily, so that a very comfortable trail was left in the rear of our column.

Old Ten-ie-ya relaxed the rigidity of his bronze features, in admiration of our method of making a trail, and assured us, that, notwithstanding the depth of snow, we would soon reach his village. We had in our imaginations pictured it as in some deep rocky canon in the mountains.

While in camp the frantic efforts of the old chief to describe the location to Major Savage, had resulted in the unanimous verdict among the "boys," who were observing him, that "it must be a devil of a place." Feeling encouraged by the hope that we should soon arrive at the residences of his Satanic majesty's subjects, we wallowed on, alternately becoming the object of a joke, as we in turn were extricated from the drifts. When we had traversed a little more than half the distance, as was afterwards proved, we met the Yosemites on their way to our rendezvous on the South Fork.

As they filed past us, the major took account of their number, which was but seventy-two. As they reached our beaten trail, satisfaction was variously expressed, by grunts from the men, by the low rippling laughter from the squaws, and by the children clapping their hands in glee at the sight. On being asked where the others of his band were, the old Sachem said, "This is all of my people that are willing to go with me to the plains. Many that have been with me are from other tribes. They have taken wives from my band ; all have gone with their wives and children to the Tuolumne and to the Monos." Savage told Ten-ie-ya that he was telling him that which was not true. The Indians could not cross the mountains in the deep snow, neither could they go over the divide of the Tuolumne. That he knew they were still at his village or in hiding places near it. Ten-ie-ya assured the major he was telling him the truth, and in a very solemn manner declared that none of his band had been left behind—that all had gone before his people had left. His people had not started before because of the snow storm.

With a belief that but a small part of Ten-ei-ya's band was with this party, Major Savage decided to go on to the Indian village and ascertain if any others could be found or traces of them discovered. This decision was a satisfactory one and met with a hearty approval as it was reported along the line.

This tribe had been estimated by Pon-wat-chee and Cow-chit-tee, as numbering more than two hundred; as about that number usually congregated when they met together to "*cache*" their acorns in the valley, or for a grand annual hunt and drive of game; a custom which secured an abundant supply for the feast that followed.

At other times they were scattered in bands on the sunny slopes of the ridges, and in the mountain glens. Ten-ie-ya had been an unwilling guide thus far, and Major Savage said to him: "You may return to camp with your people, and I will take one of your young men with me. There are but few of your people here. Your tribe is large. I am going to your village to see your people, who will not come with you. They *will* come with me if I find them."

Savage then selected one of the young "braves" to accompany him. Ten-ie-ya replied, as the young Indian stepped forward by his direction, "I will go with my people; my young man shall go with you to my village. You will

not find any people there. I do not know where they are.
My tribe is small—not large, as the white chief has said.
The Pai-utes and Mono's are all gone. Many of the people
with my tribe are from western tribes that have come to
me and do not wish to return. If they go to the plains and
are seen, they will be killed by the friends of those with
whom they had quarreled. I have talked with my people
and told them I was going to see the white chiefs sent to
make peace. I was told that I was growing old, and it was
well that I should go, but that young and strong men can
find plenty in the mountains; therefore why should they
go? to be yarded like horses and cattle. My heart has been
sore since that talk, but I am now willing to go, for it is
best for my people that I do so."

The Major listened to the old Indian's volubility for
awhile, but interrupted him with a cheering "Forward
march!" at which the impatient command moved briskly
forward over the now partly broken trail, leaving the chief
alone, as his people had already gone on.

We found the traveling much less laborious than before,
and it seemed but a short time after we left the Indians
before we suddenly came in full view of the valley in
which was the village, or rather the encampments of
the Yosemities. The immensity of rock I had seen in my
vision on the Old Bear Valley trail from Ridley's Ferry
was here presented to my astonished gaze. The mystery
of that scene was here disclosed. My awe was increased by
this nearer view. The face of the immense cliff was shad-
owed by the declining sun; its outlines only had been seen
at a distance. This towering mass

> "Fools our fond gaze, and greatest of the great,
> Defies at first our Nature's littleness,
> Till, growing with (to) its growth, we thus dilate
> Our spirits to the size of that they contemplate."

That stupendous cliff is now known as "El Capitan" (the Captain), and the plateau from which we had our first view of the valley, as Mount Beatitude.

It has been said that "it is not easy to describe in words the precise impressions which great objects make upon us." I cannot describe how completely I realized this truth. None but those who have visited this most wonderful valley, can even imagine the feelings with which I looked upon the view that was there presented. The grandeur of the scene was but softened by the haze that hung over the valley,—light as gossamer—and by the clouds which partially dimmed the higher cliffs and mountains. This obscurity of vision but increased the awe with which I beheld it, and as I looked, a peculiar exalted sensation seemed to fill my whole being, and I found my eyes in tears with emotion.

During many subsequent visits to this locality, this sensation was never again so fully aroused. It is probable that the shadows fast clothing all before me, and the vapory clouds at the head of the valley, leaving the view beyond still undefined, gave a weirdness to the scene, that made it so impressive; and the conviction that it was utterly indescribable

EL CAPITAN.
(3,300 feet in height.)

added strength to the emotion. It is not possible for the same intensity of feeling to be aroused more than once by the same object, although I never looked upon these scenes except with wonder and admiration.

Richardson, in his admirable work, "Beyond the Mississippi," says: "See Yosemite and die! I shall not attempt to describe it; the subject is too large and my capacity too small. * * * Painfully at first these stupendous walls confuse the mind. By degrees, day after day, the sight of them clears it, until at last one receives a just impression of their solemn immensity. * * * Volumes ought to be and will be written about it."

Mr. Richardson has expressed in graphic language the impressions produced upon nearly all who for the first time behold this wonderful valley. The public has now, to a certain degree, been prepared for these scenes.

They are educated by the descriptions, sketches, photographs and masterly paintings of Hill and Bierstadt; whereas, on our first visit, our imagination had been misled by the descriptive misrepresentations of savages, whose prime object was to keep us from their safe retreat, until we had expected to see some terrible abyss. The reality so little resembled the picture of imagination, that my astonishment was the more overpowering.

To obtain a more distinct and *quiet* view, I had left the trail and my horse and wallowed through the snow alone to a projecting granite rock. So interested was I in the scene before me, that I did not observe that my comrades had all moved on, and that I would soon be left indeed alone. My situation attracted the attention of Major Savage,—who was riding in rear of column,—who hailed me from the trail below with, "you had better wake up from that dream up there, or you may lose your hair; I have no faith in Ten-ie-ya's statement that there are no Indians about here.

We had better be moving; some of the murdering devils may be lurking along this trail to pick off stragglers." I hurriedly joined the Major on the descent, and as other views presented themselves, I said with some enthusiasm, " If my hair is now required, I can depart in peace, for I have here seen the power and glory of a Supreme being; the majesty of His handy-work is in that 'Testimony of the Rocks.' That mute appeal—pointing to El Capitan—illustrates it, with more convincing eloquence than can the most powerful arguments of surpliced priests." " Hold up, Doc! you are soaring too high for me; and perhaps for yourself. This is rough riding; we had better mind this devilish trail, or we shall go *soaring* over some of these slippery rocks." We, however, made the descent in safety. When we overtook the others, we found blazing fires started, and preparations commenced to provide supper for the hungry command; while the light-hearted "boys" were indulging their tired horses with the abundant grass found on the meadow near by, which was but lightly covered with snow.

Mr. J. M. Hutchings has recently cited Elliott's History of Fresno County and dispatches from Major Savage as proof that it was May 5th or 6th, 1851, that the Maripcsa Battalion first entered the Yosemite. As a matter of fact, our adjutant was not with us when the discovery was made in March, nor was there ever but two companies in the Yosemite at any time, Boling's and part of Dill's. Captain Dill himself was detailed for duty at the Fresno, after the expedition in March, as was also the adjutant. In making out his report, Mr. Lewis must have ignored the first entry of the valley by the few men who discovered it, and made his first entry to appear as the date of the discovery. This may or may not have been done to give importance to the operations of the battalion. I have never seen the report.

CHAPTER IV.

My d vout astonishment at the supreme grandeur of the
scenery by which I was surrounded, continued to engross
my mind. The warmth of the fires and preparations for
supper, however, awakened in me other sensations, which
rapidly dissipated my excitement. As we rode up, Major
Savage remarked to Capt. Boling, "We had better move on
up, and hunt out the "Grizzlies" before we go into camp
for the night. We shall yet have considerable time to look
about this hole before dark." Captain Boling then reported
that the young guide had halted here, and poured out
a volley of Indian lingo which no one could understand,
and had given a negative shake of his head when the course
was pointed out, and signs were made for him to move on.
The Captain, not comprehending this performance, had followed the trail of the Indians to the bank of the stream
near by, but had not ventured further, thinking it best to
wait for Major Savage to come up. After a few inquiries,
the Major said there was a ford below, where the Indians
crossed the Merced; and that he would go with the guide
and examine it. Major Savage and Captains Boling and
Dill then started down to the crossing. They soon returned, and we were ordered to arrange our camp for the
night. Captain Boling said the Merced was too high to

ford. The river had swollen during the day from the melting of the snow, but would fall again by morning.

The guide had told the Major there was no other way up the valley, as it was impossible to pass the rocks on the south side of the stream. From this, it was evident the Major had never before seen the valley, and upon inquiry, said so. One of our best men, Tunnehill, who had been listening to what the Captain was saying, very positively remarked : "I have long since learned to discredit everything told by an Indian. I never knew one to tell the truth. This imp of Satan has been lying to the Major, and to me his object is very transparent. He knows a better ford than the one below us." A comrade laughingly observed : "Perhaps you can find it for the Major, and help him give us an evening ride; I have had all the exercise I need to-day, and feel as hungry as a wolf." Without a reply, Tunnehill mounted his little black mule and left at a gallop. He returned in a short time, at the same rapid gate, but was in a sorry plight. The mule and rider had unexpectedly taken a plunge bath in the ice-cold waters of the Merced. As such mishaps excited but little sympathy, Tunnehill was greeted with : "Hallo! what's the matter, comrade?" "Where do you get your washing done?" "Been trying to cool off that frisky animal, have you?" "Old Ten-ie-ya's Cañon is not in as hot a place as we supposed, is it?" "How about the reliability of the Indian race?" To all these bantering jokes, though in an uncomfortable plight, Tunnehill, with great good nature, replied : "I am all right! I believe in orthodox immersion, but this kind of baptism has only *confirmed* me in previous convictions." The shivering mule was rubbed, blanketed, and provided for, before his master attended to his own comfort, and then we learned that, in his attempt to explore a way across the Merced, his mule was swept off its feet, and both were carried for some distance down the raging torrent.

After supper, guards stationed, and the camp fires plentifully provided for, we gathered around the burning logs of oak and pine, found near our camp. The hearty supper and cheerful blaze created a general good

BRIDAL VEIL FALL.
(630 feet in height.)

feeling. Social converse and anecdotes—mingled with jokes—were freely exchanged, as we enjoyed the solace of our pipes and warmed ourselves preparatory to seeking further refreshment in sleep. While thus engaged, I retained a full consciousness of our locality; for being in close proximity to the huge cliff that had so attracted my attention, my mind was frequently drawn away from my comrades. After the jollity of the camp had somewhat subsided, the valley became the topic of conversation around our camp fire. None of us at that time, surmised the extreme vastness of those cliffs; although before dark, we had seen El Capitan looking down upon our camp, while the "Bridal Veil" was being wafted in the breeze. Many of us *felt* the mysterious grandeur of the scenery, as defined by our limited opportunity to study it. I had—previous to my descent with the Major—observed the towering height above us of the old "Rock Chief," and noticing the length of the steep descent into the valley, had at least some idea of its solemn immensity.

It may appear *sentimental*, but the coarse jokes of the careless, and the indifference of the practical, sensibly jarred my more devout feelings, while this subject was a matter of general conversation; as if a sacred subject had been ruthlessly profaned, or the visible power of Deity disregarded. After relating my observations from the "Old Bear Valley Trail," I suggested that this valley should have an appropriate name by which to designate it, and in a tone of pleasantry, said to Tunnehill, who was drying his wet clothing by our fire, "You are the first white man that ever received any form of baptism in this valley, and you should be considered the proper person to give a baptismal name to the valley itself." He replied, "If whisky can be provided for such a ceremony, I shall be happy to participate; but if it is to be another cold water affair, I have no desire to take a hand. I have done enough in that line for tonight." Timely jokes and ready repartee for a time changed the subject, but in the lull of this exciting pastime, some one remarked, "I like Bunnell's suggestion of giving this

valley a name, and to-night is a good time to do it." "All
right—if you have got one, show your hand," was the response of another. Different names were proposed, but
none were satisfactory to a majority of our circle. Some
romantic and foreign names were offered, but I observed
that a very large number were canonical and Scripture
names. From this I inferred that I was not the only one
in whom religious emotions or thoughts had been aroused
by the mysterious power of the surrounding scenery.

As I did not take a fancy to any of the names proposed,
I remarked that "an American name would be the most
appropriate;" that "I could not see any necessity for going
to a foreign country for a name for American scenery—the
grandest that had ever yet been looked upon. That it would
be better to give it an Indian name than to import a strange
and inexpressive one; that the name of the tribe who had
occupied it, would be more appropriate than any I had
heard suggested." I then proposed "that we give the
valley the name of Yo-sem-i-ty, as it was suggestive, euphonious, and certainly *American;* that by so doing, the
name of the tribe of Indians which we met leaving their
homes in this valley, perhaps never to return, would be per-
etuated." I was here interrupted by Mr. Tunnehill, who
impatiently exclaimed: "Devil take the Indians and their
ames! Why should we honor these vagabond murderers
y perpetuating their name?" Another said: "I agree with
Tunnehill; —— the Indians and their names. Mad An-
hony's plan for me! Let's call this Paradise Valley." In
reply, I said to the last speaker, "Still, for a young man
with such *religious tendencies* they would be good objects
on which to develop your Christianity." Unexpectedly, a
earty laugh was raised, which broke up further discus
ion, and before opportunity was given for any others to
object to the name, John O'Neal, a rollicking Texan of

Capt. Boling's company, vociferously announced to the whole camp the subject of our discussion, by saying, "Hear ye! Hear ye! Hear ye! A vote will now be taken to decide what name shall be given to this valley." The question of giving it the name of Yo-sem-i-ty was then explained; and upon a *viva voce* vote being taken, it was almost unanimously adopted. The name that was there and thus adopted by us, while seated around our camp fires, on the first visit of a white man to this remarkable locality, is the name by which it is now known to the world.

At the time I proposed this name, the signification of it (a grizzly bear) was not generally known to our battalion, although "the grizzlies" was frequently used to designate this tribe. Neither was it pronounced with uniformity. For a correct pronunciation, Major Savage was our best authority. He could speak the dialects of most of the mountain tribes in this part of California, but he confessed that he could not readily understand Ten-ie-ya, or the Indian guide, as they appeared to speak a Pai-ute jargon.

Major Savage checked the noisy demonstrations of our "Master of Ceremonies," but approvingly participated in our proceedings, and told us that the name was Yo-sem-i-ty, as pronounced by Ten-ie-ya, or O-soom-i-ty, as pronounced by some other bands; and that it signified a full-grown grizzly bear. He further stated, that the name was given to old Ten-ie-ya's band, because of their lawless and predatory character.

As I had observed that the different tribes in Mariposa County differed somewhat in the pronunciation of this name, I asked an explanation of the fact. With a smile and a look, as if he suspected I was quizzing him, the Major replied: "They only differ, as do the Swedes, Danes and Norwegians, or as in the different Shires of England; but you know well enough how similar in sound words may be of entirely different meaning, and how much depends on accent. I have found this to be the greatest difficulty a learner has to contend with."

After the name had been decided upon, the Major narrated some of his experiences in the use of the general "sign language"—as a Rocky Mountain man—and his practice of it when he first came among the California Indians, until he had acquired their language. The Major regarded the Kah-we-ah, as the parent language of the San-Joaquin Valley Indians, while that in use by the other mountain tribes in their vicinity, were but so many dialects of Kah-we-ah, the Pai-ute and more Northern tribes. When we sought our repose, it was with feelings of quiet satisfaction that I wrapped myself in my blankets, and soundly slept.

I consider it proper, to digress somewhat from a regular narrative of the incidents of our expedition, to consider some matters relative to the name "Yosemity." This was the form of orthography and pronunciation originally in use by our battalion. Lieutenant Moore, of the U. S. A. in his report of an expedition to the Valley in 1852, substituted *e* as the terminal letter, in place of *y*, in use by us; no doubt thinking the use of *e* more scholarly, or perhaps supposing Yosemite to be of Spanish derivation. This orthography has been adopted, and is in general use, but the proper pronunciation, as a consequence, is not always attainable to the general reader.

Sometime after the name had been adopted, I learned from Major Savage that Ten-ei-ya repudiated the name for the Valley, but proudly acknowledged it as the designation of his band, claiming that "when he was a young chief, this name had been selected because they occupied the mountains and valleys which were the favorite resort of the Grizzly Bears, and because his people were expert in killing them. That his tribe had adopted the name because those who had bestowed it were afraid of 'the Grizzlies' and feared his band."

It was traditionary with the other Indians, that the band to which the name Yosemite had been given, had originally been formed and was then composed of outlaws or refugees from other tribes. That nearly all were descendants of the neighboring tribes on both sides of "Kay-o-pha," or "*Skye Mountains;*" the "High Sierras."

Ten-ie-ya was asked concerning this tradition, and responded rather loftily: "I am the descendant of an Ah-wah-ne-chee chief. His people lived in the mountains and valley where my people have lived. The valley was then called Ah-wah-nee. Ah-wah-ne-chee signifies the dwellers in Ahwahnee."

I afterwards learned the traditional history of Ten-ie-ya's ancestors. His statement was to the effect, that the Ah-wah-ne-chees had many years ago been a large tribe, and lived in territory now claimed by him and his people. That by wars, and a fatal black-sickness (probably small-pox or measles), nearly all had been destroyed. The survivors of the band fled from the valley and joined other tribes. For years afterward, the country was uninhabited; but few of the extinct tribe ever visited it, and from a superstitious fear, it was avoided. Some of his ancestors had gone to the Mono tribe and been adopted by them. His father had taken a wife from that tribe. His mother was a Mono woman, and he had lived with her people while young. Eventually, Ten-ie-ya, with some of his father's tribe had visited the valley, and claimed it as their birth-right. He thus became the founder of the new tribe or band, which has since been called the "Yosemite."

It is very probable that the statement of Major Savage, as to the origin of the name as applicable to Ten-ie-ya's band, was traditional with his informants, but I give credit to Ten-ie-ya's own history of his tribe as most probable.

From my knowledge of Indian customs, I am aware that it is not uncommon for them to change the names of persons or localities after some remarkable event in the history of either. It would not, therefore, appear strange that Ten-ie-ya should have adopted another name for his band. I was unable to fix upon any definite date at which the Ah-wah-ne-cliees became extinct as a tribe, but from the fact that some of the Yosemites claimed to be direct descendants, the time could not have been as long as would be inferred from their descriptions. When these facts were communicated to Captain Boling, and Ah-wah-ne was ascertained to be the *classical* name, the Captain said that name was all right enough for history or poetry, but that we could not now change the name Yosemite, nor was it desirable to do so. I made every effort to ascertain the signification of Ah-wah-ne, but could never fully satisfy myself, as I received different interpretations at different times. In endeavoring to ascertain from Ten-ie-ya his explanation of the name, he, by the motion of his hands, indicated depth.

It is not uncommon for the mountain men and traders, to acquire a mixed jargon of Indian dialects, which they mingle with Spanish, French or English in their talk to an extent sometimes amusing. The Indians readily adopt words from this lingo, and learn to Anglicize Indian names in conversation with "Americans." This, when done by the Mission Indians, who perhaps have already made efforts to improve the Indian name with Mission Spanish, tends to mislead the inquirer after "*pure*" *Indian names.*

The Mission Indians after deserting, introduced and applied Spanish names to objects that already had Indian designations, and in this way, new words are formed from corrupted Mission Spanish, that may lead to wrong interpretations. I learned from Russio, the chief interpreter, that sometimes more than one word was used to express the same object, and often one word expressed different objects. As an illustration of corrupted Spanish that passes for Indian, the words Oya (olla) and Hoya, may be taken. Oya signifies a water pot, and Hoya, a pit hole. From these words the Mission Indians have formed "Loya," which is used to designate camp grounds where holes in the rocks may be found near, in which to pulverize acorns, grass seeds, &c., as well as to the "Sentinal Rock," from its fancied resemblance to a water pot, or long water *basket.* Another source of difficulty, is that of representing by written characters the echoing guttural sounds of some Indian words. While being aware of this, I can safely assert that Yosemite, is purer and better Indian than is Mississippi, ("Me-ze-se-be," the river that runs every where; that is, "Endless river) or many other names that are regarded as good if not *pure Indian.**

* According to the Rev. S. G. Wright, of Leach Lake, Minnesota Reservation, and "*Wain-ding*" (the source of the wind), the best interpreters of the Chippewa perhaps now living, but few, if any, of the Chippewa names for our lakes and rivers have been preserved in their purity.

Our interpretors were, or had been, Mission Indians, who rendered the dialects into as good Spanish as they had at command, but rather than fail in their office, for want of words, they would occasionally insert one of their own coining. This was done, regardless of the consequences, and when chided, declared it was for our benefit they had done so.

Attempts were made to supersede the name we had given the valley, by substituting some fancied improvements. At first, I supposed these to be simply changes rung on Yosemite, but soon observed the earnestness of the sponsors in advocating the new names, in their magazine and newspaper articles. They claimed to have acquired the *correct name* from their Indian guides, employed on their visits to the Yosemite.

In 1855 Mr. J. M. Hutchings, of San Francisco, visited the Yosemite, and published a description of it, and also published a lithograph of the Yosemite Fall. Through his energetic efforts, the valley was more fully advertised. He ambitiously gave it the name of Yo-Hamite, and tenaciously adhered to it for some time ; though Yosemite had already crystalized.

The Rev. Doctor Scott, of San Francisco, in a newspaper article—disappointing to his admirers—descriptive of his travels and sojourn there, endeavored to dispossess both Mr. Hutchings and myself of our names, and *named* the valley Yo-Amite : probably as a *peace* offering to us both.

I did not at first consider it good policy to respond to these articles. I had no desire to engage in a newspaper controversy with such influences against me; but after solicitations from Mr. Ayers, and other friends, I gave the facts upon which were based editorials in the "California Chronicle," "Sacramento Union," the Mariposa and other papers.

By invitation of Mr. Hutchings, I had a personal interview with him in San Francisco, relative to this matter, and at his request furnished some of the incidents connected with our expedition against the Indians, as hereinbefore narrated. These he published in his magazine, and afterwards in his "Scenes of Wonder and Curiosity in California."

This statement of facts was signed by myself, and certified to by two members of the State legislature—James M. Roan and George H. Crenshaw—as follows: "We, the undersigned, having been members of the same company, and through most of the scenes depicted by Doctor Bunnel', have no hesitation in saying that the article above is correct."

Mr. Hutchings says: "We cheerfully give place to the above communication, that the public may learn how and by whom this remarkable valley was first visited and named; and, although we have differed with the writer and others concerning the name given, as explained in several articles that have appeared at different times in the several newspapers of the day, in which Yo-Hamite was preferred; yet as Mr. Bunnell was among the first to visit the valley, we most willingly accord to him the right of giving it whatsoever name he pleases."

Mr. Hutchings then goes on to explain how he obtained the name Yo-Hamite from his Indian guide Kos-sum; that its correctness was affirmed by John Hunt, previous to the publication of the lithograph of the great falls, etc., and during this explanation, says: "Up to this time we had never heard or known any other name than Yosemite;" and farther on in a manly way says: "Had we before known that Doctor Bunnell and his party were the first whites who ever entered the valley (although we have the honor of being *the first in later years to visit it and call public at-*

tention to it), we should long ago have submitted to the name Doctor Bunnell had given it, as the discoverer of the valley."

After my interview with Mr. Hutchings—for I had never heard the word Yo-Hamite until it was published by him—I asked John Hunt, the Indian trader referred to, where he had got the word furnished to Mr. Hutchings. John, with some embarrassment, said, that "Yo-Hem-i-te was the way his Indians pronounced the name." I asked what name? "Why, Yosemite," said John. But, I replied, you know that the Indian name for the valley is Ah-wah-ne! and the name given by us was the name of Ten-ie-ya's band? "Of course, (said John,) but my Indians now apply the word Yo-Hemite to the valley or the territory adjacent, though their name for a bear is Osoomity." John Hunt's squaw was called, and asked by him the meaning of the word, but confessed her ignorance. Mr. Cunningham was also consulted, but could give us no certain information; but surmised that the word had been derived from "Le-Hamite 'The Arrowwood.'" Another said possibly from "Hem-nock," the Kah-we-ah word for God. As to Yo-Amite, insisted on by Doctor Scott, I made no effort to find an interpretation of it.

CHAPTER V.

THE date of our discovery and entrance into the Yosemite
was about the 21st of March, 1851. We were afterward
assured by Ten-ie-ya and others of his band, that this was
the first visit ever made to this valley by white men. Ten-
ie-ya said that a small party of white men once crossed the
mountains on the North side, but were so guided as not to
see it; Appleton's and the People's Encyclopedias to the
contrary notwithstanding. *

It was to prevent the recurrence of such an event, that
Ten-ie-ya had consented to go to the commissioner's camp
and make peace, intending to return to his mountain home
as soon as the excitement from the recent outbreak subsided. The entrance to the Valley had ever been carefully
guarded by the old chief, and the people of his band. As
a part of its traditionary history, it was stated: "That
when Ten-ie-ya left the tribe of his mother and went to
live in Ah-wah-ne, he was accompanied by a very old Ah-

---

* Captain Joe Walker, for whom "Walker's Pass" is named, told me
that he once passed qu'te near the valley on one of his mountain trips;
but that his Ute and Mono guides gave such a dismal account of the
canons of both rivers, that he kept his course near to the divide until
reaching Bull Creek, he descended and went into camp, not seeing the
valley proper.

wah-ne-chee, who had been the great 'medicine man' of his tribe."

It was through the influence of this old friend of his father that Ten-ie-ya was induced to leave the Mono tribe, and with a few of the descendants from the Ah-wah-nee-chees, who had been living with the Monos and Pai-Utes, to establish himself in the valley of his ancestors as their chief. He was joined by the descendants from the Ah-wah-ne-chees, and by others who had fled from their own tribes to avoid summary Indian justice. The old "medicine man" was the counselor of the young chief. Not long before the death of this patriarch, as if endowed with prophetic wisdom, he assured Ten-ie-ya that while he retained possession of Ah-wah-ne his band would increase in numbers and become powerful. That if he befriended those who sought his protection, no other tribe would come to the valley to make war upon him, or attempt to drive him from it, and if he obeyed his counsels he would put a spell upon it that would hold it sacred for him and his people alone; none other would ever dare to make it their home. He then cautioned the young chief against the horsemen of the lowlands (the Spanish residents), and declared that, should they enter Ah-wah-ne, his tribe would soon be scattered and destroyed, or his people be taken captive, and he himself be the last chief in Ah-wah-ne.

For this reason, Ten-ie-ya declared, had he so rigidly guarded his valley home, and all who sought his protection. No one ventured to enter it, except by his permission; all feared the "witches" there, and his displeasure. He had "made war upon the white gold diggers to drive them from the mountains, and prevent their entrance into Ah-wah-ne."

The Yo-sem-i-tes had been the most warlike of the mountain tribes in this part of California; and the Ah-wah-ne-chee and Mono members of it, were of finer build and lighter color than those commonly called "California Digger Indians." Even the "Diggers" of the band, from association and the better food and air afforded in the mountains, had become superior to their inheritance, and as a tribe, the Yosemites were feared by other Indians.

The superstitious fear of annihilation had, however, so depressed the warlike ardor of Ten-ie-ya, who had now become an old man, that he had decided to make efforts to conciliate the Americans, rather than further resist their occupancy of the mountains; as thereby, he hoped to save his valley from intrusion. In spite of Ten-ie-ya's cunning, the prophecies of the "old medicine" man have been mostly fulfilled. White horsemen have entered Ah-wah-ne; the tribe has been scattered and destroyed. Ten-ie-ya was the last chief of his people. He was killed by the chief of the Monos, not because of the prophecy; nor yet because of our entrance into his territory, but in retribution for a crime against the Mono's hospitality. But I must not, Indian like, tell the latter part of my story first.

After an early breakfast on the morning following our entrance into the Yosemite, we equipped ourselves for duty; and as the word was passed to "fall in," we mounted and filed down the trail to the lower ford, ready to commence our explorations.

The water in the Merced had fallen some during the night, but the stream was still in appearance a raging torrent. As we were about to cross, our guide with earnest gesticulations asserted that the water was too deep to cross, that if we attempted it, we would be swept down into the cañon. That later, we could cross without difficulty. These assertions angered the Major, and he told the guide that he lied; for he knew that later in the day the snow would melt.

Turning to Captain Boling he said: "I am now positive that the Indians are in the vicinity, and for that reason the guide would deceive us." Telling the young Indian to remain near his person, he gave the order to cross at once.

The ford was found to be rocky; but we passed over it without serious difficulty, although several repeated their morning ablutions while stumbling over the boulders.

The open ground on the north side was found free from snow. The trail led toward "El Capitan," which had from the first, been the particular object of my admiration.

At this time no distinctive names were known by which to designate the cliffs, waterfalls, or any of the especial objects of interest, and the imaginations of some ran wild in search of *appropriate* ones. None had any but a limited idea of the height of this cliff, and but few appeared conscious of the vastness of the granite wall before us; although an occasional ejaculation betrayed the feelings which the imperfect comprehension of the grand and wonderful excited. A few of us remarked upon the great length of time required to pass it, and by so doing, probably arrived at more or less correct conclusions regarding its size.

Soon after we crossed the ford, smoke was seen to issue from a cluster of manzanita shrubs that commanded a view of the trail. On examination, the smoking brands indicated that it had been a picket fire, and we now felt assured that our presence was known and our movements watched by the vigilant Indians we were hoping to find. Moving rapidly on, we discovered near the base of El Capitan, quite a large collection of Indian huts, situated near Pigeon creek. On making a hasty examination of the village and vicinity, no Indians could be found, but from the generally undisturbed condition of things usually found in an Indian camp, it was evident that the occupants had but recently left; appearances indicated that some of the wigwams or huts had been occupied during the night   Not far from the camp, upon posts, rocks, and in trees, was a large *caché* of acorns and other provisions.

As the trail showed that it had been used by Indians go-

HALF DOME.
(4,737 feet in height.)

ing up, but a short halt was made. As we moved on, a smoke was again seen in the distance, and some of the more eager ones dashed ahead of the column, but as we reached the ford to which we were led by the main trail leading to the right, our dashing cavaliers rejoined us and again took their places. These men reported that "fallen rocks" had prevented their passage up on the north side, and that our only course was to cross at the ford and follow the trail, as the low lands appeared too wet for rapid riding. Recrossing the Merced to the south-side, we found trails leading both up and down the river. A detachment was sent down to reconnoitre the open land below, while the main column pursued its course. The smoke we had seen was soon discovered to be rising from another encampment nearly

NORTH DOME AND ROYAL ARCHES,
(3,568 feet in height.)

south of the "Royal Arches;" and at the forks of the Ten-ie-ya branch of the Merced, near the south-west base of the "Half Dome," still another group of huts was brought to view.

These discoveries necessitated the recrossing of the river, which had now again become quite swollen; but by this time our horses and ourselves had become used to the icy waters, and when at times our animals lost their footing at the fords, they were not at all alarmed, but vigorously swam to the shore.

Abundant evidences were again found to indicate that the huts here had but just been deserted; that they had been occupied that morning. Although a rigid search was made, no Indians were found. Scouting parties in charge of Lieutenants Gilbert and Chandler, were sent out to examine each branch of the valley, but this was soon found to be an impossibe task to accomplish in one day. While exploring among the rocks that had fallen from the "Royal Arches" at the southwesterly base of the North Dome, my attention was attracted to a huge rock stilted upon some smaller ones. Cautiously glancing underneath, I was for a moment startled by a living object. Involuntarily my rifle was brought to bear on it, when I discovered the object to be a female; an extremely old squaw, but with a countenance that could only be likened to a vivified Egyptian mummy. This creature exhibited no expression of alarm, and was apprently indifferent to hope or fear, love or hate. I hailed one of my comrades on his way to camp, to report to Major Savage that I had discovered a peculiar living ethnological curiosity, and to bring something for it to eat. She was seated on the ground, hovering over the remnants of an almost exhausted fire. I replenished her supply of fuel, and waited for the Major. She neither spoke or exhibited any curiosity as to my presence.

Major Savage soon came, but could elicit nothing of importance from her. When asked where her companions were, she understood the dialect used, for she very curtly replied "You can hunt for them if you want to see them"! When asked why she was left alone, she replied "I am too old to climb the rocks"! The Major—forgetting the gallantry due her sex—inquired "How old are you?" With an ineffably scornful grunt, and a coquettish leer at the Major, she maintained an indignant silence. This attempt at a smile, left the Major in doubt as to her age. Subse-

CATHEDRAL ROCKS
(2,660 feet in height.)

quently, when Ten-ie-ya was interrogated as to the age of this old squaw, he replied that "No one knows her age. That when he was a boy, it was a favorite *tradition* of the *old* members of his band, that when she was a child, the peaks of the Sierras were but little hills." This free interpretation was given by the Major, while seated around the camp fire at night. If not *reliable*, it was excessively amusing to the "Boys," and added to the Major's popularity. On a subsequent visit to the Valley, an attempt was made to send the old creature to the commissioner's camp; she was placed on a mule and started. As she could not bear the fatigue, she was left with another squaw. We learned that she soon after departed "to *the happy land in the West.*"

The detachment sent down the trail reported the discovery of a small rancheria, a short distance above the "Cathedral Rocks," but the huts were unoccupied. They also reported the continuance of the trail down the left bank. The other detachments found huts in groups, but no Indians. At all of these localities the stores of food were abundant.

Their *cachés* were principally of acorns, although many contained bay (California laurel), Piñon pine (Digger pine), and chinquepin nuts, grass seeds, wild rye or oats (scorched), dried worms, scorched grasshoppers, and what proved to be the dried larvæ of insects, which I was afterwards told were gathered from the waters of the lakes in and east of the Sierra Nevada. It was by this time quite clear that a large number of Ten-ie-ya's band was hidden in the cliffs or among the rocky gorges or cañons, not accessible to us from the knowledge we then had of their trails and passes. We had not the time, nor had we supplied ourselves sufficiently to hunt them out. It was therefore decided that the best policy was to destroy their huts and stores, with a view of starving them out, and of thus compelling them to come in and join with Ten-ie-ya and the people with him on the reservation. At this conclusion the destruction of their property was ordered, and at once commenced. While this work was in progress, I indulged my curiosity in examining the lodges in which had been left their home property, domestic, useful and ornamental. As compared with eastern tribes, their supplies of furniture of all kinds, excepting baskets, were meagre enough.

These baskets were quite numerous, and were of various patterns and for different uses. The large ones were made either of bark, roots of the Tamarach or Cedar, Willow or

Tule. Those made for gathering and transporting food supplies, were of large size and round form, with a sharp apex, into which, when inverted and placed upon the back, everything centres. This form of basket enables the carriers to keep their balance while passing over seemingly impassable rocks, and along the verge of dangerous precipices. Other baskets found served as water buckets. Others again of various sizes were used as cups and soup bowls; and still another kind, made of a tough, wiry grass, closely woven and cemented, was used for kettles for boiling food. The boiling was effected by hot stones being continually plunged into the liquid mass, until the desired result was obtained.

The water baskets were also made of "wire-grass;" being porous, evaporation is facilitated, and like the porous earthen water-jars of Mexico, and other hot countries, the water put into them is kept cool by evaporation. There were also found at some of the encampments, robes or blankets made from rabbit and squirrel skins, and from skins of water-fowl. There were also ornaments and musical instruments of a rude character. The instruments were drums and flageolets. The ornaments were of bone, bears' claws, birds' bills and feathers. The thread used by these Indians, I found was spun or twisted from the inner bark of a species of the asclepias or milk-weed, by ingeniously suspending a stone to the fibre, and whirling it with great rapidity. Sinews are chiefly used for sewing skins, for covering their bows and feathering their arrows. Their fish spears were but a single tine of bone, with a cord so attached near the centre, that when the spear, loosely placed in a socket in the pole, was pulled out by the struggles of the fish, the tine and cord would hold it as securely as though held by a barbed hook.

There were many things found that only an Indian could

possibly use, and which it would be useless for me to attempt to describe; such, for instance, as stag-horn hammers, deer prong punches (for making arrow-heads), obsidian, pumice-stone and salt brought from the eastern slope of the Sierras and from the desert lakes. In the hurry of their departure they had left everything. The numerous bones of animals scattered about the camps, indicated their love of horse-flesh as a diet.

Among these relics could be distinguished the bones of horses and mules, as well as other animals, eaten by these savages. Deers and bears were frequently driven into the valley during their seasons of migration, and were killed by expert hunters perched upon rocks and in trees that commanded their runways or trails; but their chief dependence for meat was upon horseflesh.

Among the relics of stolen property were many things recognized by our "boys," while applying the torch and giving all to the flames. A comrade discovered a bridle and part of a riata or rope which was stolen from him with a mule *while waiting for the commissioners to inquire into the cause of the war with the Indians!* No animals of any kind were kept by the Yosemites for any length of time except dogs, and they are quite often sacrificed to gratify their pride and appetite, in a dog feast. Their highest estimate of animals is only as an article of food. Those stolen from the settlers were not kept for their usefulness, except as additional camp supplies. The acorns found were alone estimated at from four to six hundred bushels.

During our explorations we were on every side astonished at the colossal representations of cliffs, rocky cañons and water-falls which constantly challenged our attention and admiration.

Occasionally some fragment of a garment was found, or

other sign of Indians, but no trail could be discovered by *our* eyes. Tired and almost exhausted in the fruitless search for Indians, the footmen returned to the place at which they had left their horses in the cañons, and in very thankfulness caressed them with delight.

In subsequent visits, this region was thoroughly explored and names given to prominent objects and localities.

While searching for hidden stores, I took the opportunity to examine some of the numerous sweat-houses noticed on the bank of the Merced, below a large camp near the mouth of the Ten-ie-ya branch. It may not be out of place to here give a few words in description of these conveniences of a permanent Indian encampment, and the uses for which they are considered a necessity.

The remains of these structures are sometimes mis aken for Tumuli. They were constructed of poles, bark, grass and mud. The frame-work of poles is first covered with bark, reeds or grass, and then the mud—as tenacious as the soil will admit of—is spread thickly over it. The structure is in the form of a dome, resembling a huge round mound. After being dried by a slight fire, kindled inside, the mud is covered with earth of a sufficient depth to shed the rain from without, and prevent the escape of heat from within. A small opening for ingress and egress is left; this comprises the extent of the house when complete, and ready for use. These sweat-baths are used as a luxury, as a curative for disease, and as a convenience for cleansing the skin, when necessity demands it, although the Indian race is not noted for cleanliness.

As a luxury, no Russian or Turkish bath is more enjoyed by civilized people, than are these baths by the Mountain Indians. I have seen a half dozen or more enter one of these rudely constructed sweat-houses, through the small aperture left for the purpose. Hot stones are taken in, the aperture is closed until suffocation would seem impending, when they would crawl out reeking with perspiration, and with a shout, spring like acrobats into the cold waters of the stream. As a remedial agent for disease, the same course is pursued, though varied at times by the burning and inhalation of resinous boughs and herbs.

In the process for cleansing the skin from impurities, hot air alone is generally used. If an Indian had passed the usual period for mourning for a relative, and the adhesive pitch too tenaciously clung to his no longer sorrowful countenance, he would enter, and re-enter the heated house, until the cleansing had become complete.

The mourning pitch is composed of the charred bones and ashes of their dead relative or friend. These remains of the funeral pyre, with the charcoal, are pulverized and mixed with the resin of the pine. This hideous mixture is usually retained upon the face of the mourner until it wears off. If it has been well compounded, it may last nearly a year; although the young—either from a super-abundance of vitality, excessive reparative powers of the skin, or from powers of will—seldom mourn so long. When the bare surface exceeds that covered by the pitch, it is not a scandalous disrespect in the young to remove it entirely; but a mother will seldom remove pitch or garment until both are nearly worn out.

In their camps were found articles from the miners' camps, and from the unguarded "ranchman." There was no lack of evidence that the Indians who had deserted their villages or wigwams, were truly entitled to the *soubriquet* of "the Grizzlies," "the lawless."

Although we repeatedly discovered fresh trails leading from the different camps, all traces were soon lost among the rocks at the base of the cliffs. The debris or talus not only afforded places for temporary concealment, but provided facilities for escape without betraying the direction. If by chance a trail was followed for a while, it would at last be traced to some apparently inaccessible ledge, or to the foot of some slippery depression in the walls, up which we did not venture to climb. While scouting up the Ten-ie-ya cañon, above Mirror Lake, I struck the fresh trail of quite a large number of Indians. Leaving our horses, a few of us followed up the tracks until they were lost in the ascent up the cliff. By careful search they were again found and followed until finally they hopelessly disappeared.

Tiring of our unsuccessful search, the hunt was abandoned, although we were convinced that the Indians had in some way passed up the cliff.

During this time, and while descending to the valley, I partly realized the great height of the cliffs and high fall. I had observed the height we were compelled to climb before the Talus had been overcome, though from below this appeared insignificant, and after reaching the summit of our ascent, the cliffs still towered above us. It was by instituting these comparisons while ascending and descending, that I was able to form a better judgment of altitude; for while entering the valley,—although, as before stated, I had observed the towering height of El Capitan,—my mind had been so preoccupied with the marvelous, that comparison had scarcely performed its proper function.

The level of the valley proper now appeared quite distant as we looked down upon it, and objects much less than full size. As night was fast approaching, and a storm threatened, we returned down the trail and took our course for the rendezvous selected by Major Savage, in a grove of oaks near the mouth of "Indian Cañon."

While on our way down, looking across to and up the south or Glacier Cañon, I noticed its beautiful fall, and planned an *excursion* for the morrow. I almost forgot my fatigue, in admiration of the solemn grandeur within my view; the lofty walls, the towering domes and numerous water-falls; their misty spray blending with the clouds settling down from the higher mountains.

The duties of the day had been severe on men and horses, for beside fording the Merced several times, the numerous branches pouring over cliffs and down ravines from the melting snow, rendered the overflow of the bottom lands so constant that we were often compelled to splash through the water-courses that later would be dry. These torrents of cold water, commanded more especial attention, and excited more *comment* than did the grandeur of the cliffs and water-

GLACIER FALL.
(550 feet in height.)

falls. We were not a party of tourists, seeking recreation, nor philosophers investigating the operations of nature. Our business there was to find Indians who were endeavoring to escape from our *charitable* intentions toward them. But very few of the volunteers seemed to have any appreciation of the wonderful proportions of the enclosing granite rocks; their curiosity had been to see the stronghold of the enemy, and the *general* verdict was that it was gloomy enough.

Tired and wet, the independent scouts sought the camp and reported their failures. Gilbert and Chandler came in with their detachments just at dark, from their tiresome explorations of the southern branches. Only a small squad of their commands climbed above the Vernal and Nevada falls; and seeing the clouds resting upon the mountains above the Nevada Fall, they retraced their steps through the showering mist of the Vernal, and joined their comrades, who had already started down its rocky gorge. These men found no Indians, but they were the first discoverers of the Vernal and Nevada Falls, and the Little Yosemite. They reported what they had seen to their assembled comrades at the evening camp-fires. Their names have now passed from my memory—not having had an intimate personal acquaintance with them—for according to my recollection they belonged to the company of Capt. Dill.

While on our way down to camp we met Major Savage with a detachment who had been burning a large *caché* located in the fork, and another small one below the mouth of the Ten-ie-ya branch. This had been held in reserve for possible use, but the Major had now fired it, and the flames were leaping high. Observing his movements for a few moments we rode up and made report of our unsuccessful efforts. I briefly, but with some enthusiasm, described my view from the cliff up the North Cañon, the Mirror Lake view of the Half Dome, the Fall of the South Cañon and the view of the distant South Dome. I volunteered a suggestion that some new tactics would have to be devised before we should be able to corral the "Grizzlies" or "smoke them out." The Major looked up from the charred mass of burning acorns, and as he glanced down the smoky val-

ley, said: "This affords us the best prospect of any yet dis.
covered; just look!" "Splendid!" I promptly replied,
Yo-sem-i-te must be beautifully grand a few weeks later,
when the foliage and flowers are at their prime, and the
rush of water has somewhat subsided. Such cliffs and water-falls I never saw before, and I doubt if they exist in any
other place."

VERNAL FALL.
(350 feet in height.)

I was surprised
and somewhat ir-
ritated by the
hearty laugh with
which my reply
was greeted. The
Major caught the
expression of my
eye and shrugged
his shoulders as
he hastily said: "I
suppose that is all
right, Doctor,
about the water-
falls, &c., for there
are enough of
them here for one
locality, as we
have all discover-
ed; but my re-
mark was not in
reference to the
scenery, but the
prospect of the
Indians being starved out, and of their coming in to sue for
peace. We have all been more or less wet since we rolled up
our blankets this morning, and this fire is very enjoyable, but

the prospect that it offers to my mind of *smoking out* the Indians, is more agreeable to me than its warmth or all the scenery in creation. I know, Doc., that there is a good deal of iron in you, but there is also considerable sentiment, and I am not in a very sentimental mood." I replied that I did not think that any of us felt very much like making love or writing poetry, but that Ten-ie-ya's remark to him about the "Great Spirit" providing so bountifully for his people, had several times oc-curred to me since entering here, and that no doubt to Ten-ie-ya, this

NEVADA FALL.
(600 feet in height.)

was a veritable Indian paradise. "Well," said the Major, "as far as that is con-cerned, although I have not carried a Bible with me since I became a mount-ain-man, I remember well enough that Satan entered paradise and did all the mischief he could, but I intend to be a bigger devil in this Indian paradise than old Satan ever was; and when I leave, I don't intend to *crawl* out, either. Now Doc. we will go to camp but let me say while upon the subject, that we are in no condition to judge fairly of this valley. The annoyances and disappointments of a fruitless search, together with the certainty of a snow-storm approaching, makes all this beautiful scenery appear to me gloomy enough. In a word, it is what we supposed it to be before seeing it, a h—— a place. The valley, no doubt, will always be a wonder for its grouping of cliffs and water-falls, but hemmed in by walls of rock, your vision turned in, as it were, upon yourself—a residence here would be anything but desirable for me. Any one of the Rocky Mountain parks would be preferable, while the ease with which buffalo, black-tail and big-horn could be provided in the "Rockies" would, in comparison, make your Indian paradise anything but desirable, even for these Indians."

The more practical tone and views of the Major dampened the ardor of my fancy in investing the valley with all desirable qualities, but as we compared with each other the experiences of the day, it was very clear that the half had not yet been seen or told, and that repeated views would be required before any one person could say that he had seen the Yosemite. It will probably be as well for me to say here that though Major Savage commanded the first expedition to the valley, he never revisited it, and died without ever having seen the Vernal and Nevada Falls, or any of the views belonging to the region of the Yosemite, except those seen from the valley and from the old Indian trail on our first entrance.

We found our camp had been plentifully supplied with dry wood by the provident guard, urged, no doubt, by the threatening appearances of another snow-storm. Some rude shelters of poles and brush were thrown up around the fires, on which were placed the drying blankets, the whole serving as an improvement on our bivouac accomodations. The night was colder than the previous one, for the wind was coming down the cañons of the snowy Sierras. The fires were lavishly piled with the dry oak wood, which sent out a glowing warmth. The fatigue and exposure of the day were forgotten in the hilarity with which supper was devoured by the hungry scouts while steaming in their wet garments. After supper Major Savage announced that "from the very extensive draft on the commissary stores just made, it was necessary to return to the 'South Fork.'" He said that it would be advisable for us to return, as we were not in a condition to endure delay if the threatened storm should prove to be a severe one; and ordered both Captains Boling and Dill to have their companies ready for the march at daylight the next morning.

While enjoying the warmth of the fire preparatory to a night's rest, the incidents of our observations during the day were interchanged. The probable heights of the cliffs was discussed. One *official* estimated "El Capitan" at 400 feet!! Capt. Boling at 800 feet; Major Savage was in no mood to venture an opinion. My estimate was a sheer perpendicularity of at least 1500 feet. Mr. C. H. Spencer, son of Prof. Thomas Spencer, of Geneva, N. Y.,— who had traveled quite extensively in Europe,—and a French gentleman, Monsieur Bouglinval, a civil engineer, who had joined us for the sake of adventure, gave me their opinions that my estimate was none too high; that it was probable that I was far below a correct measurement, for when there was so much sameness of height the judgment could not very well be assisted by comparison, and hence instrumental measurements alone could be relied on. Time has demonstrated the correctness of their opinions. These gentlemen were men of education and practical experience in observing the heights of objects of which measurement had been made, and quietly reminded their auditors that it was difficult to measure such massive objects with the eye alone. That some author had said : " But few persons have a correct judgment of height that rises above sixty feet."

I became somewhat earnest and enthusiastic on the subject of the valley, and expressed myself in such a positive manner that the "*enfant terrible*" of the company derisively asked if I was given to exaggeration before I became an "Indian fighter." From my ardor in description, and admiration of the scenery, I found myself nicknamed "Yosemity" by some of the battalion. It was customary among the mountain men and miners to prefix distinctive names. From this hint I became less *expressive*, when conversing on matters relating to the valley. My self-respect caused me to talk less among my comrades generally, but with intimate friends the subject was always an open one, and my estimates of heights were never reduced.

Major Savage took no part in this camp discussion, but on our expressing a design to revisit the valley at some future time, he assured us that there was a probability of our being fully gratified, for if the renegades did not voluntarily come in, another visit would soon have to be made by the battalion, when we could have opportunity to measure the rocks if we then desired. That we should first escort our "captives" to the commissioners' camp on the Fresno; that by the time we returned to the valley the trails would be clear of snow, and we would be able to explore to our satisfaction. Casting a quizzing glance at me, he said: " The rocks will probably keep, but you will not find all of these immense *water-powers*."

Notwithstanding a little warmth of discussion, we cheerfully wrapped ourselves in our blankets and slept, until awakened by the guard; for there had been no disturbance during the night. The snow had fallen only to about the depth of an inch in the valley, but the storm still continued.

By early dawn "all ready" was announced, and we started back without having seen any of the Indian race except our useless guide and the old squaw. Major Savage rode at the head of the column, retracing our trail, rather than attempt to follow down the south side. The water was relatively low in the early morning, and the fords were passed without difficulty. While passing El Capitan I felt like saluting, as I would some dignified acquaintance.

The *cachés* below were yet smouldering, but the lodges had disappeared.

At our entrance we had closely followed the Indian trail over rocks that could not be re-ascended with animals. To return, we were compelled to remove a few obstructions of poles, brush and loose rocks, placed by the Indians to prevent the escape of the animals stolen and driven down. Entire herds had been sometimes taken from the ranches or their ranges.

After leaving the valley, but little difficulty was encountered. The snow had drifted into the hollows, but had not to any extent obscured the trail, which we now found quite hard. We reached the camp earlier in the day than we had reason to expect. During these three days of absence from headquarters, we had discovered, named and partially explored one of the most remarkable of the geographical wonders of the world.

CHAPTER VI.

ON our arrival at the rendezvous on the South Fork the officer in charge reported: "We are about out of grub." This was a satisfactory cause for a hurried movement; for a short allowance had more terrors for men with our appetites than severe duties; and most of us had already learned that, even with prejudice laid aside, our stomachs would refuse the hospitalities of the Indians, if it were possible for them to share with us from their own scanty stores. The Major's experience prompted him at once to give the order to break camp and move on for the camp on the Fresno.

Our mounted force chafed at the slowness of our march; for the Indians could not be hurried. Although their cookery was of the most primitive character, we were very much delayed by the time consumed in preparing their food.

While traveling we were compelled to accommodate our movements to the capacities or inclinations of the women and children. Captain Dill, therefore, with his company was sent on ahead from the crossing of the South Fork, they leaving with us what food they could spare. When

Dill reached the waters of the Fresno about one hundred "*captives*" joined him. These Indians voluntarily surrendered to Captain Dill's company, which at once hurried them on, and they reached the commissioners at the Fresno.

Captain Boling's company and Major Savage remained with the "Grand Caravan," keeping out scouts and hunters to secure such game as might be found to supply ourselves with food. We had no anxiety for the safety or security of our "captives;" our own subsistence was the important consideration; for the first night out from Bishop's camp left us but scanty stores for breakfast. Our halting places were selected from the old Indian camping grounds, which were supplied with hoyas (holes or mortars). These permanent mortars were in the bed-rock, or in large detached rocks that had fallen from the cliffs or mountains. These "hoyas" had been formed and used by past generations. They were frequent on our route, many of them had long been abandoned; as there was no indications of recent uses having been made of them. From their numbers it was believed that the Indians had once been much more numerous than at that date.

By means of the stone pestles with which they were provided, the squaws used these primitive mills to reduce their acorns and grass seeds to flour or meal. While the grists were being ground, others built the fires on which stones were heated.

When red hot, these stones were plunged into baskets nearly filled with water; this is continued until the water boils. The stones are then removed and the acorn meal, or a cold mixture of it, is stirred in until thin gruel is made; the hot stones are again plunged into the liquid mass and and again removed. When sufficiently cooked, this "Atola" or porridge, was poured into plates or moulds of sand, prepared for that purpose. During the process of cooling, the excess of water leaches off through the sand, leaving the woody fibre tannin and unappropriated coarse meal in distinctive strata; the edible portion being so defined as to be easily separated from the refuse and sand. This preparation was highly prized by them, and contrary to preconceived ideas and information, all of the Indians I asked assured me that the *bitter* acorns were the best when cooked. This compound of acorn meal resembles corn starch blanc mange in color, but is more dense in consistency. Although it was free from grit, and comparatively clean, none of us were able to eat it, and we were quite hungry. From this, I was led to conclude that to relish this Indian staple, the taste must be acquired while very young.

Old Ten-ie-ya's four wives, and other squaws, were disposed to be quite hospitable when they learned that our supply of provisions was exhausted. None of the command, however, ventured to sample their acorn-jellies, grass-seed mush, roasted grasshoppers, and their other delicacies; nothing was accepted but the Piñon pine nuts, which were generally devoured with a relish and a regret for the scarcity.

Certain species of worms, the larvæ of ants and some other insects, common mushrooms and truffles, or wood-mushrooms, are prized by the Indian epicure, as are eels shrimps, oysters, frogs, turtles, snails, etc., by his white civilized brother. Are we really but creatures of education ?

The *baskets* used by the Indians for boiling their food and other purposes, as has been before stated, are made of a tough mountain bunch-grass, nearly as hard and as strong as wire, and almost as durable. So closely woven are they, that but little if any water can escape from them. They are made wholly impervious with a resinous compound resembling the vulcanized rubber used by dentists. This composition does not appear to be in the least affected by hot water. The same substance, in appearance at least, is used by Mountain Indians in attaching sinews to bows, and feathers and barbs to arrows.

I endeavored to ascertain what the composition was, but could only learn that the resin was procured from small trees or shrubs, and that some substance (probably mineral) was mixed with it, the latter to resist the action of heat and moisture. I made a shrewd guess that pulverized lava and sulphur (abundant east of the High Sierras) was used, but for some cause I was left in ignorance. The Indians, like all ignorant persons, ascribe remarkable virtues to very simple acts and to inert remedies. Upon one occasion a doctor was extolling the virtues of a certain root, ascribing to it almost miraculous powers; I tried in vain to induce him to tell me the name of the root. He stated that the secret was an heir-loom, and if told, the curative power of the plant would disappear; but he kindly gave me some as a preventive of some imaginary ill, when lo ! I discovered the famous remedy to be the cowslip.

After a delayed and hungry march of several days, we halted near sundown within a few miles of the Commissioner's headquarters, and went into camp for the night. The Indians came straggling in at will from their hunts on the way, their trophies of skill with their bows being the big California squirrels, rabbits or hares and quail. Our more expert white hunters had occasionally brought in ven_ ison for our use. We had ceased to keep a very effective guard over our " captives; " none seemed necessary, as all appeared contented and satisfied, almost joyous, as we neared their destination on the Fresno.

The truth is, we regarded hostilities, so far as these Indians were concerned, as ended. We had voted the peace policy a veritable success. We had discussed the matter in camp, and contrasted the lack of spirit exhibited by these people with what we knew of the warlike character of the Indians of Texas and of the Northwestern plains. In these comparisons, respect for our captives was lost in contempt. "The noble red man" was not here represented. The only ones of the Pacific Slope, excepting the Navahoes, Pimas and Maricopahs, that bear any comparison with the Eastern tribes for intelligence and bravery, are the You-mahs of the Colorado river, the Modocs, and some of the Rogue and Columbia river tribes, but none of these really equal the Sioux and some other Eastern tribes.

Hardly any attention had been paid to the captives during the preceding night, except from the guard about our own camp; from a supposition that our services could well be spared. Application was therefore made by a few of us, for permission to accompany the Major, who had determined to go on to the Fresno head-quarters. When consent was given, the wish was so generally expressed, that Captain Boling with nine men to act as camp guard, volunteered to remain, if Major Savage would allow the hungry "boys" to ride with him. The Major finally assented to the proposition, saying: "I do not suppose the Indians can be driven off, or be induced to leave until they have had the feast I promised them; besides, they will want to see some of the commissioner's finery. I have been delighting their imaginations with descriptions of the presents in store for them."

When the order was passed for the hungry squad to fall in, we mounted with grateful feelings towards Captain Boling, and the "boys" declared that the Major was a trump, for his consideration of our need. With the prospect of a good "square" meal, and the hope of a genial "smile" from our popular commissary, the time soon passed, and the distance seemed shortened, for we entered the Fresno camp before our anticipations were cloyed. Head-quarters was well supplied with all needful comforts, and was not totally deficient in luxuries. Our Quarter-Master and Commissary was active in his duties, and as some good women say of their husbands, "He was a good provider." We had no reason to complain of our reception; our urgent requirements were cheerfully met. The fullness of our entertainment did not prevent a good night's rest, nor interfere with the comfortable breakfast which we enjoyed. While taking coffee, the self denial of Captain Boling and his volunteer guard was not forgotten. Arrangements were made to furnish the best edible and potable stores, that could be secured from our conscientious and prudent commissary. We were determined to give them a glorious reception; but—the Captain did not bring in his captives! Major Savage sent out a small detachment to ascertain the cause of the delay. This party filled their haversacks with comforts for the "Indian guard." After some hours of delay, the Major became anxious to hear from Captain Boling, and began to be suspicious that something more serious than the loss of his animals, was the cause of not sending in a messenger, and he ordered out another detachment large enough to meet any supposed emergency. Not far from camp, they met the Captain and his nine men (the *"Indian guard"*) and *one* Indian, with the relief party first sent out. Our jovial Captain rode into "Head-quarters" looking more crest fallen than he had ever been seen before. When asked by the Major where he had left the Indians, he blushed like a coy maiden and said: "They have all gone to the mountains. but the one I have with me."

Af er Captain Boling had made his report to the Major, and made all explanations to the commissioners, and when he had refreshed himself with an extra ration or two of th potable liquid, that by special stipulation had been reserved for the "Indian Guard," something of his old humor returned to him, and he gave us the details of his annoyances by the breach of trust on the part of "our prisoners."

The Captain said: "Soon after you left us last night, one of my men, who was out hunting when we camped, came in with a deer he had killed just at the dusk of the evening. From this we made a hearty supper, and allowed the youth who had helped to bring in the deer to share in the meat. The Indian cooked the part given to him at our fire, and ate with the avidity of a famished wolf. This excited comment, and anecdotes followed of the enormous appetites displayed by some of them. The question was then raised, 'how much can this Indian eat at one meal?' I suggested that a fair trial could not be had with only one deer. Our hunter said he would give him a preliminary trial, and when deer were plenty we could then test his full capacity, if he should prove a safe one to bet on. He then cut such pieces as we thought would suffice for our breakfast, and, with my approval, gave the remainder to his boy, who was anxiously watching his movements. I consented to this arrangement, not as a test of his capacity, for I had often seen a hungry Indian eat, but as a reward for his services in bringing in the deer on his shoulders. He readily re-commenced his supper, and continued to feast until every bone was cracked and picked. When the last morsel of the venison had disappeared he commenced a doleful sing-song, 'Way-ah-we-ha-ha, Wah-ah-we-ha-ha' to some unknown deity, or, if I was to judge from my ear of the music, it must have been his prayer to the devil, for I have heard that it is a part of their worship. His song was soon echoed from the camp where all seemed contentment. After *consoling* himself in this manner for some time he fell asleep at our fire.

"The performance being over, I told my men to take their sleep and I would watch, as I was not sleepy; if I wanted them I would call them. I then thought, as Major Savage had declared, the Indians could scarcely be driven off, until they had had their feast and the presents they expected to have given them. I sat by the fire for a long time cogitating on past events and future prospects, when thinking it useless to require the men to stand guard, I told them to sleep. Moving about and seeing nothing but the usual appearance, I decided it to be unneccessary to exercise any further vigilance, and told one of the men, who was partially aroused by my movements, and who offered to get up and stand guard, that he had better lie still and sleep. Toward morning I took another round, and finding the Indian camp wrapped in apparently profound slumber, I concluded to take a little sleep myself, until daylight. This now seems unaccountable to me, for I am extremely cautious in my habits. Such a breach of military discipline would have subjected one of my men to a court-martial. I confess myself guilty of neglect of duty ; I should have taken nothing for granted.

"No one can imagine my surprise and mortification when I was called and told that the Indian camp was entirely deserted, and that none were to be seen except the one asleep by our camp fire. My indifference to placing a guard over the Indian camp will probably always be a mystery to me, but it most likely saved our lives, for if we had attempted to restrain them, and you know us well enough to believe we would not have let them off without a fight: they would probably have pretty well used us up. As it was, we did not give them up without an effort. We saddled our horses and started in chase, thinking that as while with us, their women and children would retard their progress, and that we would soon overtake them. We took the young brave with us, who had slept by our fire. He knew nothing of the departure of his people, and was very much alarmed, as he expected we would at once kill him. I tried to make him useful in following their trail; he by signs, gave me to understand he did not know where they had gone, and seemed unwilling to take the trail when I pointed it out to him. He evidently meant to escape the first opportunity. I kept him near me and treated him kindly, but gave him to understand I should shoot him if he tried to leave me.

"We pursued until the trail showed that they had scattered in every direction in the brushy ravines and on the rocky side of a mountain covered with undergrowth, where we could not follow them with our animals. Chagrined and disgusted with myself for my negligence, and my inability to recover any part of my charge, and considering farther pursuit useless, we turned about and took the trail to headquarters with our one captive."

Major Savage took the youngster under his charge, and flattered him by his conversations and kindly treatment. The Commissioners lionized him somewhat; he was gaily clothed and ornamented, loaded with presents for his own family relations, and was given his liberty and permitted to leave camp at his leisure, and thus departed the last of the "grand caravan" of some three hundred and fifty "captives," men, women and children, which we had collected and escorted from the mountains.

The sight of the one hundred brought to them by Captain Dill, and his report that we were coming with about three hundred and fifty more, aroused sanguine hopes in the commission that the war was over, and that their plans had been successful. "Now that the *prisoners* have fled," we asked, "What will be done?"

To a military man, this lack of discipline and precaution —through which the Indians escaped—will seem unpardonable; and an officer who, like our Captain, should leave his camp unguarded, under any circumstances, would be deemed disgracefully incompetent. In palliation of these facts, it may not occur to the rigid disciplinarian that Captain John Boling and the men under him—or the most of them, had not had the advantages of army drill and discipline. The courage of these mountain-men in times of danger was undoubted; their caution was more apt to be displayed in times of danger to others, than when they themselves were imperiled.

In this case Captain Boling was not apprehensive of danger to those under his charge. His excessive good nature and good will toward his men prompted him to allow, even to command them, to take the sleep and rest that an irregular diet, and the labor of hunting while on the march, had seemed to require. No one had a keener sense of his error than himself. The whole command sympathized with him —notwithstanding the ludicrous aspect of the affair—their finer feelings were aroused by his extreme regrets. They determined that if opportunities offered, he should have their united aid to wipe out this stigma. Major Savage was deceived by the child-like simplicity with which the Indians had been talking to him of the feast expected, and of the presents they would soon receive from the commissioners. He did not suppose it possible that they would make an attempt to escape, or such a number would not have been left with so small a guard. We had men with us who knew what discipline was, who had been trained to obey orders without hesitation. Men who had fought under Col. Jack Hays, Majors Ben McCullough and Mike Chevallia, both in Indian and Mexican warfare, and they considered themselves well posted. Even these men were mistaken in their opinions. The sudden disappearance of the Indians, was as much a surprise to them as to our officers.

With a view to solving this mystery Vow-ches-ter was

were congregated, and when questioned the Chief said that during the night Chow-chilla runners had been in the camp, and to him in person with their mouths filled with lies; they had probably gone to the camp of those who were coming in, and they were induced to leave. Evidently he felt assured of the fact; but until questioned, his caution, Indian-like, kept him silent. Vow-ches-ter's sincerity and desire for peace was no longer doubted. Those who were suspicious of his friendship before were silenced, if not convinced, when he volunteered to go out and bring in such of the fugitives as he could convince of the good will of the commissioners. The young Indian had not yet left the camp, but was found relating his adventures and good fortune, and was directed to accompany Vow-ches-ter on his mission of good will. The Chief was instructed to give positive assurances of protection against hostilities, if any were threatened by the Chow-chillas. He was also instructed to dispatch runners to aid his efforts, and was told to notify all that the commissioners would not remain to be trifled with; if they wished peace they must come in at once. That if the commissioners should go away, which they soon would do on their way south, no further efforts for peace would be made. That the mountain men and soldiers of the whites were angry, and would no longer take their word for peace, but would punish them and destroy their supplies. After a few days Vow-ches-ter came back with about one hundred of the runaways; these were followed by others, until ultimately, nearly all came back except Ten-ie-ya and his people. All then in camp expressed a readiness to meet for a grand council and treaty.

The reasons given by those who returned for their flight, were that just before daylight on the morning of their departure Chow-chilla runners (as had been surmised by

Vow-ches-ter) came to their camp with the report that they were being taken to the plains, where they would all be killed in order to evade the promises to pay for their lands, and for revenge.

In reply to the statements that they had been treated by the whites as friends, the Chow-chillas answered sneeringly that the whites were not fools to forgive them for killing their friends and relatives, and taking their property, and said their scouts had seen a large mounted force that was gathering in the foot-hills and on the plains, who would ride over them if they ventured into the open ground of the reservation, or encampment at the plains. This caused great alarm. They expected destruction from the whites, and in the excitement caused by the Chow-chillas, threatened to kill Captain Boling and his men, and for that purpose reconnoitered the Captain's camp. The Chow-chillas dissuaded them from the attempt, saying: "The white men always sleep on their guns, and they will alarm the white soldiers below by their firing, and bring upon you a mounted force before you could reach a place of safety."

The young fellow that was asleep in Boling's camp was not missed until on the march; his appearance among them gaily clothed, after being kindly treated, very much aided Vow-ches-ter in his statement of the object of the council and treaty to be held. The runaways told the commissioners that they felt very foolish, and were ashamed that they had been so readily deceived; they also expressed a wish that we would punish the Chow-chillas, for they had caused all the trouble. The reception they received soon satisfied them that they had nothing to fear. They were given food and clothing, and their good fortune was made known to other bands, and soon all of the tribes in the vicinity made treaties or sent messengers to express their willingness to do so, excepting the Chow-chillas and Yosemites. Even

Ten-ie-ya was reported to have ventured into the Indian quarter, but taking a look at the gaudy colored handker-chiefs and shirts offered him in lieu of his ancient and well-worn guernsey that he habitually wore, he scoffingly refused the offers. Turning towards his valley home, he sorrowfully departed; his feelings apparently irritated by the evidences of vanity he saw in the gaudy apparel and weak contentment of those he was leaving behind him. Major Savage, who it was supposed would be the Indian agent at the end of the war, was absent at the time of Ten-ie-ya's visit, but "the farmer" showed the old chief all proper respect, and had endeavored to induce him to await the Major's return, but failed.

Major Savage, though still in command of the battalion, now devoted most of his time to the commissioners; and the energy with which our campaigns had opened, seemed to be somewhat abating. The business connected with the treaties was transacted principally through his interpretation, though at times other interpreters were employed. The mission interpreters only translated the communications made in the Indian dialects into Spanish; these were then rendered into English by Spanish interpreters employed by the commission.

A pretty strong detail of men was now placed on duty at head-quarters on the Fresno, principally drawn from Captain Dill's Company. Adjutant Lewis had really no duties in the field, nor had he any taste or admiration for the snowy mountains—*on foot*. His reports were written up at head-quarters, as occasion required, and often long after the events had transpired to which they related. I was an amused observer upon one occasion, of Major Savage's method of making out an *official* report, Adjutant Lewis virtually acting only as an amanuensis.

CHAPTER VII.

MAJOR SAVAGE now advised a vigorous campaign against
the Chow-chillas. The stampeding of our captives was one
of the incentives for this movement; or at least, it was for
this reason that Captain Boling and his company most
zealously advocated prompt action. The commissioners
approved of the plan, and decided that as the meddlesome
interference of these Indians prevented other bands from
coming in, it was necessary, if a peace policy was to be
maintained with other tribes, that this one be made to feel
the power they were opposing; and that an expedition of
sufficient strength to subdue them, should be ordered immediately to commence operations against them. Accordingly, a force composed of B. and C. companies, Boling's
and Dill's, numbering about one hundred men, under command of Major Savage, started for the San Joaquin River.
The route selected was by way of "Coarse Gold Gulch," to
the head waters of the Fresno, and thence to the North
Fork of the San Joaquin.

The object in taking this circuitous route, was to sweep
the territory of any scattered bands that might infest it.

We made our first camp on the waters of "Coarse Gold Gulch," in order to allow the scouts time to explore in advance of the command. No incident occurred here to claim especial notice, but in the morning, while passing them, I made a hasty examination of one of the "Figured Rocks" to the left of the trail.

I saw but little of interest, for at the time, I doubted the antiquity of the figures. Subsequently, in conversation with Major Savage he said that the figures had probably been traced by ancient Indians, as the present tribes had no knowledge of the representations. I afterwards asked Sandino and other Mission Indians concerning them, but none could give me any information. The scouts sent out were instructed to rendezvous near a double fall on the north fork of the San Joaquin in a little valley through which the trail led connecting with that of the north fork, as grass would there be found abundant.

Major Savage was familiar with most of the permanent trails in this region, as he had traversed it in his former prospecting tours. As we entered the valley selected for our camping place, a flock of sand-hill cranes rose from it with their usual persistent yells; and from this incident, their name was affixed to the valley, and is the name by which it is now known.

The scouts, who were watching on the trail below, soon discovered and joined us. "It is a little early for camping," the Major said; "but at this season, good grass can only be found in the mountains in certain localities. Here there is an abundance, and soap root enough to wash a regiment."

We fixed our camp on the West side of the little valley, about half a mile from the double falls. These falls had nothing peculiarly attractive, except as a designated point for a rendezvous.

The stream above the falls was narrow and very rapid, but below, it ran placidly for some distance through rich meadow land. The singularity of the fall was in its being double; the upper one only three or four feet, and the lower one, which was but a step below, about ten or twelve feet. In my examination of the locality, I was impressed with the convenience with which such a water-power could be utilized for mechanical purposes, if the supply of water would but prove a permanent one.

From this camp, new scouts were sent out in search of Indians and their trails; while a few of us had permission to hunt within a mile of camp. While picketing our animals, I observed the flock of sand-hill cranes again settling down some way above us, and started with Wm. Hays to get a shot at them. We were not successful in getting within range; having been so recently alarmed, they were suspiciously on the look out, and scenting our approach, they left the valley. Turning to the eastward, we were about entering a small ravine leading to the wooded ridge on the Northwest side of the Fork, when we discovered two deer ascending the slope, and with evident intention of passing through the depression in the ridge before us.

They were looking *back* on their trail, assurance enough that *we* had not been seen. We hurriedly crept up the ravine to head them off, and waited for their approach. Hays became nervous, and as he caught a glimpse of the leader, he hastily said, "Here they come—both of them—I'll take the buck!" Assenting to his arrangement, we both fired as they rose in full view. The doe fell almost in her tracks. The buck made a bound or two up the ridge and disappeared. While loading our rifles Hays exclaimed, as if in disgust, "A miss, by jingoes! that's a fact." I replied, not so, old fellow, you hit him hard; he switched his tail desperately; you will see him again." We found him dead in the head of the next ravine, but a few rods off. Hanging up our game to secure it until our return with horses, we started along the slope of the ridge toward camp. Hays was in advance, stopping suddenly, he pointed to some immense tracks of grizzlies, which in the soft, yielding soil appeared like the foot prints of huge elephants, and then hastily examining his rifle and putting a loose ball in his mouth (we had no fixed ammunition in those days, except the old paper cartridges), started on the tracks. At first I was amused at his excited, silent preparations and rapid step, and passively accompanied him. When we had reached a dense under-growth, into which the trail led, and which he was about to enter, I halted and said : "I have followed this trail as far as I design to go. Hays, it is madness for us to follow grizzlies into such a place as that." Hays turned, came back, and said in an excited manner, "I didn't suppose you would show the white feather with a good rifle in your hands; Chandler gives you a different character. You don't mean to say you are afraid to go in there with me; we'll get one or two, sure.

I was at first inclined to be angry, but replied, "Hays, I am much obliged to you for the good opinion you have had of me, but I know what grizzlies are. *I am afraid of grizzlies unless I have every advantage of them;* and don't think it would be any proof of courage to follow them in there." Hays reached out his hand as he said: "If that is your corner stake, we will go back to camp." We s' ook hands, and that question was settled between us. Afterwards Hays told of his experience among Polar bears, and I rehearsed some of mine among cinnamon and grizzly bears, and he replied that after all he thought "we had acted wisely in letting the latter remain undisturbed. When in the brush they seemed to know their advantage, and were more likely to attack, whereas at other times, they would get out of your way, if they could." I replied by asking: "Since you know their nature so well, why did you want to follow them into the brush?" He retorted, "Simply because I was excited and reckless, like many another man."

Taking the back trail, we soon reached camp, and with our horses brought in the game before dark. While entering camp, several of our men rushed by with their rifles. Looking back across the open valley on our own trail, I saw a man running toward us as if his life depended on his speed. His long hair was fairly streaming behind as he rushed breathless into camp, without hat, shoes or gun. When first seen, the "boys" supposed the Chow-chillas were after him, but no pursuers appeared in sight. As soon as he was able to talk, he reported that he had left the squad of hunters he had gone out with, and was moving along the edge of a thicket on his way to camp, when he struck the trail of three grizzlies. Having no desire to encounter them, he left their trail, but suddenly came upon them while endeavoring to get out of the brush.

Before he could raise his rifle, they rushed toward him. He threw his hat at the one nearest, and started off at a lively gait. Glancing back, he saw two of them quarreling over his old hat; the other was so close that he dare not shoot, but dropped his gun and ran for life.

Fortunate'y, one of his shoes came off, and the bear stopped to examine and tear it in pieces, and here no doubt discontinued the chase, as he was not seen afterwards, though momentarily expected by the hunter in his flight to camp.

The hero of this adventure was a Texan, that was regarded by those who knew him best as a brave man, but upon this occasion he was without side arms, and, as he said, " was taken at a disadvantage." The Major joked him a little upon his *continued* speed, but " Texas Joe" took it in good part, and replied that the Major, "or any *other* blank fool, would have run just as he did." A few of us went back with Joe, and found his rifle unharmed. The tracks of his pursuers were distinctly visible, but no one evinced any desire to follow them up.

We considered his escape a most remarkable one.

A little after dark all the scouts came in, and reported that no Indians had been seen, nor very fresh signs discovered, but that a few tracks were observed upon the San Joaquin trail.

The news was not encouraging, and some were a little despondent, but as usual, a hearty supper and the social pipe restored the younger men to their thoughtless gayety. My recollections bring to mind many pleasant hours around the camp-fires of the "Mariposa Battalion." Many of the members of that organization were men of more than ordinary culture and general intelligence; but they had been led out from civilization into the golden tide, and had acquired a reckless air and carriage, peculiar to a free life in the mountains of California.

The beauty of the little valley in which we were camped had so attracted my attention, that while seated by the camp-fire in the evening, enjoying my meal, I spoke of it in the general conversation, and found that others had discovered a "claim" for a future rancho, if the subjection of the Indians should make it desirable. The scouts mentioned the fact of there being an abundance of game as far as they had been, but that of course they dare not shoot, lest the Indians might be alarmed. These men were provided with venison by Hays and myself, while many a squirrel, jack rabbit, quail and pigeon was spitted and roasted by other less fortunate hunters. Our deer were divided among immediate friends and associates, and Captain Boling slyly remarked that "the Major's appetite is about as good as an Indian's." Major Savage seemed to enjoy the conversation in praise of this region, and in reply to the assertion that this was the best hunting ground we had yet seen, said: "Where you find game plenty, you will find Indians not far off. This belt of country beats the region of the Yosemite or the Poho-no Meadows for game, if the Indians tell the truth; and with the exception of the Kern River country, it is the best south of the Tuolumne River. It abounds in grizzlies and cinnamon bears, and there are some black bears. Deer are very plenty, and a good variety of small game—such as crane, grouse, quail, pigeons, road-runners, squirrels and rabbits—besides, in their season, water fowl. This territory of the Chow-chillas has plenty of black oak acorns (their favorite acorn), and besides this, there are plenty of other supplies of bulbous roots, tubers, grasses and clover. In a word, there is everything here for the game animals and birds, as well as for the Indians."

I now thought I had a turn on the Major, for he was quite enthusiastic, and I said: "Major, you have made out another Indian Paradise; I thought you a skeptic." With a smile as if in remembrance of our conversation in the Yosemite, he replied: "Doc, I don't believe these Chow-chilla devils will leave here without a fight, for they seem to be concentrating; but we are going to drive them out with a 'flaming brand.' I think we shall find some of them to-morrow, if we expect good luck." Turning to Captain Boling he continued, "Captain, we must make an early move in the morning; and to-morrow we must be careful not to flush our game before we get within rifle-shot. You had better caution the guards to be vigilant, for we may have a visit from their scouts to-night, if only to stampede our horses."

Taking this as a hint that it was time to turn in, I rolled myself in my blankets. My sleep was not delayed by any thoughts of danger to the camp,—though I would have

Captain Boling crossed the North Fork below the falls, but after a few horses had passed over the trail, the bottom land became almost impassable. As I had noticed an old trail that crossed just above the falls, I shouted to the rear guard to follow me, and started for the upper crossing, which I reached some little distance in advance. Spurring my mule I dashed through the stream. As she scrambled up the green sod of the slippery shore I was just opening my mouth for a triumphant whoop, when the sod from the overhanging bank gave way under the hind feet of the mule, and, before she could recover, we slipped backwards into the stream, and were being swept down over the falls. Comprehending the imminent peril, I slipped from my saddle with the coil of my "riata" clasped in hand (fortunately I had acquired the habit of leaving the rope upon the mule's neck), and, by an effort, I was able to reach the shore with barely length of rope enough to take one turn around a sappling and then one or two turns around the rope, and by this means I was able to arrest the mule in her progress, with her hind legs projecting over the falls, where she remained, her head held out of the water by the rope. I held her in this position until my comrades came up and relieved me, and the mule from her most pitiable position. This was done by attaching another rope, by means of which it was drawn up the stream to the shore, where she soon recovered her feet and was again ready for service. Not so my medicines and surgical instruments, which were attached to the saddle.

While Captain Boling was closing up his scattered command, I took the opportunity to examine my damaged stores and wring out my blankets. Being thus engaged, and out of sight of the main column, they moved on without us. I hastily dried my instruments, and seeing that my rifle had also suffered, I hastily discharged and reloaded it. We

doubtedly discovered our rapid approach, and in their haste
to report the fact, had neglected to remove this rope, by
means of which, the crossing was made. The Indians of
Northern climes are equally expert in crossing streams.
In winter, they sprinkle sand upon the smooth ice, in order
to cross their unshod ponies. The discovery of the rope being reported to Captain Boling, he proposed to utilize it by
establishing a temporary ferry of logs. On examination, the
rope was found to be too slender to be of practical use, but
was employed to convey across a stronger one, made from
our picket ropes or "riatas," tied together and twisted.

· Two of our best swimmers crossed the river above the
narrows, and pulled our rope across by means of the bark
one. To protect the men on the opposite side, Captain
Middleton, Joel H. Brooks, John Kenzie and a few other
expert riflemen, stood guard over them. A float was made
of dry logs while the rope was being placed in position, and
this was attached to the one across the stream by means of
a rude pulley made from the crotch of a convenient sapling.
By this rude contrivance, we crossed to and fro without accident. The horses and baggage were left on the right
bank in charge of a small but select camp guard. As we
commenced the ascent of the steep aclivity to the table
above, where we had seen the Indians apparently awaiting
our approach, great care was taken to keep open order.
We momentarily expected to receive the fire of the enemy.
The hill-side was densely covered with brush, and we cautiously threaded our march up through it, until we emerged
into the open ground at the crest of the hill. Here, not
an Indian was in sight to welcome or threaten our arrival.
They had probably fled as soon as they witnessed our crossing. Captain Boling felt disappointed; but immediately
sent out an advance skirmish line, while we moved in
closer order upon the village in sight, which we afterwards

found to be that of Jose Rey. Arrived there, we found it forsaken. This village was beautifully situated upon an elevated table lying between the South Fork and the main river. It overlooked the country on all sides except the rear, which could have only been approached through the rugged cañons of the forks. It would therefore have been impossible for us to surprise it. We found that the Indians had left nothing of value but the stores of acorns near by. Captain Boling's countenance expressed his feelings, with regard to our lack of success. He ordered the lodges to be destroyed with all the supplies that could be discovered.

While entering the village, we had observed upon a little knoll, the remnant of what had been a large fire; a bed of live coals and burning brands of manzanita-wood still remained. The ground about it indicated that there had been a large gathering for a burial-dance and feast, and for other rites due the departed; and therefore, I surmised that there had been a funeral ceremony to honor the remains of some distinguished member of the tribe. I had the curiosity to examine the heap and found that I was correct. On raking open the ashes of the funeral-pyre, the calcined bones were exposed, along with trinkets and articles of various kinds, such as arrow-heads of different shapes and sizes, for the chase and for warfare; a knife-blade, a metal looking-glass frame, beads and other articles melted into a mass. From these indications—having a knowledge of Indian customs—I inferred that the deceased was probably a person of wealth and distinction in Indian society. Calling Sandino to the spot, I pointed out to him my discoveries. Devoutly crossing himself, he looked at the mass I had raked from the ashes, and exclaimed: "Jose Rey, ah! he is dead!" I asked how he knew that it was the body of Jose Rey that had been burned. He said: (picking up the knife-blade)

"This was the knife of Jose Rey." He then told me "that a chief's property was known to all of his people and to many other tribes. That many had been here to take part in the funeral ceremonies, and only a great chief would have so many come to do honor to his remains; besides we have known for a long time that he would die." I reported this statement to Captain Boling, who thought it was correct. It was afterwards confirmed by some of the followers of the dead chief.

Sandino was or had been a Mission Indian, and prided himself on being a good Catholic. I asked him why the Indians burnt the bodies of their dead. He replied after devoutly crossing himself, for no Indian will willingly speak of their dead. "The Gentiles (meaning the wild Indians) burn the bodies to liberate the spirit from it." After again crossing himself, "We being Christians by the favor of God, are not compelled to do this duty to our dead. They enter into the spirit-world through the virtue of the blood of Christ;" then with his face gleaming with religious fervor, he said, "Oh! is not this a great blessing—*no labor, no pain, and where all have plenty.*" On a more intimate acquaintance with Sandino, I found that he had an implicit belief in all the superstitions of his race, but that the saving grace of the blood of Christ was simply superior to their charms and incantations.

My experience among other Indians, particularly the Sioux, Chippewa, and other tribes that have long had missionaries among them, leads me to the conclusion that Sandino's views of Christianity will not be found to differ materially from those of many others *converted.* I afterwards had a much more satisfactory conversation with "Russio," who verified Sandino's statement concerning their belief, and object in burning their dead. This Chief also gave me in detail some of their traditions and mythologies, which I shall reserve for future description.

Our scouts reported that the fresh trails followed by them led to the main trail up the cañon of the river. Everything having been set on fire that would burn, we followed in pursuit toward the "High Sierras." Before starting the scouts that had gone up the South Fork cañon were called in, and we lightened our haversacks by taking a hasty but hearty lunch. We followed the trail continuously up, passed a rocky, precipitous point, that had terminated in a ridge at the rear of the village, and pursuing it rapidly for several miles, we suddenly found that the traces we had been following disappeared. We came to a halt, and retracing our steps, soon found that they had left the trail at some bare rocks, but it was impossible to trace them farther in any direction. Sandino expressed the opinion that the Indians had crossed the river; and pointing across the foaming rapids said: "They have gone there!" He was denounced by the scouts for this assertion, and they swore that "an otter would drown if he attempted to swim in such a place." Captain Boling asked: "Is he a coward afraid of an ambush, or is he trying to shield his people by discouraging our advance?" After Spencer and myself had talked with him a few moments, we both expressed our faith in his loyalty, and told the Captain that we thought he was sincere in the opinion expressed, that the Indians had crossed to the other side. I stated that I did not think it impossible for them to do so, as they were all most excellent swimmers. That I had seen the Yumas of the Colorado river dive, time after time, and bring up fish caught with their bare hands, and perform other seemingly impossible feats. I would not, therefore, denounce Sandino without some proof of treachery. Captain Boling was not convinced, however, by my statements. It was decided that the Chow-chil-las had not crossed the river, and that we should probably find their trail further on.

With scouts in advance, we resumed our march up the cañon. The trail was rough, and, in places, quite precipitous; but we followed on until reaching a point in the canon where we should expect to find "*signs*," for there was no choice of routes, but this only trail up the cañon had not been used by any one; and the advance were found awaiting the Captain's arrival at the gorge. The Captain was puzzled, and ordered a halt. A council was held, about as satisfactory as the other had been, but all agreed in the conclusion that the Indians had beaten us in wood craft, and had artfully thrown us from their trail; though their signal fires were still to be seen at intervals on the high rocky points of the river. This was a common mode of communication among them. By a peculiar arrangement of these fires during the night, and by the smoke from them during the day, they are able to telegraph a system of secret correspondence to those on the look out. An arrow, shot into the body of a tree at a camp ground, or along a trail; or the conspicuous arrangement of a bent bush or twig, often shows the direction to be traveled. A bunch of grass, tied to a stick and left at the fork of a stream or trail, or at a deserted camp, performed the same service. Upon the treeless deserts or plains, a mark upon the ground, by camp or trail, gave the required information; thus proving that these people possess considerable intelligent forethought.

After looking at the signal fires for some time, Captain Boling said: "Gentlemen, there is one thing I can beat these fellows at, and that is in building fires. We will go back to the crossing, and from there commence a new campaign. We will build fires all over the mountains, so that these Indians will no longer recognize their own signals. We will make ours large enough to burn all the acorns and other provender we can find. In a word, we are forced into a mode of warfare unsuited to my taste or manhood, but this campaign has convinced me of the utter folly of attempting to subdue them unless we destroy their supplies of all kinds. Gentlemen, you can take my word for it, they do not intend to fight us, or they would have tried to stop us at the crossing, where they had every advantage."

There is no point in the mountains more easy to defend than their village. It was located most admirably. If they had the fight in them, that was claimed by Major Savage and the Indians at head-quarters, we could never have crossed the river or approached their village. Their courage must have died with Jose Rey. His courage must have been supposed to be that of the tribe. They have become demoralized, being left without the energy of the chief. Their warlike nature is a humbug. Talk about these Indians defeating and driving back the Spanish Californians, after raiding their ranches, as has been told! If they did, they must have driven back bigger cowards than themselves, who have run away without even leaving a trail by which they can be followed. I don't believe it." The Captain delivered this serio-comic discourse while seated on a rock, with most inimitable drollery; and at my suggestion that they might perhaps yet show themselves, he replied rather impatiently: "Nonsense, they will not exhibit themselves to-day!" and with this convincing remark, he ordered our return.

As we filed away from the narrow gorge, those left in rear reported "Indians!" Instinctively turning, we discovered on the *opposite* side of the river, a half dozen or more, not encumbered with any kind of garment. A halt was called, and Chandler and a number of others instantly raised their rifles for a shot. They were within range, for the cañon was here quite narrow, but the Captain promptly said: "No firing, men! I am anxious for success, but would rather go back without a captive, than have one of those

Indians killed, unless," he added after a moment's pause, "they are fools enough to shoot at us." Just at the conclusion of this order, and as if in burlesque applause of the sentiment expressed by the Captain, the savages commenced slapping their naked swarthy bodies in a derisive manner.

The laugh of our men was parried by the Captain, and although annoyed by this unexpected demonstration, he laughingly remarked that he had never before been so *peculiarly* applauded for anything he had ever said. The absurdity of the scene restored us all to a better humor. Again the order was given to march, and we resumed our course down the cañon, with the renewed demonstrations of the Indians. The orders of the Captain alone prevented a return *salute*, which would have promptly checked their offensive demonstrations.

At the precipice, which we had so guardedly passed on our way up the cañon, we came near losing our Captain. In passing this locality he made a mis-step, and slipped towards the yawning abyss at the foot of the cliff; but for a small pine that had been "moored in the rifted rock," no earthly power could have saved him from being dashed to the bottom. He fortunately escaped with some severe bruises, a lacerated elbow and a sprained wrist. This accident and our tired and disappointed condition, gave a more serious appearance to our line, and a more sombre tone to our conversations than was usual. We reached camp in a condition, however, to appreciate the supper prepared by our guard.

CHAPTER VIII.

It was not until after we had partaken of a hearty supper and produced our pipes, that the lively hum of conversation and the occasional careless laughter indicated the elastic temperament of some of the hardy, light-hearted, if not light-headed, "boys," while in camp. The guard was duly detailed, and the signal given to turn in, but not authoritatively; and tired as we were, many of us sat quite late around the camp-fires on that evening. The excitements and disappointments of our recent excursion did not prove to be promoters of sleep; some of us were too tired to sleep until we had somewhat rested from our unusual fatigue. The events of the day—the *true method of subduing Indians*, and the probable results of the plans proposed by Captain Boling for future operations in this vicinity, were the general topics of conversation among the different groups. This general inclination to discuss the "peace policy" of the commissioners and the plans of our officers, did not arise from anything like a mutinous disposition, nor from any motives having in view the least opposition to any of the measures connected with the campaign in which we were then engaged.

We had expected that this tribe would resist our invasion of their territory and show fight. In this we had been disappointed. The self-confident and experienced mountain men, and the ex-rangers from the Texan plains, felt annoyed that these Indians had escaped when almost within range of our rifles. Our feelings—as a military organization—were irritated by the successful manner in which they had eluded our pursuit, and thrown us from their trail. *We had been outwitted by these ignorant Indians;* but as individuals, no one seemed inclined to acknowledge it; our lack of success was attributed to the restraints imposed on the free movements of our organization by orders of the commissioners. Although none designed to censure our Captain for his failure, the free speech intimations, that we might have been successful, if Major Savage had remained to aid us with his knowledge, was not soothing to the Captain's already wounded pride. The popularity of Captain Boling was not affected by our camp-fire discussion. Had a charge, or intimation even, been made by any one of incapacity or neglect of duty in our free expressions, the personal safety of the individual would have been immediately endangered; although no excess of modesty was observed in expressing opinions. Lieut. Chandler was at our own fire, and our officers talked over the solution of the enigma in a quiet conversational tone. The usual cheerful countenance of the Captain had a more serious expression. His attention was as much attracted to the groups around us, as to the remarks of Lt. Chandler.

The energetic Lieutenant was our most rigid disciplinarian when on duty. His fearless impetuosity in the execution of all his duties, made him a favorite with the more reckless spirits; his blunt and earnest manner excited their admiration; for, though possessed of a sublime egotism, he was entirely free from arrogance. Instead of his usual cheerful and agreeable conversation, he was almost morosely taciturn; he refilled his capacious mouth with choice Virginia, and settled back against the wood-pile. After listening to us for a while, he said: "I am heartily sick of this Quaker-style of subduing Indians. So far,—since our muster-in— we have had plenty of hard work and rough experience, with no honor or profit attending it all. We might as well be armed with clubs like any other police." There was none in our group disposed to dispute the assertion of Chandler. As a body, we were anxiously desirous of bringing the Indian troubles to a close as soon as it could be practically accomplished. Many of us had suffered pecuniarily from the depredations of these Mountain tribes, and had volunteered to aid in subduing them, that we might be able to resume our mining operations in peace. Many of us had left our own profitable private business to engage in these campaigns for the public good, expecting that a vigorous prosecution of the war would soon bring it to a close. I will here say that some sensational newspaper correspondents took it upon themselves to condemn this effort made by the settlers to control these mountain tribes, which had become so dangerous; charging the settlers with having excited a war, and to have involved the government in an unneccessary expense, for the purpose of reaping pecuniary benefits; and that our battalion had been organized to afford occupation to adventurous idlers, for the pay afforded. Knowing the ignorance that obtains in regard to real Indian character, and the mistaken philanthropy that would excuse and probably even protect and lionize murderers, because they were *Indians;* but little attention was at first paid to these falsely slanderous articles, until one was published, so personally offensive, and with such a false basis of statement, that Captain Boling felt it his duty to call for the name of its author. His name was given by the editor of the paper on a formal demand being made. The Captain then *intimated* through a friend, that a public retraction of the article was desirable. In due time, the Captain received a very satisfactory apology, and a slip of a published retraction of the offensive correspondence. The investigation developed the fact that the writer—who was an Eastern philanthropist—had been played upon by certain parties in Stockton, who had failed to get the contract to supply the battalion.

At an adjoining fire a long-haired Texan was ventilating his professed experience in the management of Indians "down thar." Observing that Captain Boling was within hearing of his criticism, he turned, and without any intentional disrespect, said: "Cap., you orter a let me plunk it to one o' them red skins up in the cañon thar. I'd a bin good for one, sure; and if I'd a had my way o' treatin' with Injuns, Cap., I reckon I'd a made a few o' them squawk by this time."

Captain Boling was suffering from his bruises and sprained wrist, and he evidently was not pleased to hear these liberal criticisms, but knowing the element by which he was surrounded, he did not forget the policy of conciliating it in order to prevent any feelings of discontent from arising so soon after having assumed full command. He therefore quickly replied: "I have no especial regard for these Chow-chillas; you are probably aware of that, Jack; but the orders and instructions of the Commissioners will have to be disregarded if we shoot them down at sight. It would have been almost like deliberate murder to have killed those naked Indians to-day, because, Jack, you know *just* what you can do with that rifle of yours. If you had fired you knew you was sure to kill; but the Indians did not know the danger there was in coming inside your range. It was lucky for the cowards that you did not shoot." This allusion to the Texan's skill with his rifle disposed of the subject as far as he was concerned, for he " turned in," while a broad grin showed his satisfaction as he replied, " I reckon you're about on the right trail now, Cap," and disappeared under his blanket.

Captain Boling sat for some time apparently watching the blazing logs before him. He took no part in the discussion of Indian affairs, which continued to be the engrossing subject among the wakeful ones, whose numbers gradually diminished until Spencer and one or two others beside myself only remained at our fire. The Captain then said: " I do not despair of success in causing this tribe to make peace, although I cannot see any very flattering prospects of our being able to corral them, or force an immediate surrender. They do not seem inclined to fight us, and we cannot follow them among the rocks in those almost impassable cañons with any probability of taking them. Bare-footed they rapidly pass without danger over slippery rocks that we, leather-shod, can only pass at the peril of our lives. My mishap of to-day is but a single illustration of many that would follow were we to attempt to chase them along the dizzy heights they pass over. Being lightly clad, or not at all, they swim the river to and fro at will, and thus render futile any attempt to pursue them up the river, unless we divide the force and beat up on both sides at the same time. I have thought this matter over, and have reached the conclusion that, unless some lucky accident throws them into our hands, I see but one course to pursue, and that is to destroy their camps and supplies, and then return to head-quarters."

After having had the bandages arranged on his swollen arm he bade us good night, and sought such repose as his bruised limbs and disappointed ambition would permit. Having ended our discussions, we came to the sage conclu-

sion that Captain Boling was in command, and duty required our obedience to his orders. Satisfied with this decision, we readily dropped off to sleep.

The next morning the usual jocular hilarity seemed to
prevail in camp. A refreshing slumber had seemingly given
renewed vigor to the tired explorers of the rough trail up
the cañon. The camp guard assigned to duty at "our ferry" were on duty during the night, so that the breakfast call
was promptly responded to with appetites unimpaired.
Captain Boling's arm was dressed and found to be somewhat
improved in appearance, though very sore. He would not
consent to remain in camp, and ordered his horse to be saddled after breakfast. Before the morning sun had risen we
were in our saddles, endeavoring to explore the region north
of the San Joaquin. Small detachments were detailed from
both companies to explore, on foot, up the South Fork, and
the territory adjacent. Upon the return of this command,
their report showed that quite a large number of Indians
had passed over that stream, though none were seen. A
considerable supply of acorns was found and destroyed by
this expedition; but after they left the oak table-land, near
the fork, they reported the country to the east to be about
as forbidding as that on the main river. Captain Boling
detailed a few footmen to scatter over the country on the
north side, to burn any *cachés* they might find, while we on
horseback swept farther north, towards the Black Ridge.
We found the soil soft and yielding, and in places it was
with difficulty that our weak, grass-fed animals could pass
over the water-soaked land, even after we had dismounted.
I thought this boggy ground, hard enough later in the season, another obstacle to a successful pursuit, and so expressed
myself to the Captain. I told him that in '49 I stayed over
night with Mr. Livermore of the Livermore Pass, and that
now I fully comprehended why he thought the mountain

tribes could not be entirely subdued, because, as he said, "they will not fight except sure of victory, and cannot be caught."

Mr. Livermore said he had followed up several raiding parties of Indians who were driving off stock they had stolen from the Ranchos, but only upon one occasion did they make a bold stand, when his party was driven back, overcome by numbers. Captain Boling was silent for some time, and then said: "Perhaps after all I have done these Indians injustice in calling them cowards; probably they feel that they are not called upon to fight and lose any of their braves, when by strategy they can foil and elude us. Human nature is about alike in war as in other things; it is governed by what it conceives to be its interest."

CACHES OR INDIAN ACORN STOREHOUSES.

There were in the country we passed over, some beautiful mountain meadows and most luxuriant forests, and some of the sloping table lands looked like the ornamental parks of an extensive domain. These oak-clad tables and ridges, were the harvest fields of the San Joaquin Indians, and in their vicinity we found an occasional group of deserted huts. These, with their adjacent supplies of acorns, were at once given to the flames. The acorns found and destroyed by the scouting parties, were variously estimated at from eight hundred to one thousand bushels; beside the supply of Piñon pine-nuts and other supplies hoarded for future use. The pine-nuts were not all destroyed by fire; most of them were confiscated, and served as a dessert to many a roast.

From the total amount of acorns estimated to have been destroyed, their supplies were comparatively small, or the number of Indians on the San Joaquin had been, as in other localities, vastly overrated. Our search was thoroughly made—the explorations from day to day, extending from our camps over the whole country to an altitude above the growth of the oaks. During these expeditions, not an Indian was seen after those noticed on the upper San Joaquin; but fresh signs were often discovered and followed, only to be traced to the rocky cañons above where, like deceptive "*ignes fatui*," they disappeared.

Being allowed the largest liberty as surgeon to the expedition, I had ample time to examine the various things found in their camps, and obtain from Sandino all the information I could concerning them. The stone arrow-heads and their manufacture, especially interested me. I found considerable quantities of the crude material from which they were made, with many other articles brought from other localities, such as resin, feathers, skins, pumice-stone, salt, etc., used in the manufacture of their implements of war, and for the chase as well as for domestic uses.

At this time but few guns were in the possession of these mountain tribes. Their chief weapons of war and for the chase were bows and arrows. With these they were very expert at short range, and to make their weapons effective were disposed to lay in ambush in war, and upon the trails of their game. Their bows were made from a species of yew peculiar to the West, from cedar and from a spinated evergreen tree, rare in Southern California, which, for want of scientific classification, I gave the name of "nutmeg pine." It bears a nut resembling in general appearance that agreeable spice, while the covering or pulpy shell looks very much like mace. The nut is, however, strongly impregnated with resin. The leaves are long, hard, and so sharp that the points will pierce the flesh like sharp steel. The wood is stronger and more elastic than either the yew, cedar or fir. It is susceptible of a fine polish. I made a discovery of a small cluster of this species of tree at the foot of the cascades in the cañon, two miles below the Yosemite valley, while engaged in a survey of that locality.*

The shafts of their arrows are made of reeds, and from different species of wood, but the choicest are made of what is called Indian arrow-wood (Le Hamite). This wood is only found in dark ravines and deep rocky cañons in the mountains, as it seems to require dampness and shade. Its scarcity makes the young shoots of a proper growth a very valuable article of barter between the mountain tribes and those of the valleys and plains. A locality in the Yosemite valley once famous for its supply of this arrow-wood, was the ravine called by the Yosemites " Le-Hamite," (as we might say "the oaks," or " the pines,") but which is now designated as " Indian Cañon."

Their arrow-shafts are first suitably shaped, and then polished between pieces of pumice stone. This stone was also used in fashioning and polishing their bows, spear-shafts and war clubs. Pumice stone is found in abundance in the volcanic regions of California and Oregon, and east of the Sierra Nevada. The quality of the best observed by me, was much finer and lighter than that seen in the shops as an article of commerce. The arrow heads are secured to the shaft by threads of sinew, and a species of cement used

---

* I have learned through the kindness of Dr. A. Kellogg, of the California Academy of Sciences, that this tree is now known as the " *Torreya Californica.*"

for that and other purposes. The arrow-heads made and in most common use by the California Indians, as well as by many other tribes in the mountain ranges of the West and Southwest, are of the same shape and general appearance, and of similar material, with the exception of obsidian and old junk bottles, as the arrow heads found in all parts of the United States. They have been generally supposed to have been made and used by the pre-historic races that once inhabited this continent. The bow and arrows were in common use by the aborigines when America was first discovered, and their use has been continued to the present time among the tribes whose limited territories were not to any extent intruded upon by the whites.

The Indians of California, unlike those of Southern Mexico and South America, who use the woorara (strychnos toxifera), poison their arrow-heads with the poison of the rattlesnake. Some animal's liver is saturated with the poison and left until it reaches a state of thorough decomposition, when the barbs are plunged into the festering mass, withdrawn and dried. The gelatinous condition of the liver causes the poison to adhere to the stone, and the strength of the poison is thus preserved for some days. Only those arrow-heads that are inserted into a socket, and held in place by cement, are thus poisoned. These are easily detached after striking an object (the concussion shattering the cement, and the play of the shaft loosening the barb), and are left to rankle in the wound.

According to Russio, however, this practice is now seldom resorted to, except in revenge for some great or fancied injury, or by the more malignant of a tribe, Indian policy seeming to discountenance a former custom.

The introduction of fire arms among them, has been from the frontiers of civilization. The "*flint,*" or more properly cherty rock, when first quarried, is brittle and readily split and broken into the desired shapes required, even with the rude implements used by the Indians; though it is not probable that any but themselves could use them, as considerable skill seems to be required. The tool commonly used in the manufacture of arrow-heads, is a species of hammer or pick, made by fastening the sharp prong of a deer's horn to a long stick.

With these instruments of various sizes laminated pieces of rock are separated, such as slate, with quartz in filtrations, and scales are chipped from rocks, volcanic and other glass, with a skill that challenges admiration. Stone hammers, or pieces of hard stone, were secured by withes and used in some of the processes of flaking; and I have been assured that steel implements have been stolen from the miners and used for the same purpose, but I never saw them used. Arrow-heads were found, made from bones, from chert, obsidian or volcanic glass, and even old junk bottles, obtained for the purpose, during their gushing days, from the deserted camps of the libative miners.

The most approved fire-arms are now found among many of the western tribes, where but a few years ago bows and arrows were in common use. Although these hereditary implements of war and of the chase are almost wholly discarded, occasionally an old-fashioned Indian may be seen, armed with his bow and arrows, his fire-stick a foot long, occupying the hole punctured in the lobe of one ear, and his reed-pipe filling the like position in the other, while his skunk-skin pouch contained his kin-ne-kin-nick, a piece of spunk and dry charred cedar, on which a light was obtained by rapid friction with his fire-stick. This method of procuring fire, has, even among the Indians, been superseded by the flint and steel, and they in turn by the labor-saving friction matches.

I have, however, recently witnessed the process of lighting a fire by this primitive process, among the priests of the Winnebago and other eastern tribes, who still use and preserve the fire-stick in making fire for their sacred rites, during which they chant in a traditionary Indian dead language, an interpretation of which they do not pretend they are able to make. The priests told me that bad spirits would interfere with their ministrations if they did not preserve the customs of their fathers, and that the dead language made their ceremonies all the more impressive and awe-inspiring to their auditors.

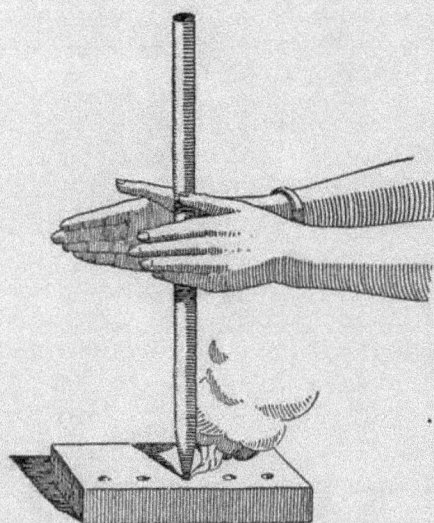

During our explorations up the San Joaquin and branches, the rapidly melting snow on the mountains above flooded the streams which we were required to cross in our excursions, and we were often compelled from this cause to leave our horses and proceed on foot; hence our work was toilsome and slow.

FIRE STICK AS USED.

As soon as Captain Boling was satisfied that we had accomplished, in this locality, all that could be expected of his command, we started for head-quarters. The route selected for our return was by way of "Fine Gold Gulch," and down the San Joaquin to a camp opposite the site of Fort Miller, that was about being established for the protection of the settlers. This was done upon recommendation of the commissioners.

CHAPTER IX.

A FEW days after our return from the campaign against
the Chow-chil-las, a small delegation from a Kah-we-ah band
on King's river was sent in by Captain Kuykendall, whose
energy had subdued nearly all of the Indians in his department. The chief of this band informed Major Savage that
Tom-kit and Frederico, successors in authority to Jose Rey,
had visited his camp, and had reported that they were very
hungry. They came, they said, to hold a council. The
chief told the Major that he had advised them to come in
with him and make a treaty, but they refused. They said
the white man's "medicine" was too powerful for them;
but if their great chief had not died, he would have driven
the white men from the mountains, for he was "a heap
wise." The white soldiers had killed their great chief; they
had killed many of their best warriors; they had burned up
their huts and villages and destroyed their supplies, and
had tried to drive their people from their territory, and
they would kill their women and children if they did not
hide them where they could not be found; and much more
in a similar vein.

A small supply of acorns had been given these fugitives,

and when the chief left, they had promised to return and hear what the commissioners had said. Major Savage reported this, and with the commissioners' approval, decided to return with the Kah-we-ah chief and meet in counsel with the Chow-chil-las. He took with him sufficient "beef" on foot to give the Indians a grand feast, which lasted several days; during which time arrangements were completed for treaties with all of the remaining bands of the Kah-we-ah tribe, and with the Chow-chillas. The result of the Major's negotiations were in the highest degree satisfactory. Captain Boling, however, claimed some of the honor, for, said he, I defeated the Chow-chillas by *firing at long range.*

This once turbulent and uncompromising tribe became the most tractable of the mountain Indians. They were superior in all respects to those of most other tribes. They had intimate relations with the Monos, a light colored race as compared with the Valley or Kah-we-ah tribe, and were very expert in the manufacture and use of the bow and arrow. The Mono's had intermarried with the Chow-chil-las, and they aided them in their intercourse with the Pah-u-tes in their barter for salt, obsidian, lava and other commodities. The Chow-chil-las now being disposed of, and a treaty signed by the other tribes, it was decided by the commissioners that our next expedition should be against the Yo-sem-i-tes. This had been recommended by Major Savage as the only practical method of effecting any terms with their old Chief. Every inducement had been offered them that had been successful with the others; but had been treated with contempt. The liberal supplies of beef they refused, saying they preferred horse-flesh. The half-civilized garbs and gaudy presents tendered at the agency were scorned by Ten-ie-ya as being no recompense for relinquishing the freedom of his mountain home. Major Savage announced that the expedition would start as soon as the floods had somewhat subsided, so that the streams could be crossed. As for ourselves, we had learned to take advantage of any narrow place in a stream, and by means of ropes stretched for feet and hands, we crossed without difficulty streams that we could not ford with horses. As this delay would allow an opportunity for some of the battalion to see to such private business as required their attention, short furloughs were granted to those most anxious to improve this occasion.

While the companies of Captains Boling and Dill were exploring the vicinities of the Merced and San Joaquin in search of Indians, Captain Kuykend.ll, with the able support of his Lieutenants and his company, were actively engaged in the same duties south of the San Joaquin. Captain Kuykendall vigorously operated in the valleys, foot-hills and mountains of the King's and Kah-we-ah rivers, and those of the smaller streams south. The Indians of Kern river, owing to the influence of a mission Chief, "Don-Vincente," who had a plantation at the Tehon pass, remained peaceful, and were not disturbed. The success of Captain Kuykendall's campaigns enabled the commissioners to make treaties with all the tribes within the Tulare valley, and those that occupied the region south of the San Joaquin river.

Owing to lapse of time since these events, and other causes, I am unable to do justice to him, or the officers and men under him. My personal recollections of the incidents of his explorations, were acquired while exchanging stories around camp fires. Operating as they did, among the most inaccessible mountains in California, with but one company, they successfully accomplished the duties assigned them.

It was supposed that some of the tribes and bands among whom they were sent were extremely hostile to the whites, and that they would combine and resist their approach; but after a single engagement on King's river, the Indians were put to flight without the loss of a man, and could not be induced to hazard another like encounter. The plans of operation were similar to those of Captains Boling and Dill: the destruction of the camps of all who refused to come in and have a talk with the commissioners. Captain Kuykendall's company found these people almost without fire-arms and civilized clothing of any kind, and depending wholly on their bows and arrows. Except in the vicinity of King's and Kah-we-ah rivers, the savages were scattered over a large range of country. Their camps were generally in the valleys and among the foot-hills; when alarmed, they fled to the rocky cañons among the mountains. In one of our conversations, during a visit of Captain Kuykendall to the Fresno, he said: "When we first started out, we learned from our scouts and guides, that a large body of Indians had collected well up on King's river. Making a rapid march, we found, on arriving in sight, that they were inclined to give us battle. We at once charged into their camp, routed and killed a number, while others were ridden down and taken prisoners. We followed the fugitives, making a running fight, until compelled to leave our horses, when they eluded pursuit. Not yet discouraged, we followed on toward the head waters of the Kah-we-ah, seeing occasionally, upon a ridge just ahead of us, groups of Indians; but upon our reaching *that* locality, they were resting on the *next ridge;* and as we came into view, turned their backs upon us, applauding our efforts to overtake them, in a very *peculiar* manner. They fled into a worse country than anything before seen in our explorations, and I soon perceived the folly of attempting to follow them longer. As to this region east and southeast of the termination of our pursuit, I have only this to say, that it is simply indescribable. I did not see any '*dead Indians*' after leaving the village, and during the pursuit, although some of the boys were sure they had 'fetched their man.' It is certain that a number were killed in the assault, but how many, we were unable to ascertain, for upon our return, as usual, the dead had been carried off. We lost no men in the fight, and had but one wounded. The wound was very painful, having been inflicted by one of the glass arrowheads that it is designed shall be left rankling in the wound; but after that was extracted, the wound soon healed without serious results."

After this chase on foot into the "High Sierras," the operations of Capt. Kuykendall were more limited, for, as he had stated, he regarded it as the height of folly to attempt to follow the lightly-armed and lighter clad "hostiles" with cavalry, into their rocky mountain retreats. In the saddle, except a few sailors in his company, his men felt at home, and were willing to perform any amount of severe duty, however dangerous or difficult it might be, but on foot, the Texans, especially, were like "Jack ashore, without anything to steer by." When required to take a few days, provisions and their blankets on their backs, their efforts, like those of our command, were not very effective, so far as catching the natives was concerned. These foot expeditions were designed by the officers to keep the enemy alarmed, and in the cold regions, while their supplies were being destroyed by the mounted force ranging below. By this strategy, Captain Kuykendall kept his men constantly occupied, and at the same time displayed his genius as a soldier.

His foot expeditions were generally made by a few enthusiastic scouts, who were as much induced to volunteer to perform this duty from a love of nature as from a desire to fight. Here were found

> "The palaces of Nature, whose vast walls
> Have pinnacled in clouds their snowy scalps,
> And throned eternity in icy halls
> Of cold sublimity, where forms and falls
> The avalanche—the thunderbolt of snow!
> All that expands the spirit, yet appals,
> Gather around these summits, as to show
> How earth may pierce to Heaven, yet leave vain man below."

The stories told by the men in Kuykendall's command were received with doubts, or as exaggerations. Their descriptions represented deeper valleys and higher cliffs than had been seen and described by scouts of the other companies. It was intimated by us, who had previously described the region of the Yosemite, "that the man who told the first story in California stood a poor chance." Having read Professor J. D. Whitney's reports of that region, I can better appreciate the reports of Captain Kuykendall and those under him, of the character of the mountain territory to which they had been assigned. Mr. Whitney, State Geologist, in speaking of the geological survey of this vicinity, says: "Of the terrible grandeur of the region embraced in this portion of the Sierra, it is hardly possible to convey any idea. Mr. Gardner, in his notes of the view from Mount Brewer, thus enumerates some of the most striking features of the scene: 'Cañons from two to five thousand feet deep, between thin ridges topped with pinnacles sharp as needles; successions of great crater-like amphitheatres, with crowning precipices, over-sweeping snow-fields and frozen lakes, everywhere naked and shattered granite without a sign of vegetation, except where a few gnarled and storm-beaten pines * * * cling to the rocks in the deeper cañons; such were the elements of the scene we looked down upon, while cold gray clouds were drifting overhead.'"

This description applies more properly to the territory east of any point reached by Captain Kuykendall, but it verifies the statements made by him and those of some of his men.

While on our second expedition to the Yosemite, some of Captain Kuykendall's company, who had come to headquarters and had been allowed the privileges, volunteered to accompany our supply train, as they said : "To see what kind of a country we were staying in." One, an enthusiastic lover of nature, said on his return : "The King's river country, and the territory southeast of it, beats the Yosemite in terrific grandeur, but in sublime beauty you have got us." As the furloughs granted to the members of B. and C. companies expired, all promptly reported for duty, and preparations were completed for another campaign against the Yosemites.

Captain Dill, with part of his company, was retained on duty at headquarters, while Lt. Gilbert with a detachment of C. Company, was ordered to report for duty to Captain Boling. Dr. Pfifer was placed in charge of a temporary hospital, erected for the use of the battalion. Surgeon Bronson had resigned, preferring the profits received from his negro slaves, who were then mining on Sherlock's creek to all the romance of Indian warfare. The doctor was a clever and genial gentleman, but a poor mountaineer. Doctor Lewis Leach was appointed to fill the vacancy. Doctor Black was ordered to duty with Captain Boling. Major Savage offered me a position, and it was urged upon me by Captain Boling, but having a number of men engaged in a mining enterprise, in which Spencer and myself were interested, we had mutually agreed to decline all office. Beside this, when Mr. Spencer and myself entered into service together, it was with the expectation that we would soon be again at liberty. But once in the service, our personal pride and love of adventure would not allow us to become *subordinate* by accepting office.

As it was the design of Major Savage to make a thorough search in the territory surrounding the Yosemite, if we failed in surprising the inhabitants in their valley, a few scouts and guides were provided for the expedition to aid in our search among the " High Sierras," so distinctively named by Prof. Whitney. Among our ample supplies ropes were furnished, by order of Major Savage, suitable for floats, and for establishing bridges where needed. These bridges were suggested by myself, and were useful as a support while passing through swift water, or for crossing narrow but rushing torrents. This was accomplished expeditiously by simply stretching "*taut*" two ropes, one above the other, the upper rope, grasped by the hands, serving to secure the safe passage of the stream. Where trees were not found in suitable position to make the suspension, poles were lashed together so as to form *shears*, which served for trestles. I also suggested that snow-shoes could probably be used with advantage on our mountain excursions. The use of these I found entirely unknown, except to Major Savage and a few other eastern men. My experience favored their use, as I had often found it easier to travel *over* deep snow than to wallow through it. My suggestion caused a "*heap*" of merriment, and my friend Chandler laughed until he became "*powerful weak*," and finally I was assailed by so many shafts of witty raillery from my southern comrades, that I was willing to retreat, and cry out, ' hold, enough!' "

The services of Major Savage being indispensable to the Commissioners, it was decided that the expedition would be under the command of Captain Boling. In making this announcement, the Major said: he expected Ten-ie-ya and his people would come in with us if he was formally invited, and a sufficient escort provided. Captain Boling very seriously assured the Major, that if the Yosemites accepted the invitation, he should endeavor to make the trip a *secure* one; there should be no neglect on the part of the escort if suitable *supplies* were provided for subsistence. Major Savage laughingly replied that as the expedition would be under the especial command of Captain Boling, he had no fears that ample supplies would not be provided.

Our preparations being made, we again started for the Merced in search of the Yosemites. It was the design of Capt. Boling to surprise the Indians if possible, and if not, to cut off the escape of their women and children, the capture of whom, would soon bring the warriors to terms. With this plan in view, and leaving Chandler virtually in command of the column, we made a rapid march direct for their valley, crossing the streams without much difficulty, and without accident.

The advance, consisting of Captain Boling with a small detachment, and some of the scouts, quietly entered the valley, but no Indians were seen. A few new wigwams had been built on the south side near the lower ford, to better guard the entrance as was supposed. Without halting, except to glance at the vacant huts, the advance rode rapidly on, following a trail up the south side, which our Pohonochee guide informed the captain was a good trail.

On entering the valley and seeing the deserted wigwams I reached the conclusion that our approach had been heralded. As my military ardor subsided, my enthusiastic love of the beautiful returned to me, and I halted a moment to take a general view of the scenery; intending also to direct the column up the south side. While waiting for Chandler, I examined the huts, and found several bushels of scorched acorns that had been divested of their covering, as if for transportation. I knew that the natives had no more fondness for burnt acorns than Yankees have for burnt beans, and the interpreter Sandino, who was with me at this

—no got much eat; acorns, fire burn—pull 'em out." In one of the huts we found a young dog, a miserable cur that barked his affright at our approach, and fled into the brush near by. I told Lt. Chandler of the directions left for his guidance, and as he expressed his intention to bring up the rear of the column into closer order, I received permission to move slowly on with his advance, consisting of Fire-baugh, Spencer, French, Fisher, Stone, a few others and myself. We were soon overtaken by Chandler, who had given his orders to the rear-guard. As we rode along, I reported the conclusions of Sandino and my knowledge of the fact that nearly all the acorns had been burnt. I also told him what Sandino had previously said, that the Indians took the shells off the acorns they carried over the mountains, and from this cause, thought the hulled acorns found were designed for a distant transportation. Again referring the matter to Sandino, who was called up for the purpose, he said, "No fire when take off skin; no like 'em; Yosemite close by, want 'em acorn." Upon telling Chandler that Sandino's opinion was that the acorns found were saved from some of the burning supplies fired at our first visit, and that the Yosemites were transporting them to some mountain retreat, the Lieutenant could not credit it, and said that "Sandino's opinions are unreliable."

Sandino was not popular, either with our officers or with the "boys." Captain Boling doubted his integrity, while Chandler said he was a most arrant coward and afraid of the wild Indians. Chandler was right; but, nevertheless, Sandino told us many truths. At times his timidity and superstition were very annoying; but if reproved, he became the more confused, and said that many questions made his head ache; *a very common answer to one in search of knowledge among Indians.* Sandino had been sent along by the Major as our interpreter, but a Spanish interpreter was necessary to make him of any use. As a scout he was inferior—almost useless. We afterwards found that Sandino's surmises were true. It was evident that the fire had been extinguished at some of the large heaps, and many acorns saved, though in a damaged condition.

As we rode on up the valley, I became more observant of the scenery than watchful for signs, when suddenly my attention was attracted by shadowy objects flitting past rocks and trees on the north side, some distance above El Capitan. Halting, I caught a glimpse of Indians as they passed an open space opposite to us. Seeing that they were discovered, they made no further efforts to hide their movements, but came out into open view, at long rifle range. There were five of them. They saluted us with taunting gestures, and fearlessly kept pace with us as we resumed our march. The river was here a foaming impassable torrent. The warriors looked with great indifference on our repeated efforts to discover a fording place. As we approached a stretch of comparatively smooth water, I made known to Chandler my intention of swimming the stream to capture them. His answer was: "Bully for you, Doc; take 'em, if you can, alive, but take 'em *anyhow*." I started with Spencer, Firebaugh, French, young Stone and two others, for a sloping bank where our animals would most willingly enter the stream; but Stone spurred passed me as we reached the bank, and when Firebaugh's mulish mustang refused the water, though given the spur, and all the other mules refused to leave the horse, Stone backed his mule over the bank, and we swam our mules after the "boy leader" across the Merced.

The Indians, alarmed by this unexpected movement, fled up the valley at the top of their speed. By the time we had crossed, they had nearly reached a bend in the river

found the trail obstructed by a mass of what then appeared to be recently fallen rocks. Without hesitation, we abandoned our mules, and continued the pursuit on foot, up to the

KOUSEWORTH & CO. PHOTO.

THE THREE BROTHERS.
(3,850 feet in height.)

rocky spur known as the "Three Brothers," where entering the Talus, they disappeared. Find them, we could not. The obstructing rocks on the old north side trail were known as "We-äck," "The Rocks," and understood to mean the "fallen rocks," because, according to traditions they had fallen *upon* the old trail. The modern trail for horses crossed the stream a short distance below, where there was a very good ford in a lower stage of water, but at this time, the early part of May, the volume of water rushing down the Merced was astonishing. We had crossed readily enough in the heat of excitement; but it was with feelings of reluctance that we re-entered the cold water and swam our mules back to where a few of our comrades had halted on the south side.

Mr. Firebaugh, having failed to get his mustang to follow us, had run him up on the south side as if to cut off the fugitives, and saw them hide behind a ledge of rocks.

When informed of the situation, Capt. Boling crossed to the north side and came down to the ledge where the scouts were hidden; but the Captain could scarcely at first credit Firebaugh's statement, that he had seen them climb up the cliff. Our Indian scouts were sent up to hunt out the hidden warriors, and through the means of fair promises, if they came down voluntarily, Captain Boling succeeded in bringing in the five Indians. Three of the captives were known to us, being sons of Ten-ie-ya, one of whom was afterwards killed; the other two were young braves, the wife of one being a daughter of the old chief. The Indian name for the three rocky peaks near which this capture was made was not then known to any of our battalion, but from the strange coincidence of three brothers being made prisoners so near them, we designated the peaks as the "Three Brothers." I soon learned that they were called by the Indians "Kom-po-pai-zes," from a fancied resemblance of the peaks to the heads of frogs when sitting up *ready to leap*. A fanciful interpretation has been given the Indian name as meaning "mountains playing leap-frog," but a literal translation is not desirable.

They hear the plaintive bull-frog to his mistress trilling sweet;
They see the green-robed sirens plunge down in waters deep.
But leap these mountains may not; they watch, with clouded brow,
Return of young Ten-ie-ya—heard not his death's pow-wow.

CHAPTER X.

WHILE Captain Boling was engaged in capturing the Indians we had "treed" on the north side of the valley, scouting parties were sent out by Lieut. Chandler. They spread over the valley, and search was made in every locality that was accessible. Discovering fresh signs on a trail I had unsuccessfully followed on my first visit, I pursued the traces up to a short distance below Mirror Lake. Being alone I divided my attention between the wonders of the scenery and the tracks I was following, when suddenly I was aroused by discovering a basket of acorns lying by the trail. Seeing that it was a common carrying basket, such as was generally used by the squaws in "packing," I at first came to the conclusion that it had been thrown off by some affrighted squaw in her haste to escape on my approach. Observing another on a trail leading toward the Talus, I felt confident that I had discovered the key to the hiding-place of the Indians we were in search of. Securing my mule with the "riata" I continued the search, and found several baskets before reaching the walls of the cliff, up which, in a kind of groove, the trail ascended. By this time I began to be suspicious, and thought that there was too much method in this distribution of acorns along the trail for frightened squaws to have made, and it now occurred to me what Sandino had said of acorns being hulled for transportation up the cliffs; and these *had not been hulled!*

Before reaching the Talus, I observed that the foot-prints were large, and had been made by the males, as the toes did not turn in, as was usual with the squaws; and it now began to appear to me, that the acorns were only left to lead us into some trap; for I was aware that "warriors" seldom disgraced themselves by "packing," like squaws. Taking a look about me, I began to feel that I was venturing too far; my ambitious desire for further investigation vanished, and I hastened back down the trail. While descending, I met Lt. Gilbert of C company, with a few men. They too had discovered baskets, dropped by the "*scared Indians*," and were rushing up in hot pursuit, nearly *capturing* me. I related my discoveries, and told the Lieutenant of my suspicions, advising him not to be too hasty in following up the "*lead.*" After I had pointed out some of the peculiarities of the location above us, he said with a sigh of disappointment, "By George! Doc. I believe you are right—you are more of an Indian than I am any way; I reckon we had better report this to the Captain before we go any further." I replied, "I am now going in to report this strategy to Captain Boling, for I believe he can make some flank movement and secure the Indians, without our being caught in this trap." But while we were descending to the trail, I seriously thought and believed, that Lt. Gilbert and his men as well as myself, had had a narrow escape. The bit of history of the rear guard of Charlemagne being destroyed by the Pyrenians flashed through my mind, and I could readily see how destructive such an attack might become.

After taking the precaution to secrete the baskets on the main trail, Lt. Gilbert, with his scouts, continued his explorations in other localities, saying as he left that he would warn all whom he might see "not to get into the trap." I mounted my mule and rode down the valley in search of Captain Boling, and found him in an oak grove near our old camp, opposite a cliff, now known as " Hammo" (the lost arrow). I here learned the particulars of his successful capture of the five scouts of Ten-ie-ya's band, and at his request asked them, through Sandino, who had come over with the "*kitchen mules*," why they had so exposed themselves to our view. They replied that Ten-ie-ya knew of our approach before we reached the valley. That by his orders they were sent to watch our movements and report to him. That they did not think we could cross the Merced with our horses until we reached the upper fords; and therefore, when discovered, did not fear. They said that Ten-ie-ya would come in and "have a talk with the white chief when he knows we are here."

After repeated questioning as to where their people were, and where the old chief would be found if a messenger should be sent to him, they gave us to understand that they were to meet Ten-ie-ya near To-co-ya, at the same time pointing in the direction of the "North Dome." Captain Boling assured them that if Ten-ie-ya would come in with his people he could do so with safety. That he desired to make peace with him, and did not wish to injure any of them. The young brave was the principal spokesman, and he replied : "Ten-ie-ya will come in when he hears what has been said to us."

Having acquired all the information it was possible to get from the Indians, Capt. Boling said that in the morning he would send a messenger to the old chief and see if he would come in. When told this the young "brave" appeared to be very anxious to be permitted to go after him, saying: "He is there now," pointing towards the "North Dome," "another day he will be on the 'Skye Mountains,' or anywhere," meaning that his movements were uncertain.

Capt. Boling had so much confidence in his statements, that he decided to send some of the scouts to the region of the North Dome for Ten-ie-ya; but all efforts of our allies and of ourselves, failed to obtain any further clue to Ten-ie-ya's hiding-place, for the captives said that they dare not disclose their signals or countersign, for the penalty was death, and none other would be answered or understood by their people. I here broke in upon the captain's efforts to obtain *useful knowledge* from his prisoners, by telling him of the discovery of baskets of acorns found on the trail; and gave him my reasons for believing it to be a design to lead us into an ambush—that the Indians were probably on the cliff above. I volunteered the suggestion that a movement in that direction would surprise them while watching the trap set for us.

Captain Boling replied: " It is too late in the day for a job of that kind; we will wait and see if Ten-ie-ya will come in. I have made up my mind to send two of our prisoners after him, and keep the others as hostages until he comes. To make a sure thing of this, Doctor, I want you to take these two," pointing to one of the sons and the son-in-law of Ten-ie-ya, " and go with them to the place where they have said a trail leads up the cliff to Ten-ie-ya's hiding place. You will take care that they are not molested by any of our boys while on this trip. Take any one with you in camp, if you do not care to go alone."

Taking a small lunch to break my fast since the morning meal, I concluded to make the trip on foot; my mule having been turned loose with the herd. Arming myself, I started alone with the two prisoners which Capt. Boling had consigned to my guardianship. I kept them ahead of me on the trail, as I always did when traveling with any of that race. We passed along the westerly base of the North Dome at a rapid gait, without meeting any of my comrades, and had reached a short turn in the trail around a point of rocks, when the Indians suddenly sprang back, and jumped behind me. From their frightened manner, and cry of terror, I was not apprehensive of any treachery on their part. Involuntarily I cried out, "Hallo! what's up now?" and stepped forward to see what had so alarmed them. Before me, stood George Fisher with his rifle leveled at us. I instantly said: "Hold on George! these Indians are under my care!" He determinedly exclaimed without change of position, "Get out of the way, Doctor, those Indians have got to die." Just behind Fisher was Sergeant Cameron, with a man on his shoulders. As he hastily laid him on the ground, I was near enough to see that his clothing was soiled and badly torn, and that his face, hands and feet were covered with blood. His eyes were glazed and bloodshot, and it was but too evident that he had been seriously injured. From the near proximity of the basket trail, I instantly surmised they had been on the cliff above. The scene was one I shall long remember.

It seemed but a single motion for Cameron to deposit his burden and level his rifle. He ordered me to stand aside if I valued my own safety. I replied as quietly as I could, "Hold on, boys! Captain Boling sent me to guard these Indians from harm, and I shall obey orders." I motioned the Indians to keep to my back or they would be killed. Cameron shouted: "They have almost killed Spencer, and have got to die. As he attempted to get sight, he said: "Give way, Bunnell, I don't want to hurt you." This I thought *very condescending*, and I replied with emphasis: "These Indians are under my charge, and I shall protect them. If you shoot you commit murder." The whole transaction thus far seemingly occupied but a moment's time, when to the surprise of us all, Spencer called my name. I moved forward a little, and said to them, "Throw up your rifles and let me come into to see Spencer." "Come in! *you* are safe," replied Fisher—still watching the Indians with a fierce determination in his manner. Spencer raised himself in a sitting position, and at a glance seemed to take in the situation of affairs, for he said: "Bunnell is right; boys, don't shoot; mine is but the fortune of war;" and telling Cameron to call me, he again seemed to fall partly into stupor. As I again moved towards them with the Indians behind me, they with some reluctance, put up their rifles. Fisher turned his back to me as he said with sarcasm, "Come in with your friends, Doctor, and thank Spencer for their safety." They relieved their excitement with volleys of imprecations. Cameron said that I "was a —— sight too high-toned to suit friends that had always been willing to stand by me."

This occurrence did not destroy good feeling toward each other, for we were all good friends after the excitement had passed over.

I examined Spencer and found that, although no bones were broken, he was seriously bruised and prostrated by the shock induced by his injuries. Fisher started for camp to bring up a horse or mule to carry Spencer in. I learned that they had fallen into the trap on the "basket trail," and that Spencer had been injured while ascending the cliff as I had suspected. He had, unfortunately, been *trailed in*, as I had been. The particulars Cameron related to me and in my hearing after we had arrived in camp. As the Indians represented to me that the trail they proposed to take up the cliff was but a little way up the north branch, I concluded to go on with them, and then be back in time to accompany Spencer into camp. Speaking some cheering words to Spencer I turned to leave, when Cameron said to him: "You ain't dead yet, my boy." Spencer held out his hand, and as he took it Cameron said, with visible emotion, but emphatic declaration : "We will pay them back for this if the chance ever comes; Doc. is decidedly too conscientious in this affair." I escorted the Indians some way above "Mirror Lake," where they left the trail and commenced to climb the cliff.

On my return I found that Cameron had already started with Spencer; I soon overtook them and relieved him of his burden, and from there carried Spencer into camp. We found Fisher vainly trying to catch his mule. The most of the horses were still out with the scouts, and all animals in camp had been turned loose. Sergt. Cameron, while Fisher was assisting me in the removal of Spencer's clothing and dressing his wounds, had prepared a very comfortable bed, made of boughs, that the kind-hearted boys thoughtfully brought in; and after he was made comfortable and nourishment given him, the Sergeant related to Captain Boling the details of their adventure, which were briefly as follows: Cameron and Spencer while on their way back to camp discovered the baskets on the trail. Feeling certain that they had discovered the hiding-place of the Indians, as we had done, they concluded to make a reconnoisance of the vicinity before making a report of their discovery. Elated at their success, and unsuspicious of any unusual danger, they followed the trail that wound up the cliff, along jutting rocks that in places projected like cornices, until the converging walls forced them to a steep acclivity grooved in the smooth-worn rock. Not daunted by the difficult assent, they threw off their boots and started up the slippery gutter, when suddenly a huge mass of granite came thundering down towards them. But for a fortunate swell or prominence just above they would both have been swept into eternity; as it was, the huge rock passed over their heads; a fragment, however, struck Spencer's rifle from his hand and hurled him fifty feet or more down the steep wall, where he lay, entirely senseless for a time, while a shower of rocks and stones was passing over him, the shape of the wall above sending them clear of his body.

Cameron was in advance, and fortunately was able to reach the shelter of a projecting rock. After the discharge, an Indian stretched himself above a detached rock, from which he had been watching his supposed victims. Cameron chanced to be looking that way, and instantly firing, dropped his man. No doubt he was killed, for the quantity of blood found afterward on the rock, was great. The echoing report of Cameron's rifle, brought back howls of rage from a number of rocks above, as if they were alive with demons. Anticipating another discharge from their battery, Cameron descended to the spot where Spencer had fallen, and taking him in his arms, fled out of range.

After supper, the explorers having all come in, the boys gathered around the Sergeant and importuned him to give the history of his adventures. After reflectively bringing up the scene to view, he began: "We got into mighty close quarters! Come to think of it, I don't see how we happened to let ourselves be caught in that dead-fall. I reckon we must have fooled ourselves some. The way of it was this. We went up on the south side as far as we could ride, and after rummaging around for a while, without finding anything, Spencer wanted to go up the North Cañon and get a good look at that mountain with one side split off; so I told the boys to look about for themselves, as there were no Indians in the valley. Some of them went on up the South Cañon, and the rest of us went over to the North Cañon. After crossing the upper ford, Spencer and I concluded to walk up the cañon, so we sent our animals down to graze with the herd. Spencer looked a good long while at that split mountain, and called it a 'half dome.' I concluded he might name it what he liked, if he would leave it and go to camp; for I was getting tired and hungry and said so. Spencer said 'All right, we'll go to camp.'

On our way down, as we passed that looking-glass pond, he wanted to take one more look, and told me to go ahead and he'd soon overtake me; but that I wouldn't do, so he said: "No matter, then; I can come up some other time." As we came on down the trail below the pond, I saw some acorns scattered by the side of the trail, and told Spencer there were Indians not far off. After looking about for a while Spencer found a basket nearly full behind some rocks, and in a little while discovered a trail leading up towards the cliff. We followed this up a piece, and soon found several baskets of acorns. I forgot about being hungry, and after talking the matter over we decided to make a sort of reconnoisance before we came in to make any report. Well, we started on up among the rocks until we got to a mighty steep place, a kind of gulch that now looked as if it had been scooped out for a stone battery. The trail up it was as steep as the roof on a meeting-house, and worn so slippery that we couldn't get a foot-hold. I wanted to see what there was above, and took off my boots and started up. Spencer did the same and followed me. I had just got to the swell of the steepest slope, where a crack runs across the face of the wall, and was looking back to see if Spencer would make the riffle, when I heard a crash above me, and saw a rock as big as a hogshead rolling down the cliff toward us. I sprang on up behind a rock that happened to be in the right place, for there was no time to hunt for any other shelter.

I had barely reached cover when the bounding rock struck with a crash by my side, and bounded clear over Spencer, who had run across the crevice and was stooping down and steadying himself with his rifle. A piece of the big rock that was shattered into fragments and thrown in all directions, struck his rifle out of his hands, and sent him whirling and clutching down a wall fifty feet. He lodged out of sight, where in going up we had kicked off our leathers. I thought he was killed, for he did not answer when I called, and I had no chance then to go to him, for a tremendous shower of stones came rushing by me. I expected he would be terribly mangled at first, but soon noticed that the swell in the trail caused the rocks to bound clear over him onto the rocks in the valley. I looked up to see where they came from just as an Indian stuck his head above a rock. My rifle came up of its own accord. It was a quick sight, but with me they are generally the best, and as I fired that Indian jumped into the air with a yell and fell back onto the ledge. He was hit, I know, and I reckon *he went west*. Every rock above was soon a yelling as if alive. As I expected another discharge from their stone artillery, I slid down the trail, picked up Spencer, and "vamoused the ranche," just as they fired another shot of rocks down after us. I did not stay to see where they struck after I was out of range, for my rifle and Spencer took about all of my attention until safely down over the rocks. While I was there resting for a moment, Fisher came up the trail. He heard me fire and had heard the rocks tumbling down the cliff. Thinking some one was in trouble, he was going to find out who it was.

"We concluded at first that Spencer was done for; for his heart beat very slow and he was quite dumpish. We had just started for camp with him, and met Bunnell going out with the two Indians. I reckon we would have sent them on a trip down where it is warmer than up there on the mountains, if Spencer hadn't roused himself just then. He stopped the game. He called for the Doctor; but Bunnell was as stubborn as Firebaugh's mustang and would not leave the Indians. We had to let them pass, before he would take a look at Spencer. Doc. is generally all right enough, but he was in poor business to-day. When I told him it was his own messmate, he said it didn't matter if it were his own brother. If Captain Boling will make a shooting match and put up the other three, I'll give my horse for the first three shots. Shooting will be cheap after that."

I have given the substance only of Sergt. Cameron's talk to the group around him, though but poorly imitating his style, in order to show the feeling that was aroused by Spencer's misfortune. Spencer's uniformly quiet and gentlemanly manners, made no enemies among rough comrades, who admired the courageous hardihood of "the little fellow," and respected him as a man. Many expressions of sympathy were given by the scouts who gathered around our tent, on learning of his injury. For some days after the event, he could scarcely be recognized, his face was so swollen and discolored. But what Spencer seemed most to regret, was the injury to his feet and knees, which had been cruelly rasped by the coarse granite in his descent.

The injury from this cause was so great, that he was unable to make those explorations that footmen alone could accomplish. He was an enthusiastic lover of nature, an accomplished scholar and man of the world. Having spent five years in France and Germany in the study of modern languages, after having acquired a high standing here in Latin and Greek.

We thought him peculiarly gifted, and hoped for something from his pen descriptive of the Yosemite that would endure; but he could never be induced to make any effort to describe any feature of the valley, saying: "That fools only rush in where wise men stand in awe." We were bedfellows and friends, and from this cause chiefly, perhaps, all the incidents of his accident were strongly impressed on my memory. After his full recovery his feet remained tender for a long time, and he made but one extended exploration after his accident while in the battalion.

During the camp discussion regarding my course in saving the two captives, Captain Boling and myself were amused listeners. No great pains were taken as a rule to hide one's light under a bushel, and we were sitting not far off. The Captain said that he now comprehended the extreme anxiety of the captives to see Ten-ie-ya, as doubtless they knew of his intentions to roll rocks down on any who attempted to follow up that trail; and probably supposed we would kill them if any of us were killed. As he left our tent he remarked: "These hostages will have to stay in camp. They will not be safe outside of it, if some of the boys chance to get their eyes on them."

CHAPTER XI.

ALTHOUGH our camp was undisturbed during the night, no doubt we were watched from the adjacent cliffs, as in fact all our movements were. The captives silently occupied the places by the camp fire. They were aware of Spencer's mishap, and probably expected their lives might be forfeited; for they could see but little sympathy in the countenances of those about them. The reckless demonstrations of the more frolicksome boys were watched with anxious uncertainty. The sombre expressions and *energetic* remarks of the sympathizers of Spencer induced Captain Boling to have a special guard detailed from those who were not supposed to be prejudiced against the Indians, as it was deemed all-important to the success of the campaign that Ten-ie-ya should be conciliated or captured; therefore, this detail was designed as much for the protection of the hostages as to prevent their escape. The messengers had assured the Captain that Ten-ie-ya would be in before noon, but the hostages told Sandino that possibly the messengers might not find him near To-co-ya, where they expected to meet him, as he might go a long distance away into the mountains before they would again see him. They evidently supposed that the chief, like themselves, had become alarmed at the failure of his plan to draw us into ambush, and had fled farther into the Sierras; or else doubted his coming at all, and wished to encourage the Captain to hope for the coming of Ten-ie-ya that their own chances of escape might be improved.

Sandino professed to believe their statement, telling me that they—the five prisoners—expected to have trailed us up to the scene of Spencer's disaster; failing in which—owing to our having forced them to hide near the "Frog Mountains"—they still expected to meet him on the cliff where the rocks had been rolled down, and not at To-co-ya. In this conversation, the fact appeared—derived as he said indirectly from conversations with the prisoners—that there were projecting ledges and slopes extending along the cliff on the east side of Le-hamite to To-co-ya, where Indians could pass and re-pass, undiscovered, and all of our movements could be watched. The substance of this communication I gave to Captain Boling, but it was discredited as an impossibility; and he expressed the belief that the old chief would make his appearance by the hour agreed upon with his messengers, designated by their pointing to where the sun would be on his arrival in camp. Accordingly the Captain gave orders that no scouts would be sent out until after that time. Permission, however, was given to those who desired to leave camp for their own pleasure or diversion.

A few took advantage of this opportunity and made excursions up the North Cañon to the "basket trail," with a view of examining that locality, and at the same time indulging their curiosity to see the place where Cameron and Spencer had been trailed in and entrapped by the Indians. Most of the command preferred to remain in camp to repair damages, rest, and to amuse themselves in a general way. Among the recreations indulged in, was shooting at a target with the bows and arrows taken from the captured Indians. The bow and arrows of the young brave were superior to those of the others, both in material and workmanship. Out of curiosity some of the boys induced him to give a specimen of his skill. His shots were really commendable. The readiness with which he handled his weapons excited the admiration of the lookers on. He, with apparent ease, flexed a bow which many of our men could not bend without great effort, and whose shots were as liable to endanger the camp as to hit the target. This trial of skill was witnessed by Captain Boling and permitted, as no trouble was anticipated from it.

After this exercise had ceased to be amusing, and the most of those in camp had their attention engaged in other matters, the guard, out of curiosity and for pastime, put up the target at long range. To continue the sport it was necessary to bring in the arrows used, and as it was difficult to find them, an Indian was taken along to aid in the search. The young brave made a more extended shot than all others. With great earnestness he watched the arrow, and started with one of the guard, who was unarmed, to find it. While pretending to hunt for the "lost arrow," he made a dash from the guard toward "Indian Cañon," and darted into the rocky Talus, which here encroached upon the valley. The guard on duty hearing the alarm of his comrade and seeing the Indian at full speed, fired at him, but without effect, as the intervening rocks and the zig-zag course he was running, made the shot a difficult one, without danger of hitting his comrade, who was following in close pursuit.

This aggravating incident greatly annoyed Capt. Boling, who was peculiarly sensitive on the subject of escaped prisoners. The verdant guard was reprimanded in terms more expressive than polite; and relieved from duty. The remaining Indians were then transferred to the special care of Lt. Chandler, who was told by Capt. Boling to "keep them secure if it took the whole command to do it." The Indians were secured by being tied back to back, with a "riata" or picket rope, and then fastened to an oak tree in the middle of the camp, and the guard—a new one—stationed where they could constantly watch. The morning passed, and the hour of ten arrived, without Ten-ie-ya. Capt. Boling then sent out Sandino and the scouts to hunt for him, and if found, to notify him that he was expected. Sandino soon came back, and reported that he had seen Ten-ie-ya and talked with him; but that he was unable to reach him from below, on account of the steepness of the ledge. Sandino reported that Ten-ie-ya was unwilling to come in. That he expressed a determination not to go to the Fresno. He would make peace with the white chief if he would be allowed to remain in his own territory. Neither he nor his people would go to the valley while the white men were there. They would stay on the mountains or go to the Monos.

When this was communicated to Capt. Boling, he gave orders for a select number of scouts to make an effort to bring in the old malcontent, *alive if possible*. Lt. Chandler, therefore, with a few Noot-chü and Po-ho-no-chee scouts, to climb above the projecting ledge, and a few of our men to cut off retreat, started up the Ten-ie-ya branch, led by Sandino as guide. After passing the "Royal Arches," Sandino let Chandler understand that he and his scouts had best go up by the Wai-ack or Mirror Lake trail, in order to cut off Ten-ie-ya's retreat; while he went back to the rock he pointed out as the place where he had seen and talked with Ten-ie-ya; and which commanded a view of our camp. This was distasteful to Chandler; but after a moment's reflection said: "Let the converted knave go back to camp;

I'll act without him, and catch the old chief if he is on the mountain, and that without resorting to Indian treachery."

While in camp Sandino had seemed to convey some message to the hostages, and when asked the purport of it had answered evasively. This had prejudiced Chandler, but it had not surprised me, nor did it appear inconsistent with Sandino's loyalty to Captain Boling; but the Indian was unpopular. As to his code of honor and his morality, it was about what should have been expected of one in his position, and as a frequent interpreter of his interpretations and sayings, I finally told the Captain and Chandler that it would be best to take Sandino for what he might be worth; as continued doubt of him could not be disguised, and would tend to make a knave or fool of him. On one occasion, he was so alarmed by some cross looks and words given him, that he fell upon his knees and begged for his life, thinking, as he said afterward, that he was to be killed.

During the night, and most of the time during the day, I was engaged in attendance on Spencer. Doctor Black understood it to be Spencer's wish that I should treat him. I gave but little attention to other matters, although I could see from our tent everything that was going on in camp. Not long after the departure of Chandler and his scouts, as I was about leaving camp in search of balsam of fir and other medicinals, I observed one of the guard watching the prisoners with a pleased and self-satisfied expression. As I glanced toward the Indians I saw that they were endeavoring to untie each other, and said to two of the detail as I passed them, "That ought to be reported to the officer of the guard. They should be separated, and not allowed to tempt their fate." I was told that it was "already known to the officers." I was then asked if I was on guard duty. The significance of this I was fully able to interpret, and passed on to the vicinity of "The High Falls."

On my return an hour afterwards, I noticed when nearing camp, that the Indians were gone from the tree to which they were tied when I left. Supposing that they had probably been removed for greater security, I gave it no further thought until, without any intimation of what had occurred during my short absence, I saw before me the dead body of old Ten-e-ya's youngest son. The warm blood still oozing from a wound in his back. He was lying just outside of our camp, within pistol range of the tree to which he had been tied.

I now comprehended the action of the guard. I learned that the other Indian had been fired at, but had succeeded in making his escape over the same ground and into the cañon where the other brave had disappeared. I found on expressing my unqualified condemnation of this cowardly act, that I was not the only one to denounce it. It was a cause of regret to nearly the whole command. Instead of the praise expected by the guard for the dastardly manner in which the young Indian was killed, they were told by Captain Boling that they had committed murder. Sergeant Cameron was no lover of Indians, but for this act his boiling wrath could hardly find vent, even when aided by some red hot expressions. I learned, to my extreme mortification, that no report had been made to any of the officers. The Indians had been permitted to untie themselves, and an opportunity had been given them to attempt to escape in order to fire upon them, expecting to kill them both; and only that a bullet-pouch had been hung upon the muzzle of one of the guard's rifles while leaning against a tree (for neither were on duty at the moment), no doubt both of the captives would have been killed.

Upon investigation, it was found that the fatal shot had been fired by a young man who had been led by an old Texan sinner to think that killing Indians or Mexicans was a duty; and surprised at Captain Boling's view of his conduct, declared with an injured air, that he "would not kill another Indian if the woods were full of them." Although no punishment was ever inflicted upon the perpetrators of the act, they were both soon sent to coventry, and feeling their disgrace, were allowed to do duty with the pack-train. Captain Boling had, before the occurrence of this incident, decided to establish his permanent camp on the south side of the Merced. The location selected was near the bank of the river, in full view of, and nearly opposite, "The Fall." This camp was head-quarters during our stay in the valley, which was extended to a much longer time than we had anticipated. Owing to several mountain storms, our stay was prolonged over a month.

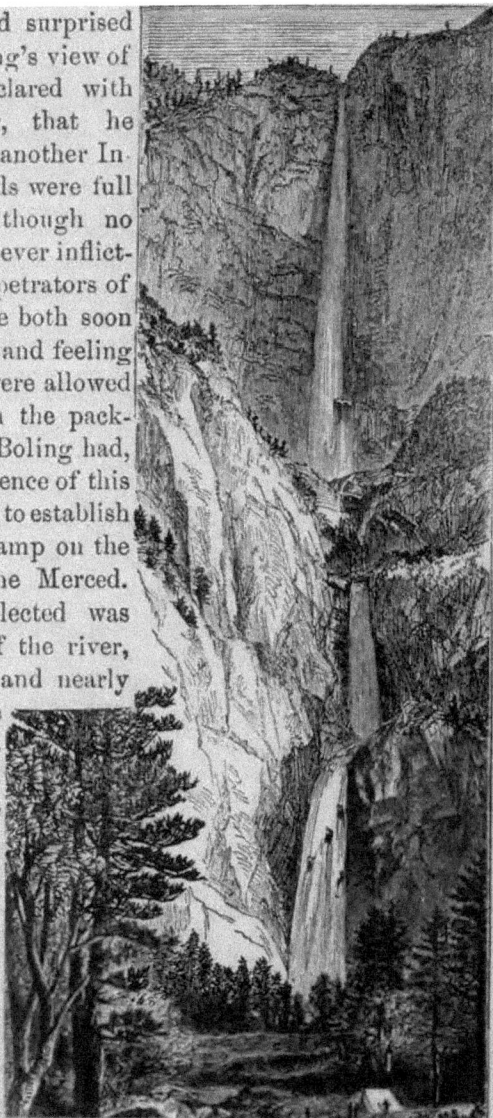

YOSEMITE FALLS.
(2,634 feet in height.)

The bottoms, or meadow land, afforded good grazing for our animals, and we were there more conveniently reached by our couriers and supply-trains from the Fresno.

From this point our excursions were made. All Indians attach great importance to securing the bodies of their dead for appropriate ceremonials, which with these was "cremation." They with others of the mountain tribes in this part of California, practiced the burning of their dead in accordance with their belief in a future state of existence, which was that if the body was burned, the spirit was released and went to "the happy land in the west." If this ceremony was omitted, the spirit haunted the vicinity, to the annoyance of the friends as well as the enemies of the deceased. Knowing this, Captain Boling felt a desire to make some atonement for the unfortunate killing of the son of Ten-ie-ya, the chief of the tribe with whom he was endeavoring to "make peace," and therefore made his arrangements to take advantage of this custom to propitiate the Indians by giving them an opportunity to remove the body of the youth. Accordingly, the order was at once given to break camp.

While the pack animals were being loaded, Lt. Chandler with his party brought in Ten-ie-ya. The Indian scouts, who were first sent out with Sandino and who knew where the talk with the chief had been held, passed on in advance and saw that he was still at his perch, watching the movements below him. Some of those out on leave discovered him also, seated on a ledge that appeared only accessible from above. The Pohonochee scouts, thinking to capture him by cutting off his retreat, followed an upper trail and reached the summit of the wall, while a few of Chandler's men, who were apprized of the situation by some of the pleasure-seekers whom they met, took a lower trail, and thus were in advance of the Indian scouts when Ten-ie-ya's retreat was reached. To their disappointment, the old chief could not be found, though at intervals fresh signs and heaps of stones were seen along the south-western slope of the mountain.

The sequel to the disappearance of Ten-ie-ya, as explained by Sandino, was simply as follows: When sent back by Chandler, Sandino resolved to make another effort to induce Ten-ie-ya to come in, lest Chandler should kill him if found. Accordingly he again climbed to the foot of the old chief's perch, and was talking with him, when some small loose stones came rolling down towards them. Seeing that his retreat above had been cut off, Ten-ie-ya at first ran along westerly, on the slope of the mountain towards Indian Cañon; but finding that he was cut off in that direction also, by the Neut-chü and Po-ho-no-chee scouts, he turned and came down a trail through an oak tree-top to the valley, which Sandino had by this time reached, and where he had been attracted by the noise made in the pursuit. Lt. Chandler had not climbed up the trail, and hearing Sandino's cry for help, and the noise above him, he was able to reach the place when Ten-ie-ya descended, in time to secure him. Ten-ie-ya said the men above him were rolling stones down, and he did not like to go up, as they broke and flew everywhere; for that reason he came down.

Ten-ie-ya accompanied his captors without making any resistance, although he strongly censured the Indians for being instrumental in his capture. They did not reach the valley in time to take part in the capture, but as Ten-ie-ya had said: "It was their cunning that had discovered the way to his hiding place."

None of the party of explorers or those under Chandler were aware of the event that had occurred during their absence. As Ten-ie-ya walked toward the camp, proudly conscious of being an object of attention from us, his eye fell upon the dead body of his favorite son, which still lay where he had fallen, without having been disturbed. He halted for a moment, without visible emotion, except a slight quivering of his lips. As he raised his head, the index to his feelings was exhibited in the glaring expression of deadly hate with which he gazed at Capt. Boling, and cast his eyes over the camp as if in search of the remains of the other son, the fellow captive of the one before him. Captain Boling expressed his regret of the occurrence, and had the circumstances explained to him, but not a single word would he utter in reply; not a sound escaped his compressed lips. He passively accompanied us to our camp on the south side of the river. It was evident that every movement of ours was closely scrutinized. Sandino was instructed to notify the chief that the body could be taken away. This permission was also received in silence.

Upon riding over to the camp ground the next morning, it was found that the body had been carried up or secreted in Indian Cañon; as all of the tracks led that way. This ravine became known to *us* as "Indian Cañon," though called by the Indians "Le-Hamite," "the arrow wood." It was also known to them by the name of "Scho-tal-lo-wi," meaning the way to "*Fall Creek*." The rocks near which we were encamped, between "Indian Cañon" and "The Falls," were now called by the Po-ho-no-chee scouts who were with us, "Hammo," or "Ummo," "The Lost Arrow," in commemoration of the event. On the morning following the capture of Ten-ie-ya, Capt. Boling tried to have a talk with him; but he would not reply to a question asked through the intepreter; neither would he converse with Sandino or the Indians with us. He maintained this moody silence and extreme taciturnity for several days afterwards.

Finding that nothing could be accomplished through the

old chief, Captain Boling gave orders to re-commence our search for his people. Scouting parties were started on foot to explore as far as was practicable on account of the snow. Although it was now May, the snow prevented a very extended search in the higher Sierras. On the first day out these parties found that, although they had made a faithful and active search, they had not performed half they had planned to do when starting. Distances were invariably under-estimated. This we afterward found was the case in all of our excursions in the mountains, where we estimated distance by the eye; and calling attention to the phenomena, I tried to have the principle applied to heights as well. The height of the mountainous cliffs, and the clear atmosphere made objects appear near, but the time taken to reach them convinced us that our eyes had deceived us in our judgment of distance. To avoid the severe labor that was imposed upon us by carrying our provisions and blankets, an attempt was made to use pack-mules, but the circuitous route we were compelled to take consumed too much time; besides the ground we were desirous of going over was either too soft and yielding, or too rocky and precipitous. We were compelled to leave the mules and continue our explorations on foot. Later in the season there would have been no difficulty in exploring the mountains on horse-back, if certain well established routes and passes were kept in view; but aside from these our Indian guides could give us little or no information. This we accounted for upon the theory that, as there was no game of consequence in the higher Sierras, and the cold was great as compared with the lower altitudes, the Indians knowledge of the "Higher Sierras" was only acquired while passing over them, or while concealed in them from the pursuit of their enemies. All scouting parties were, therefore, principally dependent upon their own resources, and took with them a supply of food and their blankets for a bivouac. In this way much time and fatigue of travel was saved. Some were more adventurous than others in their explorations. These, on returning from a scout of one or more days out, would come in ragged and foot-sore, and report with enthusiasm their adventures, and the wonders they had seen. Their descriptions around the camp fire at night were at first quite exciting; but a few nights' experience in the vicinity of the snow-line, without finding Indians, soon cooled down the ardor of all but a very few, who, from their persistent wandering explorations, were considered somewhat eccentric.

Through our Indian scouts, we learned that some of the Yosemites had gone to the Tuolumne. These were Tuolumne Indians who had intermarried with the Yosemites, and had been considered as a part of Ten-ie-ya's band. Taking their women and children, they returned to the Tuolumne tribe as soon as it was known that Ten-ie-ya had been captured; fearing he would again promise to take his band to the Fresno. Our orders prohibited us from disturbing the Tuolumne Indians; we therefore permitted them to return to their allegiance without attempting to follow them.

Ten-ie-ya was treated with kindness, and as his sorrow for the loss of his son seemed to abate, he promised to call in some of his people, and abide by their decision, when they had heard the statements of Capt. Boling. At night he would call as if to some one afar off. He said his people were not far from our camp and could hear his voice. We never heard a reply, although the calls were continued by order of Capt. Boling for many nights.

Although he was closely watched by the camp guard, he made an attempt to escape while the guard's back was momentarily turned upon him. Sergt. Cameron, who had especial charge of him at the time, saw his movement, and as he rushed from his keeper, Cameron dashed after and caught him before he was able to plunge into and swim the river.

As Ten-ie-ya was brought into the presence of Capt. Boling by Sergt. Cameron, after this attempt to escape, he supposed that he would now be condemned to be shot. With mingled fear of the uncertainty of his life being spared, and his furious passion at being foiled in his attempt to regain his liberty, he forgot his usual reserve and shrewdness. His grief for the loss of his son and the hatred he entertained toward Copt. Boling, who he considered as responsible for his death, was uppermost in his thoughts, and without any of his taciturn, diplomatic style he burst forth in lamentations and denunciations, given in a loud voice and in a style of language and manner of delivery which took us all by surprise. In his excitement, he made a correct use of many Spanish words, showing that he was more familiar with them than he had ever admitted even to Sandino; but the more emphatic expressions were such as may often be heard used by the muleteers of Mexico and South America, but are not found in the Lexicons. As he approached Capt. Boling, he began in a highly excited tone: "*Kill me*, sir Captain! Yes, *kill me*, as you killed my son; as you would kill my people if they were to come to you! You would kill all my race if you had the power. Yes, sir, American, you can now tell your warriors to kill the old chief; you have made me sorrowful, my life dark; you killed the child of my heart, why not kill the father? But wait a little; when I am dead I will call to my people to come to you, I will call louder than you have had me call; that they shall hear me in their sleep, and come to avenge the death of their chief and his son. Yes, sir, American, my spirit will make trouble for you and your people, as you have caused trouble to me and my people. With the wizards, I will follow the white men and make them fear me." He here aroused himself to a sublime frenzy, and completed his rhapsody by saying: "You may kill me, sir, Captain, but you shall not live in peace. I will follow in your foot-steps, I will not leave my home, but be with the spirits among the rocks, the water-falls, in the rivers and in the winds; wheresoever you go I will be with you. You will not see me, but you will fear the spirit of the old chief, and grow cold.* The great spirits have spoken! I am done."

Captain Boling allowed the old orator to finish his talk without interruption. Although he did not fully understand him, he was amused at his earnest style and impetuous gestures. On hearing it interpreted, he humorously replied: "I comprehended the most of what he said. The old chief has improved. If he was only reliable he would make a better interpreter than Sandino. As for speech-making, Doc., I throw up. The old Pow-wow can beat me all hollow." Ten-ie-ya earnestly watched the countenance of the good natured Captain, as if to learn his decision in the matter. The Captain observing him, quietly said: "Sergeant Cameron! the old sachem looks hungry, and as it is now about supper time, you had better give him an extra ration or two, and then see that he is so secured that he will not have a chance to escape from us again."

I watched the old incorrigible while he was delivering this eloquent harangue (which, of course, is necessarily a free translation) with considerable curiosity. Under the excitement of the moment he appeared many years younger. With his vigorous old age he displayed a *latent* power which was before unknown to us. I began to feel a sort of vene-

*It is claimed by all Indian "Medicine Men" that the presence of a spirit is announced by a *cool* breeze, and that sometimes they turn cold and shake as with an ague.

ration for him. My sympathies had before been aroused for his sorrow, and I now began to have almost a genuine respect for him; but as I passed him half an hour afterwards, the poetry of his life appeared changed. He was regaling himself on fat pork and beans from a wooden dish which had been brought to him by order of Cameron. This he seemed to enjoy with an appetite of a hungry animal. His guard had provided his wooden bowl and ladle by chipping them out of an alder tree, but failing to finish them smoothly, they could not be *properly* washed; but this fact seemed not to disturb his relish for the food. As I looked at his enjoyment of the loaded dish, I now saw only a dirty old Indian. The spiritual man had disappeared. I addressed him in Spanish, but not a word of reply; instead he pointed to his ear, thereby indicating that he was deaf to the language. Afterwards he even repudiated his "*Medicineship.*"

CHAPTER XII.

Bears and Other Game—Sickness of Captain Boling—Convalescence and Determination—A Guess at Heights—A Tired Doctor and a Used-up Captain—Surprising an Indian—Know-nothingness, or Native Americanism—A Clue and Discovery—A Short-cut to Camp, but an Unpopular Route.

CONSIDERABLE hilarty has been exhibited by modern visitors when told that the Yosemite and its environs were once the favorite resort of the grizzly bear. After these visitors have returned to New York or Boston, they tell the public not to be afraid of bears, as they were quite harmless; rather inclined to become domestic, etc. That is well enough now, perhaps, although grizzlies may yet be found; but at the date of the discovery; their trails were as large and numerous, almost, as cow-paths in a western settlement. Several bears were seen by us, and one was killed. The Yo-sem-i-tes used to capture these monsters by lying in wait for them on some rock or in some tree that commanded their thoroughfare, and after the bear had been wounded, all the dogs in the village were turned loose upon him. After being brought to bay, he was dispatched with arrows or the spear. A medium sized terrier or two will so annoy a large grizzly, keeping out of his way in the meantime, that he is apt to become stubborn and stand his ground.

In such cases, there is less danger to the hunter. I have known of two being killed in this way at short range. The approach of the hunter was disregarded by the bear. Their hams had been so bitten by the dogs that they dared not run, for fear of a fresh attack. I killed a large one as he came out of the Merced river, a little above where the town of Merced has since been built, and the same day, being in a whale-boat, I had to back from an old she-bear and her two cubs, encountered in a short turn of the river. I tried to kill these also, but my rifle had got soaked in the rain that was pouring at the time; as for the pistol shots, fired by some of the oarsmen, they only seemed to increase her speed, and that of her cubs, as they reached the shore and plunged through the willows. I had, previous to the killing of the grizzly, killed a large black bear with a rifle of small calibre, and gaining confidence, I attacked the grizzly, and was fortunate in cutting a renal-artery, from which the bear soon bled to death; but upon viewing the huge monster, I fully realized the folly of an open attack upon this kind of game, and ever afterwards, so far as I could, when alone, avoided their noted haunts. With all my caution and dread of an unexpected encounter with them, I met several face to face during mountain explorations; but invariably. they seemed as anxious to get away from me as I was that they should do so. Once while manœuvering to get a shot at a deer, a grizzly came out in full view but a few yards in advance of me. I was tempted to give him a shot, but as I had no refuge of dog or tree, if I made a poor shot, and knowing that I was not seen by the bear, I did not molest him, but felt relieved as he entered a chinquepin thicket, and if there had been *fifty of them*, no doubt they might have all gone without my *saying a word.*

I have seen a good deal of nonsense in print about bears, but will venture to give these incidents. Joel H. Brooks and John Kenzie, ex-members of "The Battalion," were the least susceptible to fear of them, of any persons I ever knew. Their skill as marksmen, was something wonder-derful. They used to go through a drill on foot, firing at some imaginary grizzly, then with a representative shot, the bear was wounded, and pursuing them; they would turn and flee, loading their rifles as they ran, and then turn and fire with deliberation at the imaginary bear in pursuit.

This theory of bear hunting, they determined to put in-to practice, and after the close of the Indian war, and the disbanding of the battalion, they established themselves in a camp near the Tehon Pass, a locality even more famous for bears than the Yosemite. They were successful, killed a number, and were daily acquiring more confidence in the practicability of their theory and plans of attack; when one day, while Kenzie was out hunting by himself, he unexpect-edly met a huge grizzly face to face; both were for a mo-ment startled.

Contrary to the usual, and almost invariable, habit of the bear when surprised or about to attack, he did not rise upon his hind feet; but instead of affording Kenzie the ad-vantage of the usual opportunity to aim at the small, light-colored spot on his neck, which, if centered, is instant death to the animal, the bear made a direct dash for the hunter. Seeing his peril, Kenzie at once fired with all the delibera-tion the urgency of the occasion would permit. The shot proved a fatal one, but before Kenzie could avoid the fu-rious charge of the animal, he was fatally injured by blows from the terrible monster. His bowels were literally torn out; he was unfortunate in being tripped by the tangled brush, or he might have escaped, as the bear fell dead with his first charge, Kenzie succeeded in dragging himself to their camp. He described the locality of the adventure, and requested Brooks to go and bring in the liver of the bear. He said it would afford him some consolation to eat more of the bear than the bear had been able to eat of him.

Brooks brought in and cooked some of the liver, fully gratifying Kenzie's whim; but it was the hunter's last poor triumph—he died soon after. Brooks swore off from this method of hunting, at least for a season, and accepted a position offered him at the Indian Agency.

Another member of our battalion killed a grizzly that for a time made him quite famous as a bear-fighter. As this man was an Indian, an attempt has been made to weave the incident into a legend, giving the honor of the combat to one of the Yosemites. The truth is, that a full-blooded Cherokee, known as "Cherokee Bob," or Robert Brown, wounded a grizzly, and to keep the bear from entering a thicket, set his dog on the game. While "Bob" was reloading his rifle, and before he could get the cap on, the bear, disregarding the dog, charged upon Bob, and bore him to the ground. The dog instantly attacked the bear, biting his hams most furiously. The grizzly turned from Brown and caught the dog with his paw, holding him as a cat would hold a mouse. By this means Bob was released, and but slightly bruised. In an instant he drew his hunting knife and plunged it to the heart of the bear, and ended the contest. The dog was seriously injured, but Bob carried him in his arms to camp, and attended his wounds as he would a comrade's or as he might have done his own. As "Cherokee Bob's" bear fight was a reality known to his comrades, I have noticed it here.

The various routes to the Yosemite are now so constantly traveled that bears will rarely be seen. They possess a very keen scent, and will avoid all thoroughfares traveled by man, unless very hungry; they are compelled to search for food. Strange as it may appear to some, the ferocious grizzly can be more reliably tamed and domesticated than the black bear. A tame grizzly at Monterey, in 1849, was allowed the freedom of the city. Capt. Chas. M. Webber, the original proprietor of the site of Stockton, had two that were kept chained. They became very tame. One of these, especially tame, would get loose from time to time and roam at will over the city. The new inhabitants of Stockton seemed not to be inspired by that faith in his docility and uprightness of character that possessed the owner, for they found him ravenously devouring a barrel of sugar that belonged to one of the merchants, and refused to give up any portion of it. This offended the grocer, and he sent word to Mr. Webber to come and remove his truant thief. The Captain came, paid for the damaged sugar, and giving him, like a spoiled child, some of the sweets he had confiscated to induce him to follow, led the bear home. But bruin remembered his successful foray, and breaking his chain again and again, and always returning to the merchant's premises for sugar, Mr. Webber rid himself and the community of the annoyance by disposing of his grizzlies.

During a hunt in company with Col. Byron Cole, Messrs. Kent, Long and McBrien of San Francisco, I caught a good sized cub, and Mr. Long, with a terrier dog, caught another; the mother of which was killed by the unerring aim of McBrien. These cubs were taken by Cole and McBrien to San Francisco on their return, and sent to New York. I was told that they became very tame. I hope they did, for the comfort and security of their keepers; for in my first efforts to tame a grizzly, I became somewhat prejudiced against bear training as an occupation. Not long after my experience, I heard of poor Lola Montez being bitten by one she was training at Grass Valley for exhibition in Europe; and I now lost all faith in their reported docility and domestic inclinations. The California lion, like the wolf, is a coward, and deserves but little notice. Among the visitors to the Yosemite, some will probably be interested in knowing where to find the game: fish, birds and animals, that may yet remain to gratify the sportsmen's love of the rod and the chase. Most of the game has been killed or driven off by the approach of civilization. Deer and occasionally a grizzly, cinnamon or black bear may be found on the slopes of the Tuolumne, Merced, Fresno and San Joaquin, and on all the rivers and mountains south of these streams. The cinnamon bear of California is much larger than the common brown bear of the Rocky Mountains.

The *blue* black-tailed deer of California are distinct from the black tuft-tailed deer of the eastern ranges; a very marked difference will be observed in their horns and ears. This distinction has been noticed by naturalists; but the species are often confounded in newspaper correspondence. The habits of the California deer are more goat-like; they are wilder, and more easily startled than the "mule-eared" deer of the Rockies, and when alarmed, they move with the celerity of the white-tailed Virginia deer. The bare, tuft-tailed and big-eared Rocky Mountain deer, seem but little alarmed by the report of a gun; and their curiosity is nearly equal to that of the antelope.

The California deer are still abundant upon the spurs of the Sierras during their migrations to and from the foot-hills. These migrations occur during the Autumn and Spring. As the rainy season sets in, they leave the higher mountains for the foot-hills and plains, keeping near the snow line, and as the Spring advances, they follow back the receding snow to the high Sierras and the Eastern Slope, but seldom or never descend to the plain below. On account of these migratory habits, they will most likely endure the assaults of the sportsmen. The haunts of the grizzly are the same as those of the deer, for they alike prefer the bushy coverts to the more open ground, except when feeding. The deer prefer as food the foliage of shrubs and weeds to the richest grasses, and the bear prefers clover, roots, ants and reptiles; but both fatten principally on acorns, wild rye and wild oats.

California grouse are found in the vicinity of the Yosemite. During the months of July and August they were formerly found quite numerous concealed in the grass and sedges of the valley and the little Yosemite; but as they are much wilder than the prairie chicken, they shun the haunts of man, and are now only found numerous in midsummer upon or bordering on the mountain meadows and in the timber, among the pine forests, where they feed upon the pine seeds and mistletoe, which also afford them ample concealment. Their ventriloquial powers are such that while gobbling their discordant notes, they are likely to deceive the most experienced ear. It is almost impossible to feel quite sure as to which particular tree the grouse is in without seeing it. He seems to throw his voice about, now to this tree and now to that, concealing himself the while until the inexperienced hunter is deluded into the belief that the trees are full of grouse, when probably there is but one making all the noise. His attention having been diverted, the hunter is left in doubt from sheer conflicting sounds as to which particular tree he saw a bird alight in. It is generally pretty sure to *"fetch the bird,"* if you shoot into the bunch of mistletoe into which you *supposed* you saw the grouse alight.

Beside the mountain grouse and mountain quail, among the most beautiful of birds, that afford the sportsman a diversity of sport, an occasional flock of pigeons, of much larger size than those of the Atlantic States, will attract attention; though I have never seen them in very large flocks. In most of the mountain streams, and their branches, brook trout are quite abundant. They are not, however, so ravenously accommodating, as to bite just when they are wanted. I learned from the Indians that they would bite best in foaming water, when they were unable to see the angler, or the bait distinctly; their curiosity stimulating their appetites. It is important that the trout do not see the angler, and when very wary, the rod even should not be conspicuous. Below the cañon of the Yosemite, young salmon were once abundant. The Indians used to catch fish in weirs made of brush and stones; but during the extensive mining operations on the Merced and other rivers, the salmon seemed to have almost abandoned their favorite haunts, for the mud covered spawn would not hatch. Large salmon were speared by the Indians in all the rivers, with a curious bone spear of but one tine, while the smaller fry were caught in their weirs. In the Tulare lakes and in the San Joaquin, King's, Kern and other rivers, fish, frogs and turtle are abundant, and water fowl literally swarm during the winter months in many parts of California.

Among the foot-hills of the Sierra Nevada, as well as in all the lesser mountain ranges, may be found the common California blue quail, and a very curious brush or chapparel cock, known to the Spanish residents of California and Mexico as "El Paisano" (The Countryman), and as the "Correo Camino" (Road-runner), and to ornithologists as the *Geo-coc cyx Californicus.** They have received the name of "*countryman*" because of their inclination to run like country children at the sight of strangers, and that of "road-runner" from the habit of frequenting roads and trails, for the purpose of wallowing in the dust, and when alarmed darting off along the road with the speed of an ostrich or wild turkey. The object they have in wallowing in the dust is like that of the ruffled grouse, which indulge in the same practice—they sun themselves and at the same time are rid of vermin. Trusting to their legs to escape when alarmed, they take the open ground—the road—until outrunning pursuit they hide in the chapparel, and thus

---

*Known as the Mexican Pheasant, though not very good to eat.

acquire the name of "road-runner" or "chapparel cock."

I have never seen any ruffled grouse in the Sierra Nevada, but a species of these fine birds, are quite abundant in Oregon and Washington territory. I have been able to solve a question regarding them, upon which naturalists have disagreed, that is, as to how they drum. Whether the sound is produced by the wings in concussive blows upon their bodies, the air, logs or rocks? I am able to say from personal and careful observation, that the sound of "*drumming*," is made, like the sound of the "*night jar*," exclusively by a peculiar motion of the wings *in the air*. It is true, the American "pheasant" or American "partridge," commonly stands upon a log while drumming, but I have watched them while perched upon a dry small branch or twig, drum for hours most sonorously, calling upon their rivals to encounter them, and their mistresses to come and witness their gallantry. Darwin has aptly said: "The season of love, is that of battle." Notwithstanding the acuteness of observation of Mr. Darwin, he has been led into error in his statement that wild horses "do not make any danger signals." They snort and paw the earth with impatience, when they cannot discover the cause of their alarm, and almost invariably circle to the leeward of the object that disturbes them. A mule is the best of sentinels to alarm a camp on the approach of danger. Deer and elk whistle and strike the earth perpendicularly with their feet when *jumping up* to discover the cause of alarm. Deer and antelope are both so inquisitive, that if the hunter has not been seen, or has been but imperfectly seen, by dropping into the grass or brush, and raising some object to view and suddenly withdrawing it, the deer or antelope will frequently come up within a few feet of the object. Antelope are especially curious to know what disturbs them.

The coyotes, or small wolves, and the grey or tree climbing foxes of California, make a kind of barking noise, more like the bark of a small dog than the howl of a wolf, and therefore barking is not so much of "*an acquired*" art as has been supposed, though the "laughter" of dogs is more or less acquired.

The whistle of the elk is as complete a call to his mistress, and is as well understood, as though the female had said, "Whistle and I'll come to you." Elk and antelope are still to be found in California, as well as wild horses, but they are now quite timid, and resort to unfrequented ranges. The best hunting now to be found in California, except for water-fowl, is in the region of Kern River. Near its source big-horn or mountain sheep may be killed, and from along the base of the eastern slope, antelope range into the desert. Deer and bear may be found on either slope of the range, and among the broken hills south of the head of Tulare valley.

Wolves, foxes, badgers, coons, and other fur-clothed animals, are also quite numerous. I have *dared* to question some of Mr. Darwin's facts, and as I expect this to be my last literary effort (oh, ye reviewers!), I wish to remind the publishers of Webster's Dictionary that a beaver is not an "*amphibious*" animal, neither is a muscalonge "an overgrown pickerel."

A few days after we had moved camp to the south side of the Merced, Captain Boling was prostrated with an attack of pneumonia. From frequent wettings received while crossing the ice-cold torrents, and a too free use of this snow-water, which did not agree with many, he had for some days complained of slight illness, but after this attack he was compelled to acknowledge himself sick. Although the severe symptoms continued but a few days, his recovery was lingering, and confined him to camp; consequently he knew but little of his rocky surroundings.

Although regular reports were made to him by the scouting parties, he had but an imperfect conception of the labors performed by them in clambering over the rocks of the cañons and mountains. He would smile at the reports the more enthusiastic gave of the wonders discovered; patiently listen to the complaints of the more practical at their want of success in, what they termed, their futile explorations; and finally concluded to suspend operations until the fast-melting snow had so disappeared from the high mountain passes as to permit our taking a supply-train, in order to make our search thorough. The winter had been an unusually dry and cold one—so said the Indians—and, as a consequence, the accumulations of snow in the passes and lake basins had remained almost intact. A succession of mountain storms added to the drifts, so that when the snow finally began to melt, the volume of water coming from the "High Sierras" was simply prodigious—out of all proportion to the quantity that had fallen upon the plains below.

Sandino persisted in trying to make the Captain believe that most of the Yosemites had already gone through the Mono Pass, and that those remaining hidden, were but the members of Ten-ie-ya's family. This theory was not accepted by Capt. Boling, and occasional scouting parties would still be sent out. A few of us continued to make short excursions, more for adventure and to gratify curiosity, than with the expectation of discovering the hiding places of the Indians; although we kept up the form of a search. We thus became familiar with most of the objects of interest.

The more practical of our command could not remain quiet in camp during this suspension of business. Beside the ordinary routine of camp duties, they engaged in athletic sports and horse-racing. A very fair race track was cleared and put in condition, and some of the owners of fast horses were very much surprised, to see their favorites trailing behind some of the fleet-footed mules. A maltese Kentucky blooded mule, known as the "Vining Mule," distanced all but one horse in the command, and so pleased was Capt. Boling with its gracefully supple movements, that he paid Vining for it a thousand dollars in gold.

For a change of amusement, the members of our "Jockey Club" would mount their animals and take a look at such points of interest as had been designated in our camp-fire conversations as most remarkable. The scenery in the Yosemite and vicinity, which is now familiar to so many, was at that time looked upon with varied degrees of individual curiosity and enjoyment, ranging from the enthusiastic, to almost a total indifference to the sublime grandeur presented. It is doubtful if any of us could have given a very graphic description of what we saw, as the impressions then received were so far below the reality. Distance, height, depth and dimensions were invariably under-estimated; notwithstanding this, our attempts at descriptions after our return to the settlements, were received as exaggerated "yarns."

While in Mariposa, upon one occasion not very long after the discovery of Yosemite, I was solicited by Wm. T. Whitachre, a newspaper correspondent from San Francisco, to furnish him a written description of the Valley. This, of course, was beyond my ability to do; but I disinterestedly complied with his request as far as I could, by giving him some written details to work upon. On reading the paper over, he advised me to reduce my estimates of heights of cliffs and waterfalls, at least fifty per centum, or my judgment would be a subject of ridicule even to my personal friends. I had estimated El Capitan at from fifteen hundred to two thousand feet high; the Yosemite Fall at about fifteen hundred feet, and other prominent points of interest in about the same proportion.

To convince me of my error of judgment, he stated that he had interviewed Captain Boling and some others, and that none had estimated the highest cliffs above a thousand feet. He further said that he would not like to risk his own reputation as a correspondent, without considerable modification of my statements, etc. Feeling outraged at this imputation, I tore up the manuscript, and left the " newspaper man" to obtain where he could such data for his patrons as would please him. It remained for those who came after us to examine scientifically, and to correctly describe what we only observed as wonderful natural curiosities. With but few exceptions, curiosity was gratified by but superficial examination of the objects now so noted. We were aware that the valley was high up in the regions of the Sierra Nevada, but its altitude above the sea level was only guessed at. The heights of its immense granite walls was an uncertainty, and so little real appreciation was there in the battalion, that some never climbed above the Vernal Fall. They knew nothing of the beauties of the Nevada Fall, or the " Little Yosemite." We, as a body of men, were aware that the mountains, cañons and waterfalls were on a grandly extensive scale, but of the proportions of that scale we had arrived at no very definite conclusions.

During our explorations of the Sierras, we noticed the effects of the huge avalanches of snow and ice that had in some age moved over the smooth granite rocks and plowed the deep cañons. The evidences of past glacial action were frequently visible; so common, in fact, as hardly to be objects of special interest to us. The fact that glaciers in motion existed in the vast piles of snow on the Sierras, was not dreamed of by us, or even surmised by others, until discovered, in 1870, by Mr. John Muir, a naturalist and most persistent mountain explorer, who by accurate tests verified the same, and gave his facts to the world. Mr.

Muir has also brought into prominent notice, by publications in "Scribner's Monthly Illustrated Magazine," some of the beautiful lakes of the Sierras, having discovered many unknown before. Mr. Muir's descriptions combine the most delightful imagery with the accuracy of a true lover of nature. His article upon the water-auszel, "The humming-bird of the California waterfalls," in the same magazine, proves him a most accomplished observer.

All of the smaller streams that pour their tribute into the valley during the melting of the snow, become later in the season but dry ravines or mere rivulets, but the principal tributaries, running up, as they do, into the lake and snow reservoirs, continue throughout the dry season to pour their ample supply. After returning from my mountain explorations, I freely questioned Ten-ie-ya of the places we had visited. The old chief had gradually assumed his customary manner of sociability, and if convinced by outline maps in the sand that we were familiar with a locality, he would become quite communicative, and give the names of the places described in distinct words. Our English alphabet utterly fails to express the sounds of many of them, for they were as unpronounceable as Apache. This difficulty is owing more or less to the guttural termination given by the Indians.

Another important fact which causes a confusion of these names is, that owing to the poverty of their language, they use the same word, or what seems to be the same, for several objects, which by accent, comparison and allusion, or by gestures, are readily understood by them, but which it is difficult for one not familiar with the dialect to comprehend, and still more difficult to illustrate or remember. This I shall endeavor to demonstrate in giving the names applied to different localities in the valley and vicinity.

While I was endeavoring to ascertain the names of localities from Ten-ie-ya, he was allowed some privileges in camp, but was not permitted to leave his guard. The cunning old fellow watched his opportunity, and again made an attempt to escape by swimming the river; but he was again foiled, and captured by the watchfulness and surprising strength of Sergeant Cameron.

From this time Ten-ie-ya was secured by a rope which was fastened around his waist. The only liberty allowed was the extent of the rope with which he was fastened. He was a hearty feeder, and was liberally supplied. From a lack of sufficient exercise, his appetite cloyed, and he suffered from indigestion. He made application to Captain Boling for permission to go out from camp to the place where the grass was growing, saying the food he had been supplied with was too strong; that if he did not have grass he should die. He said the grass looked good to him, and there was plenty of it. Why then should he not have it, when dogs were allowed to eat it?

The Captain was amused at the application, with its irony, but surmised that he was meditating another attempt to leave us; however, he good humoredly said: "He can have a ton of fodder if he desires it, but I do not think it advisable to turn him loose to graze." The Captain consented to the Sergeant's kindly arrangements to *tether* him, and he was led out to graze upon the young clover, sorrel, bulbous roots and fresh growth of ferns which were then springing up in the valley, one species of which we found a good salad. All of these he devoured with the relish of a hungry ox. Occasionally truffles or wood-mushrooms were brought him by Sandino and our allies, as if in kindly sympathy for him, or in acknowledgment of his rank. Such presents and a slight deference to his standing as a chief, were always received with grunts of satisfaction. He was easily flattered by any extra attentions to his pleasure. At such times he was singularly amiable and conversational. Like many white men, it was evid. nt that his more liberal feelings could be the easiest aroused through his stomach.

Our supplies not being deemed sufficient for the expedition over the Sierras, and as those verdureless mountains would provide no forage for our animals, nor game to lengthen out our rations unless we descended to the lower levels, Capt. Boling sent a pack train to the Fresno for barley and extra rations. All of our Indians except Sandino and Ten-ie-ya were allowed to go below with the detachment sent along as escort for the train. While waiting for these supplies, some of the command who had been exploring up Indian Cañon, reported fresh signs at the head of that ravine. Feeling somewhat recovered in strength, Captain Boling decided to undertake a trip out, and see for himself some of our surroundings. Accordingly, the next morning, he started with some thirty odd men up Indian Cañon. His design was to explore the Scho-look or Scho-tal-lo-wi branch (Yosemite Creek) to its source, or at least the Southern exposures of the divide as far east as we could go and return at night. Before starting, I advised the taking of our blankets, for a bivouac upon the ridge, as from experience I was aware of the difficult and laborious ascent, and intimated that the excursion would be a laborious one for an invalid, if the undertaking was accomplished. The Captain laughed as he said: "Are your distances equal to your heights? If they correspond, we shall have ample time!" Of course, I could make no reply, for between us, the subject of heights had already been exhausted, although the Captain had not yet been to the top of the inclosing walls.

Still, realizing the sensitive condition of his lungs, and his susceptibility to the influences of the cold and light mountain air, I knew it would not be prudent for him to camp at the snow-line; and yet I doubted his ability to return the same day; for this reason I felt it my duty to caution him. A few others, who had avoided climbing the cliffs, or if they had been upon any of the high ridges, their mules had taken them there, joined in against my suggestion of providing for the bivouac. I have before referred to the Texan's devotion to the saddle. In it, like Camanche Indians, he will undergo incredible hardships; out of it, he is soon tired, and waddles laboriously like a sailor, until the unaccustomed muscles adapt themselves to the new service required of them; but the probabilities are against the new exercise being continued long enough to accomplish this result. Understanding this, I concluded in a spirit of jocularity to make light of the toil myself; the more so, because I knew that my good Captain had no just conception of the labor before him. By a rude process of measurement, and my practical experience in other mountains in climbing peaks whose heights had been established by measurements, I had approximately ascertained or concluded that my first estimate of from fifteen hundred to two thousand feet for the height of El Capitan, was much below the reality. I had so declared in discussing these matters. Captain Boling had finally estimated the height not to exceed one thousand feet. Doctor Black's estimate was far below this. I therefore felt assured that *a walk up* the cañon, would practically improve their judgments of height and distance, and laughed within myself in anticipation of the fun in store. On starting, I was directed to take charge of Ten-ie-ya, whom we were to take with us, and to keep Sandino near me, to interpret anything required during the trip. As we entered Indian Cañon, the old chief told the Captain that the ravine was a bad one to ascend. To this the Captain replied, "No matter, we know this ravine leads out of the valley; Ten-ie-ya's trail might lead us to a warmer locality."

Climbing over the wet, mossy rocks, we reached a level where a halt was called for a rest. As Doctor Black came up from the rear, he pointed to a ridge above us, and exclaimed, "Thank God, we are in sight of the top at last." "Yes, Doctor," said I, "that is one of the first tops." "How so?" he inquired; "Is not that the summit of this ravine?" To this I cheerfully replied, "You will find quite a number of such tops before you emerge from this cañon." Noticing his absence before reaching the summit, I learned he took the trail back, and safely found his weary way to camp. Captain Boling had over-estimated his strength and endurance. He was barely able to reach the table land at the head of the ravine, where, after resting and lunching, he visited the Falls, as he afterwards informed me. By his order I took command of nine picked men and the two Indians. With these I continued the exploration, while the party with the Captain *explored* the vicinity of the High Fall, viewed the distant mountains, and awaited my return from above.

With my energetic little squad, I led the way, old Tenieya in front, Sandino at his side, through forest openings and meadows, until we reached the open rocky ground on the ridge leading to what is now known as Mt. Hoffman. I directed our course towards that peak. We had not traveled very far, the distance does not now impress me, when as we descended toward a tributary of Yosemite creek, we came suddenly upon an Indian, who at the moment of discovery was lying down drinking from the brook. The babbling waters had prevented his hearing our approach. We hurried up to within fifty or sixty yards, hoping to capture him, but were discovered. Seeing his supposed danger, he bounded off, a fine specimen of youthful vigor. No race-horse or greyhound could have seemingly made better time than he towards a dense forest in the valley of the Scho-look. Several rifles were raised, but I gave the order "don't shoot," and compelled the old chief to call to him to stop. The young Indian did stop, but it was at a safe distance. When an attempt was made by two or three to move ahead and get close to him, he saw the purpose and again started; neither threatening rifles, nor the calls of Ten-ie-ya, could again stop his flight.

As we knew our strength, after such a climb, was not equal to the chase of the fleet youth, he was allowed to go unmolested. I could get no information from Ten-ie-ya concerning the object of the exploration; and as for Sandino, his memory seemed to have conveniently failed him. With this conclusion I decided to continue my course, and moved off rapidly. Ten-ie-ya complained of fatigue, and Sandino reminded me that I was traveling very fast. My reply to both cut short all attempts to lessen our speed; and when either were disposed to lag in their gait, I would cry out the Indian word, "We-teach," meaning hurry up, with such emphasis as to put new life into their movements.

We soon struck an old trail that led east along the southern slope of the divide, and when I abandoned my purpose of going farther towards the Tuolumne, and turned to the right on the trail discovered, Ten-ie-ya once more found voice in an attempt to dissuade me from this purpose, saying that the trail led into the mountains where it was very cold, and where, without warm clothing at night, we would freeze. He was entirely too earnest, in view of his previous taciturnity; and I told him so.

The snow was still quite deep on the elevated portions of the ridge and in shaded localities, but upon the open ground, the trail was generally quite bare. As we reached a point still farther east, we perceived the trail had been recently used; the tracks had been made within a day or two. From the appearances, we concluded they were made by Ten-ie-ya's scouts who had followed down the ridge and slope west of the North Dome to watch our movements. The tracks were made going and returning, thus showing a continued use of this locality. As the tracks diverged from the trail at this point, they led out of the direct line of any communication with the valley, and after some reflection, I was satisfied that we had struck a clue to their hiding place, and realizing that it was time to return if we expected to reach the valley before dark, we turned about and started at once on the down grade.

We found the Captain anxiously awaiting our return. He was pleased with our report, and agreed in the conclusion that the Indians were encamped not very far off. Captain Boling had suffered from fatigue and the chill air of the mountains. In speaking of a farther pursuit of our discoveries, he said: " I am not as strong as I supposed, and will have to await the return of the pack train before taking part in these expeditions."

I told Captain Boling that upon the trip, Sandino had appeared willfully ignorant when questioned concerning the country we were exploring, and my belief that he stood in fear of Ten-ie-ya; that as a guide, no dependence could be placed upon him, and that his interpretations of Ten-ie-ya's sayings were to be received with caution when given in the old chief's presence, as Ten-ie-ya's Spanish was about equal to his own. Captain Boling instructed me to tell Sandino, that in future, he need only act as interpreter. He seemed satisfied with this arrangement, and said that the country appeared different from what it was when he was a boy and had been accustomed to traverse it.

When we commenced our descent into the valley Ten-ie-ya wanted us to branch off to the left, saying he was very tired, and wanted to take the best trail. Said he, "There is a good trail through the arrow-wood rocks to the left of the cañon." I reported this to the Captain, and expressed the opinion that the old chief was sincere for once; he had grumbled frequently while we were ascending the cañon in the morning, because we were compelled to climb over the moss covered bowlders, while crossing and re-crossing the stream, and he told Sandino that we should have taken the trail along the cliff above. Captain Boling replied: "Take it, or it will be long after dark before we reach camp." Accordingly I let Ten-ie-ya lead the way, and told him to travel fast. He had more than once proved that he possessed an agility beyond his years. As his parole was at a discount, I secured a small cord about his chest and attached the other end to my left wrist to maintain *telegraphic* communication with him; but as the hidden trail narrowed and wound its crooked way around a jutting point of the cliff overlooking the valley and ravine, I slipped the loop from my wrist and ordered a halt.

Captain Boling and the men with him came up and took in the view before us. One asked if I thought a bird could go down there safely. Another wanted to know if I was aiding "Old Truthful" to commit suicide. The last question had an echo of suspicion in my own thoughts. I immediately surmised it possible the old sachem was leading us into another trap, where, by some preconcerted signal, an avalanche of rocks would precipitate us all to the bottom. I asked Ten-ie-ya if this trail was used by his people; he assured me it was, by women and children; that it was a favorite trail of his. Seeing some evidences of it having been recently used, and being assured by Sandino that it was somewhere below on this trail that Ten-ie-ya had descended to the valley when taken a prisoner, a few of us were shamed into a determination to make the attempt to go where the old chief could go.

Most of the party turned back. They expressed a willingness to fight Indians, but they had not, they said, the faith requisite to attempt to walk on water, much less air. They went down Indian Cañon, and some did not reach camp until after midnight, tired, bruised and footsore. We who had decided to take our chances, re-commenced our descent. I told Ten-ie-ya to lead on, and to stop at the word "halt," or he would be shot. I then dispatched Sandino across the narrow foot-way, which, at this point was but a few inches in width, and which was all there was dividing us from Eternity as we passed over it. Telling them both to halt on a projecting bench in view, I crossed this yawning abyss, while Sandino, aided by a very dead shot above, held the old man as if petrified, until I was able once more to resume my charge of him.

This I found was the only really dangerous place, on what was facetiously called, by those who were leaving us, "a very good trail." The last fifty or sixty feet of the descent was down the sloping side of an immense detached rock, and then down through the top of a black oak tree at the south-westerly base of the vast cliff or promontory known as the "Arrow-wood Cliff." The "Royal Arches," the "Washington Column," and the "North Dome," occupy positions east of this trail, but upon the same vast pile of granite.

I sometime afterward pointed out the trail to a few visitors that I happened to meet at its foot. They looked upon me with an incredulous leer, and tapped their foreheads significantly, muttering something about "Stockton Asylum." Fearing to trust my amiability too far, I turned and left them. Since then I have remained cautiously silent. Now that the impetuosity of youth has given place to the more deliberative counsels of age, and all dangers to myself or others are past, I repeat, for the benefit of adventurous tourists, that on the southwesterly face of the cliff overlooking the valley and Indian Cañon, there is a trail hidden from view, that they may travel if they will, and experience all the sensations that could ever have been felt, while alive, by a Blondin or LaMountain.

This portion of the cliff we designated as Ten-ie-ya's Trail, and it accords well with the scene in the Jungfrau Mountains, where Manfred, alone upon the cliffs, says:

> "And you, ye craigs, upon whose extreme edge
> I stand, and on the torrent's brink beneath
> Behold the tall pines dwindled as to shrubs,
> In dizziness of distance; when a leap,
> A stir, a motion, even a breath, would bring
> My breast upon its rocky bosom's bed
> To rest forever—wherefore do I pause?
> I feel the impulse—yet I do not plunge;
> I see the peril—yet do not recede;
> And my brain reels—and yet my foot is firm:
> There is a power upon me which withholds,
> And makes it my fatality to live."

CHAPTER XIII.

DURING our long stay in the Yosemite, I discovered that almost every prominent object and locality in and about it, had some distinctive appellation. Every peak and cliff, every cañon or ravine, meadow, stream and waterfall, had a designation by which it could be distinguished by the Yosemites. I made considerable effort to acquire these names in their native purity. Although I did not at that time learn all of them, I did in subsequent visits to the valley and to the camps of the remnants of the tribes, acquire, as I then believed, a very nearly correct pronunciation of most of them. I used all the advantages afforded by my position as one of the Spanish interpreters, and applied myself perseveringly to the task of preserving these names; for even at that early day I realized that public interest would, in time, be attached to that wonderful locality. I was ridiculed for the idea, or at least for the supposition that it probably would be awakened during my life-time.

I obtained many of the names of objects and locations from old Ten-ie-ya himself, whenever I could find him in a communicative mood. As he was reputed to be quite a linguist, speaking, besides his native Ah-wah-ne-chee, the Pai-ute, and other dialects, I regarded his authority as superior to that of either the Po-ho-no or Noot-chü Indians, who differed from him in the pronunciation of some of the names.

I was unable to converse with Ten-ie-ya except through an interpreter, but the words I noted down from the old chief's lips as they sounded to my ear at the time, getting the signification as best I could, or not at all. There is really no more sentiment or refined imagery of expression among Indians than will be found among ignorant people of any kind. But living as they do in close affinity with nature, natural objects first attract their attention, and the dominant characteristics of any object impress themselves upon their language. Hence many of their words are supposed to be representative of natural sounds. Our Po-ho-no-chee and Noot-chü scouts were familiar with the dialect in common use by the Yosemites, and they also aided me, while at times they confused, in acquiring the proper names. The territory claimed by the Po-ho-no-chees, joined that of the Yosemites on the south. During the Summer months, they occupied the region of the Po-ho-no Meadows, and the vicinity of the Pohono Lake. Their territory, however, extended to the right bank of the South Fork of the Merced. It was there we found a little band on our first expedition. Some of this band were quite intelligent, having with the Noot-chüs, worked for Major Savage. It was from them that the Major first learned that the Yosemites were a composite band, collected from the disaffected of other bands in that part of California, and what is now Nevada; and as the Major said, the dialect in common use among them was nearly as much of a mixture as the components of the band itself, for he recognized Pai-ute, Kah-we-ah and Oregon Indian words among them.

Major Savage was intimately familiar with the dialects of his Indian miners and customers, and was probably at that time the best interpreter in California of the different mountain dialects.

I consulted him freely as to the pronunciation of the names, and learned his interpretation of the meaning of them. These names, or most of them, were first given for publication by myself, as received from the Yosemites and Po-ho-no-chees; together with English names which had been given to some of the same points by the battalion. I purposely avoided all attempts at description, giving instead, a few estimates of heights. The data then furnished by myself was published in editorials, and has been mostly preserved, though in an imperfect state, from some fault in my writing or that of the proof-reader. Reference to old files of the "California Chronicle," "Sacramento Union," "California Farmer" and the Mariposa papers, will show a somewhat different orthography from that now in use.*

While in the valley I made memoranda of names and important events, which I have preserved, and which, with interpretations kindly furnished me by Mr. B. B. Travis, an excellent *modern* interpreter, I am now using to verify my recollections and those of my comrades. While acquiring these names, I employed every opportunity to make them familiar, but this proved to be a thankless task, or at least it was an impossible one. The great length of some of the names, and the varied pronunciations, made the attempt an impracticable one. I then gave attention to the substitution

---

* Mr. Winchester, connected with some eastern publication, accompanied Captain Boling and myself, in the latter part of June, 1851, as far as the Tehon Pass. During the trip I gave him a full account of the operations of the battalion, which he took notes of, and said he should publish on arriving home. His health was very poor, and I doubt if his manuscript was ever published. I never heard from him afterwards.

of suitable English names in place of the Indian words, and to supersede the fantastic and absurd ones already suggested and affixed by some of the command. It is so customary for frontiersmen to give distinctive names of their own coinage, that we had great difficulty in getting any of the Indian names adopted; and considerable judgment had to be exercised in selecting such English names as would "stick"—as would displace such names as the "Giant's Pillar," "Sam Patch's Falls," "The Devil's Night-Cap," etc., etc. Many English names were given because they were thought to be better than the Indian names, which could not be remembered or pronounced, and the meaning of which was not understood. The English names agreed upon and adopted at that time have since been retained, notwithstanding some adverse criticisms and efforts to supersede them by some fancied Indian or mythological substitute. Some of these names were the selection of my comrades—"Cloud's Rest," for one; because upon our first visit the party exploring the "Little Yosemite" turned back and hastened to camp upon seeing the clouds rapidly settling down to rest upon that mountain, thereby indicating the snow storm that soon followed.

The most of the names were however, selected by myself, and adopted by our command. This deference was awarded to my selections because I was actively interested in acquiring the Indian names and significations, and because I was considered the most interested in the scenery.

I have related in a previous chapter the incident of selecting the name "Yosemite" for the valley, not then knowing its Indian name. As the "High Fall," near which we were encamped, appeared to be the principal one of the Sierras, and was the fall *par excellence*, I gave that the name of "Yosemite Falls," and in so naming it I but followed out the idea of the Indians who called it "Choo-look" or "Scholook," which signifies in this case " The Fall." A comparison of the Yosemite Falls with those known in other parts of the world, will show that in elements of picturesque beauty, height, volume, color and majestic surroundings, the Yosemite has no rival upon earth. The Zambesi and Niagara are typical of volume, but the Yosemite is sixteen times greater in height than Niagara, and about eight times that of the Victoria Falls. The upper part of the Yosemite is more than twice the height of the Svoringvoss, of Norway, and lacks but thirty feet of being twice as high as the highest of the Southerland waterfalls, of New Zealand. The three falls of the Southerland aggregate but 1,904 feet, 730 less than the Yosemite.

The Ribbon Fall of the El Capitan has a sheer descent of 2,100 feet, but its beauty disappears with the melting snow. The other falls were only designated by the names of the streams upon which they are situated. The river Merced was spoken of as the river of Ah-wah-ne; but the three principal branches were variously designated; the main, or middle, up to the Vernal Fall, as "Yan-o-pah," the "Water Cloud" branch, and above the Vernal, as "Yo-wy-we-ack," "the twisting rock branch."

The north and south branches had their distinctive names; the north, Py-we-ack, meaning the branch of the "Glistening Rocks," and the south, Too-lool-we-ack, or more definitely, Too-lool-lo-we-ack. The modern interpretations of some of these names may be regarded as quite fanciful, though Major Savage would declare that Indian languages were so full of figures of speech that without imagination they could not be understood.

The strictly literal interpretation of this name would be inadmissable, but it is well enough to say, that to the unconscious innocence of their primitive state, the word simply represented an effort of nature in the difficult passage of the water down through the rocky gorge. It is derived from

Too-lool and We-ack, and means, ὁ ποτᾰμος, ὁς᾿ διά πετράς οὐρεῑ. This name has been published as if by authority to signify *"The Beautiful"*—how beautiful, the learned in Greek may judge.

This really beautiful fall was visited by few of our battalion, and owing to the impracticability of following up the cañon above the fall, and the great difficulty of access to it, it was left neglected; the command contenting itself with a distant view. In view of the discoveries of Mr. Muir that there were glaciers at its source, and that the cliff now known as " Glacier Point " may be said to mark the entrance to this "South Cañon," a name often confounded with "South Fork," and especially because of the impropriety of translating this Indian name, I think it advisable to call this the Glacier Fall, and, therefore, give it that name in this volume. The name of " Illeuette " is not Indian, and is, therefore, meaningless and absurd. In accordance with the customs of these mountain people of naming their rivers from the most characteristic features of their source, the North or Ten-ie-ya branch of the Merced, which comes down the North Cañon from the glistening glacial rocks at its source, was called Py-we-ack, " the river of glistening rocks," or more literally, perhaps, " the river-smoothed rocks." Whether from Pai, a river, or from Py-ca-bo, a spring, I am in doubt. If the first syllable of the name Py-we-ack be derived from Py-ca-bo, then, probably, the name signified to them "the glistening rock spring branch," as the ice-burnished rocks at the head of Lake Ten-ie-ya stand at the source of the river.

I have never been satisfied with the poetical interpretation given the name, nor with its transfer to " Yan-o-pah," the branch of the "little cloud," as rendered by Mr. Travis. But as Py-we-ack has been displaced from Lake Ten-ie-ya and its outlet, it is proper and in accordance with the custom to call the branch Ten-ie-ya also. The name of Ten-ie-ya was given to the lake at the time of its discovery. It was there we captured the remnant of the Yosemite band, as will be explained in the next chapter. The name of Ten-ie-ya Cañon, Ten-ie-ya Fork and Lake Ten-ie-ya, has for this reason superseded the original name of Py-we-ack; but in naming the lake, I preserved an Indian name that represented the central figure in all of our operations.

Wai-ack was the name for "Mirror Lake," as well as for the mountain it so perfectly reflected. The lake itself was not particularly attractive or remarkable, but in the early morning, before the breeze swept up the cañon, the reflections were so perfect, especially of what is now known as Mt. Watkins, that even our scouts called our attention to it by pointing and exclaiming: "Look at Wai-ack," interpreted to mean the "Water Rock." This circumstance suggested the name of "Mirror Lake." The name was opposed by some, upon the ground that all still water was a mirror. My reply established the name. It was that other conditions, such as light and shade, were required, as when looking into a well, the wall of the Half Dome perfecting the conditions, and that when shown another pool that was more deserving, we would transfer the name. Captain Boling approved the name, and it was so called by the battalion.

The middle or main branch was designated by the Yosemites—from the fork of the Glacial Branch up to the Vernal Fall—as Yan-o-pah, because they were compelled to pass through the spray of the Vernal, to them a "little cloud," while passing up this cañon. The Indian name of the Nevada Fall, "Yo-wy-we," or Yo-wy-ye, and that of Too-lool-lo-we-ack, afforded innumerable jests and amusing comments, and when the suggestion of naming these falls was made, it was received with rude hilarity. Names without

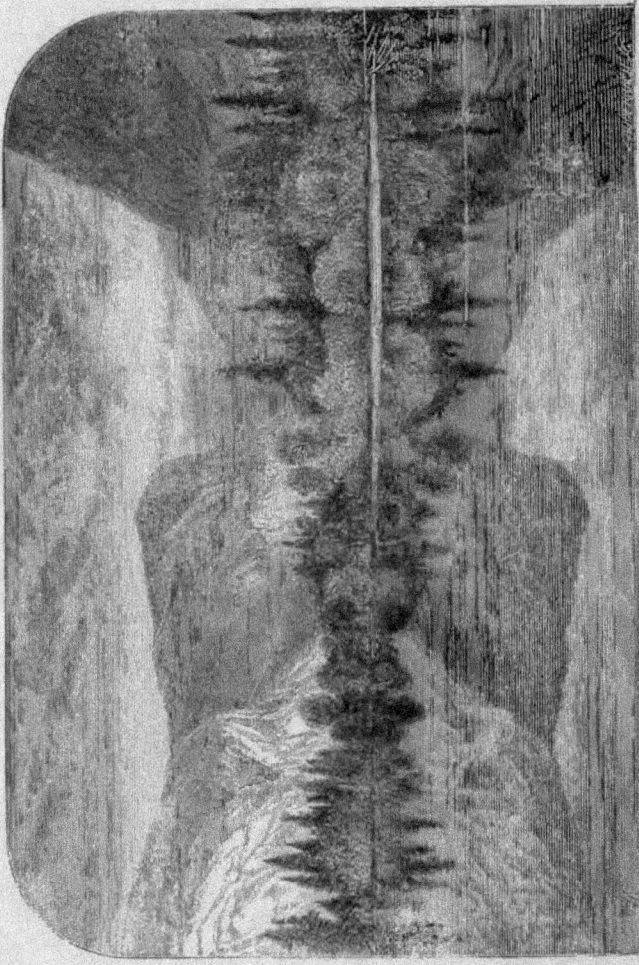

MIRROR LAKE—WATKINS' AND CLOUDS' REST.

number were presented as improvements on the originals. These names were indeed more than my own gravity would endure; Yo-wy-we being represented at first to signify the "wormy" water, from the twist or *squirm* given to the water in falling upon an obstructing rock; and therefore, after consultation with a few of my personal friends, I suggested Vernal, as an English name for Yan-o-pah, and Nevada, for that of Yo-wy-we. The Nevada Fall was so called because it was the nearest to the Sierra Nevada, and because the name was sufficiently indicative of a wintry companion for our spring.

It would be a difficult task to trace out and account for all of our impressions, or for the forms they take; but my recollection is that the cool, moist air, and newly-springing Kentucky blue-grass at the Vernal, with the sun shining through the spray as in an April shower, suggested the *sensation* of spring before the name of Vernal occurred to me; while the white, foaming water, as it dashed down Yo-wy-we from the snowy mountains, represented to my mind a vast avalanche of snow. In concluding my advocacy of these names, I represented the fact that while we were enjoying the vernal showers below, hoary-headed winter was pouring his snowy avalanches above us. Then, quoting from Byron, I said:

> The Vernal " * mounts in spray the skies, and thence again
> Returns in an unceasing shower, which round
> With its unemptied cloud of gentle rain,
> Is an eternal April to the ground,
> Making it all one emerald."

These names were given during our long stay in the valley, at a time when

> "The fragrant strife of sunshine with the morn
> Sweeten'd the air to ecstasy!"

It is agreeably complimentary for me to believe that our motives in giving English names were comprehended, and our action in the matter appreciated by others. Mr. Richardson, in "Beyond the Mississippi," shows an almost intuitive perception of our reasons for adopting the English names given to the principal falls in the Yosemite. He says: "These names are peculiarly fitting—Bridal Veil indeed looks like a veil of lace; in summer when Bridal Veil and Yosemite dwarf, Vernal still pours its ample torrent, and Nevada is always white as a snow-drift. The Yosemite is height, the Vernal is volume, the Bridal Veil is softness, but the Nevada is height, volume and softness combined. South Fork cataract, most inaccessible of all, we did not visit. In spring each fall has twenty times as much water as in summer. On the whole Yosemite is incomparably the most wonderful feature on our continent." Speaking of the Vernal Fall, Mr. Richardson says: "I saw what to Hebrew prophet had been a vision of heaven, or the visible presence of the Almighty. It was the round rainbow—the complete circle. There were two brilliant rainbows of usual form, the crescent, the bow proper. But while I looked the two horns of the inner or lower crescent suddenly lengthened, extending on each side to my feet, an entire circle, perfect as a finger ring. In two or three seconds it passed away, shrinking to the first dimensions. Ten minutes later it formed again and again, and again as suddenly disappeared. Every sharp gust of wind showering the spray over me, revealed for a moment the round rainbow. Completely drenched, I stood for an hour and a half and saw fully twenty times that dazzling circle of violet and gold on a ground-work of wet, dark rocks, gay dripping flowers and vivid grasses. I never looked upon any other scene in nature so beautiful and impressive." Mr. Richardson has with a great deal of enthusiasm given a vivid description of what appeared to me as a glowing representation of youthful spring; and to which the name of "vernal" was, I think, consistently and appropriately applied.

Mr. Hutchings, in criticising the name Vernal, has misstated the Indian name for this fall, furnished him by myself, and published in his magazine and his "Scenes of Wonder;" and while neglecting to speak in terms of the vivid green of the yielding sod, that "squirts" water, he eloquently describes the characteristics of a *vernal* shower; or the Yosemites "little water cloud," Can-o-pah ; or, if it pleases him better, Yan-o-pah. The name given by the Yosemites to the Ten-ie-ya branch of the Merced was unmistakably Py-we-ack. This name has been transferred from its original locality by some *romantic* preserver of Indian names. While passing over to Yan-o-pah, it was provided with an entirely new signification. It is indeed a laughable idea for me to even suppose that a worm and acorn-eating Indian would ever attempt to construct a name to mean "*a shower of sparkling crystals;*" his diet must have been improved by *modern* intelligent culture. The signification is certainly poetical, and is but *one step* removed from the sublime. One objection only can be raised against it; it is a little too romantic; something after the style of the tradition furnished Mr. Bancroft.*

Names were given to the numerous little streams that poured into the valley during the melting of the snow, and formed many beautiful water-falls and cascades, but I shall not attempt to describe them, as it would serve no useful purpose to give the common-place, and in some instances, very *primitive* names of these ephemeral streams. In any other mountains, in any other country, great interest would attach to them; but in the Yosemite, they are but mere suggestions to the grander objects that overshadow them.

Another witness to the propriety of the English names is Professor J. D. Whitney, State Geologist. In his admirable "Yosemite Guide Book" he says: "The names given by the early white visitors to the region, have entirely re-

* From an elaboration of legend interpreted by Stephen M. Cunningham, in 1857.

placed the native ones; and they are, in general, quite sufficiently euphonious and proper, some of them, perhaps slightly inclined to sentimentality; for if we recognize the appropriateness of the 'Bridal Veil' as a designation for the fall called Po-ho-no by the Indians, we fail to perceive why the 'Virgin's Tears' should be flowing on the opposite side of the valley."

This criticism is undoubtedly just. It seems as if some one had made an enormous stride across from the poetically sublime to ridiculous sentimentality. It is fortunate that the fall dries up early in the season!

The name of "Bridal-Veil" was suggested as an appropriate English name for the Fall of the Pohono by Warren Bær, Esq., at the time editor of the "Mariposa Democrat," while we were visiting the valley together. The appropriateness of the name was at once acknowledged, and adopted as commemorative of his visit. Mr. Bær was a man of fine culture, a son of the celebrated Doctor Bær of Baltimore.

The Pohono takes its rise in a small lake known as Lake Pohono, twelve or fifteen miles in a southernly direction from the Fall. The stream is fed by several small branches that run low early in the season.

The whole basin drained, as well as the meadows adjacent, was known to us of the battalion, as the Pohono branch and meadows.

The band who inhabited this region as a summer resort, called themselves Po-ho-no-chee, or Po-ho-na-chee, meaning the dwellers in Po-ho-no, as Ah-wah-ne-chee was understood to indicate the occupants of Ah-wah-nee. This delightful summer retreat was famous for the growth of berries and grasses, and was a favorite resort for game. The black seeds of a coarse grass found there, were used as food. When pulverized in stone mortars, the meal was made into mush and porridge. I found it impossible to obtain the literal signification of the word, but learned beyond a doubt that Po-ho-no-chee was in some way connected with the stream. I have recently learned that Po-ho-no means a daily puffing wind, and when applied to fall, stream, or meadow, means simply the fall, stream, or meadow of the puffing wind, and when applied to the tribe of Po-ho-no-chees, who occupied the meadows in summer, indicated that they dwelled on the meadows of that stream.

Mr. Cunningham says: "Po-ho-no, in the Indian language, means a belt or current of wind coming in puffs and moving in one direction." There is such a current, in its season, on the Old Millerton Road, where the dust is swept off clean. The Chow-chilla Indians call that the Po-ho-no. The Po-ho-no of the Yosemite makes its appearance where the two cascade creeks enter the canon, and this air current is daily swept up the canon to the Bridal Veil Fall, and up its stream, in puffs of great power. The water is thrown back and up in rocket-like jets, far above the fall, making it uniquely remarkable among the wonders of the valley.

Mr. Hutching's interpretation is entirely fanciful, as are most of his Indian translations."

The name for the little fall to which the name of "Virgin's Tears" has been applied, was known to us as "Pigeon Creek Fall." The Indian name is "Lung-yo-to-co-ya"; its literal meaning is "Pigeon Basket," probably signifying to them "Pigeon Nests," or *Roost*. In explanation of the name for the creek, I was told that west of El Capitan, in the valley of the stream, and upon the southern slopes, pigeons were at times quite numerous. Near the southwest base of the cliff we found a large *caché*. The supplies were put up on rocks, on trees and on posts. These granaries were constructed of twigs, bark and grass, with the tops covered in and rounded like a large basket.

If this *caché* had any connection with the name of "Pigeon Baskets," Lung-yo-to-co-ya would probably designate "The Pigeon Creek *Caché*."

After a reverential salutation, "El Capitan" must now receive my attention.

It has been stated in print that the signification of Tote-ack-ah-noo-la was "Crane Mountain," and that the name was given because of the habit sand-hill cranes had of entering the valley over this cliff. I never knew of this habit. Many erroneous statements relating to the Yosemite have appeared—some in Appleton's Encyclopædia, and one very amusing one in Bancroft's Traditions—but none appear to me more improbable.

During our long stay at our second visit, this cliff was invariably called by our scouts Tote-ack-ah-noo-la, and with some slight difference in the terminal syllable, was so called by Ten-ie-ya. This word was invariably translated to mean the "Rock Chief," or "The Captain."

Upon one occasion I asked, "Why do you call the cliff Tote-ack-ah-noo-la?" The Indian's reply was, "Because he looks like one." I then asked, "What was meant by *he?*" at the same time saying that the cliff was not a man, to be called "he." His reply was, "Come with me and see." Taking Sandino with me, I went, and as the Indian reached a point a little above and some distance out from the cliff, he triumphantly pointed to the perfect image of a man's head and face, with side whiskers, and with an expression of the sturdy English type, and asked, "Does he not look like Tote-ack-ah-noo-la?" The "Rock Chief," or "Captain," was again Sandino's interpretation of the word while viewing the likeness.

This was the first intimation that any of us had of the

reason why the name was applied, and it was *shown* in response to the question asked, why the rock had been personified.

To-tor-kon, is the name for a sand-hill crane, and ni-yul-u-ka, is the Pai-ute for head; but "crane-head" can scarcely be manufactured out of Tote-ack-ah-noo-la. It appears to me most probable that Tote-ack-ah-noo-la is derived from "ack," a rock, and To-whon-e-o, meaning chief. I am not etymologist enough to understand just how the word has been constructed, but am satisfied that the primates of the compound are rock and chief. If, however, I am found in error, I shall be most willing to acknowledge it, for few things appear more uncertain, or more difficult to obtain, than a complete understanding of the *soul* of an Indian language; principally because of the ignorance and suspicion with which a persistent and thorough research is met by the sensitively vain and jealous savages.

In leaving this subject, I would say that before it be too late, a careful and full collection of vocabularies of *all* the tongues should be made. I am aware of what has already been done by the labors of Schoolcraft, and the officers of the army in more modern times; but there is yet left a large field for persistent labor, that should be worked by the Smithsonian Institute or ethnological societies.

In adopting the Spanish interpretation, "El Capitan," for Tote-ack-ah-noo-la, we pleased our mission interpreters and conferred upon the majestic cliff a name corresponding to its dignity. When this name was approved it set aside forever those more numerous than belong to royal families. It is said by Mr. Hutchings that a profile likeness is readily traced on the angle of the cliff. The one pointed out to me was above the pine tree alcove on the southern face of the cliff, half way up its wall. It appeared to have been formed by the peculiar conformation of the rock and oxidation. The chemical stain of iron, or other mineral substance, had produced this representation, which was looked upon with superstitious awe.

" The Fallen Rocks," " The Frog Mountains," or " Three Brothers," the " Yosemite Falls," " The Lost Arrow," " Indian Cañon " and " The Arrow-wood Rocks " have already been noticed in these pages. It remains for me to briefly notice a few more objects and close this chapter. The names " North Dome," " South Dome " and " Half Dome " were given by us during our long stay in the valley from their localities and peculiar configuration. Some changes have been made since they were adopted. The peak called by us the " South Dome " has since been given the name of " Sentinel Dome," and the " Half Dome," Tis-sa-ack, represesented as meaning the " Cleft Rock," is now called by many the " South Dome."* The name for the " North Dome " is To-ko-ya, its literal signification " The Basket." The name given to the rocks now known as " The Royal Arches " is Scho-ko-ya when alluding to the fall, and means the " Basket Fall," as coming from To-ko-ya, and when referring to the rock itself it was called Scho-ko-ni, meaning the movable shade to a cradle, which, when in position, formed an arched shade over the infant's head. The name of " The Royal Arch " was given to it by a comrade who was a member of the Masonic Fraternity, and it has since been called " The Royal Arches." The " Half Dome " was figuratively spoken of as " The Sentinel " by our mission Indians, because of its overlooking the valley. The present " Sentinel " they called " Loya," a corruption of Olla (Oya), Spanish for an earthen water-pot. The mountain tribes use, instead, a long-pointed basket, shaped somewhat like that rock, which the basket is supposed to resemble.

---

*This cliff was climbed for the first time by Mr. George G. Anderson, on October 12th, 1875. It has now a stair-way running over the difficult part of the ascent.

The name of "Glacier Point" is said to be Pa-til-le-ma, a translation of which I am unable to give. Ho-yas, and

SENTINEL ROCK.
(3,043 feet in height.)

not Lo-ya, as has been stated by some, referred to certain holes in detached rocks west of the Sentinel, which afforded "milling privileges" for a number of squaws, and hence, the locality was a favorite camp ground. "The Sentinel" or "Loya," simply marked the near locality of the Ho-yas or mortars, or "*The* camp ground;" as it does now *The Hotels*. It was a common practice for visitors to confer new names on the objects of their enthusiastic admiration, and these were frequenly given to the public through letters to newspapers, while others may be found in the more enduring monuments of literature. It is a matter of no surprise that so few of them ever *stuck*. But little change has really been made in the English names for the more important objects within the valley and in its immediate vicinity. The Cathedral Rocks and spires, known as Poo-see-na-chuc-ka, meaning "Mouse-proof Rocks," from a fancied resemblance in shape to their acorn magazines or *cachès*, or a suitability for such use, have been somewhat individualized by their English names.

Of Ko-sü-kong, the name of the "Three Graces," I never learned the meaning. Ta-pun-ie-me-te is derived from Ta-pun-ie. meaning the toes, because of walking on tip-toes across, and referred to the "stepping stones" that were at the lower ford. Mr. Travis' "succession of rocks" simply indicated the *turning-off* place. There are other names that it appears unimportant for me to notice. They have been sufficiently well preserved in Professor Whitney's valuable Guide Book.

Some romantic believers in the natural tendencies of the Indians to be poetical in their expressions, twist the most vulgar common-place expressions and names into significations poetically refined, and of devotional sincerity.

Others have taken the same license in their desire to cater to the taste of those credulous admirers of the NOBLE RED MAN, the ideal of romance, the reality of whom is graded low down in the scale of humanity. Mr. Hutchings, who, were it not for his exuberant imagination, might have learned better, gives the signification of "Lung-oo-to-koo-ya" as "Long and Slender," and applies it to what he calls the Ribbon Fall. His name is better than his interpretation. Mr. H. also says that the signification of To-toc-ah-nü-la is "a Semi-Deity;" that of "Tissa-ack" "Goddess of the Valley," and that Po-ho-no means "The Spirit of the Evil Wind."

These interpretations, like the "sparkling shower of crystals" are more artistically imaginative than correct. The Pai-ute for wind, is Ni-gat, and the Kah-we-ah, is Yah-i, one or the other of which tongues were used by the Yosemites; though the Pai-ute, or a dialect of it, was given the preference.

The savages *have* a crude, undefinable idea of a Deity or Great Spirit, a Spirit of Good, who never does them harm, and whose home is in the happy land they hope to reach after death. This happy hereafter, is supposed by most on the western slope of the Sierras to be located in the West, while those on the eastern slope or within the Colorado Basin, in Arizona and in Mexico, locate it in the East. They all have a superstitious fear of evil spirits, which they believe have the power to do them great harm, and defeat their undertakings.

They do not as a rule look to the Great Spirit for immediate protection from evil, but instead, rely upon amulets, incense and charms, or "*medicine*" bags. Through these and certain ceremonies of their priests or "mediums," they endeavor to protect themselves and their families from the evil influence of spirits in and out of the flesh.

They believe that the spirits of the dead who have not, through proper ceremonies, been released from the body and allowed at once to go to the happy land, were evil spirits that were doomed to haunt certain localities. They looked with superstitious awe upon objects and localities, which to them were of mysterious character. Even familiar objects were sometimes looked upon as having been taken possession of by spirits. These spirits it was supposed could do injury to those who might venture near them without the protection afforded by their charms, or certain offerings to their priests for indulgences from the spiritual inhabitants. Streams were often said to be controlled by spirits, and for this reason, offerings of tobacco and other substances were at times thrown in as a propitiation for past offenses, or as an offering for something in expectancy. They believe that the elements are all under control, or may be used by the more powerful spirits, and, owing probably to its infrequency in California, lightning seemed to be an especial object of awe and wonder to them.

Waterfalls seemed not to engage their attention for their beauty, but because of the power they manifested; and in none of their objections made to the abandonment of their home, was there anything said to indicate any appreciation of the scenery. Their misfortunes, accidents and failures were generally believed to have resulted from evil spiritual interference, and to insure success in any undertaking, these dark or evil spirits must first be conciliated through their "medicine men," from whom they obtain absolution.

All spirits that had not been released and taken their flight to their happy Western spirit-land were considered as evil; and only the Great Spirit was believed to be very good. The Indians of the Yosemite Valley did not look upon Tote-ack-ah-nü-lah as a veritable Deity or "semi-Deity." They looked upon this cliff, and the representation of the likeness of a human face, with the same mysterious awe and superstitious feeling that they entertained for some other objects; though perhaps their reverence was in a somewhat higher degree stimulated by this imposing human appearance; and their ability, therefore, the better to personify it. They regarded this vast mountain as an emblem of some mysterious power, beyond their comprehension. From my knowledge of their *religious belief*, I have come to the conclusion that their ideas in this direction are wholly spiritual, without material representation, except as stated, through symbolic ideas, growing out of their superstitious ignorance, like some ignorant Christians. They have in imagination peopled the rocks and mountains, woods and valleys, streams and waterfalls with innumerable spiritual occupants, possessed of supernatural or spiritual powers, none of which are believed by them to equal the power of the Great Spirit whose home is in the West, and who prohibits the return of the evil ones, until a probationary existence here upon this earth shall have given them such knowledge of and disgust with evil as will fit them for the enjoyment of good.

The special inconsistency of this belief seems to be, that if one of these demons can lure any one to destruction, the victim will be compelled to take the place and occupation of the evil spirit, who is at once liberated and takes its flight to join its family or such members of it, as are already with the blessed. This idea seemed to be based upon the natural selfishness of human nature, that would gladly fix its responsibilities and sufferings upon another. A writer in his descriptions of the Yosemite says: "The savage lowers his voice to a whisper, and crouches tremblingly past Po-ho-no, while the very utterance of the name is so dreaded by him, that the discoverers of the valley obtained it with difficulty." These statements were prefaced by the assertion that "Po-ho-no is an evil spirit of the Indians' mythology." On our second visit to the valley, it will be remembered, we found huts built by the Yosemites not far from the Po-ho-no Fall.

I never found any difficulty in learning the name of this

fall, or observed any more fear of spirits exhibited at this fall than at the Yosemite fall; but in later years, for causes that will appear in the course of this narrative, the little meadow and detached rocks west of Po-ho-no, and near to the foot of the Mariposa trail; became haunted ground to the remnant of the band, for disaster and death followed the commission of crime at that locality.

Savages are seldom able to trace to themselves the cause of misfortune, and hence evil spirits must bear the burden of their complaint. For this service they are well paid through their representatives, the "medicine men." I have often been amused, and agreeably entertained while listening to their traditionary literature.

Among the Chippewa and Dahcota tribes, my likeness to a brother, who was a trader, was recognized, and many times I was honored by a prominent place being given me in their lodges and at their dances. Some of their mysteries I was not permitted to witness, but the consecration of the ground for the dance, which is performed with great ceremony, I have several times seen, and had its signification fully explained to me. The ceremony differs but little among the different tribes, and consists of invocations, burning incense, scattering down, feathers and evergreens upon the pathway or floor of the dance, lighting of the sacred fires with their ancient fire-sticks, which are still preserved among the priests, and repeating certain cabalistic words, the meaning of which they do not even pretend to understand, but which are supposed to have a most potent influence. They also have their pantomimes and romances, which they repeat to each other like children. This legendary literature is largely imaginative, but I found the California Indians less poetical in thought and feeling than eastern tribes, and less musical, though perhaps as primitively figurative in expression.

Though seemingly unimpressed by their sublime surroundings, their figures and comparisons, when not objectionable, were beautiful, because natural. The Pai-ute and Mono Colony originally established by Ten-ie-ya, was the result of a desire to improve their physical condition. They were attached to this valley as a home. The instinctive attraction that an Indian has for his place of nativity is incomprehensible; it is more than a religious sentiment; it is a passion. Here, sheltered in a measure from the storms of winter, and the burning heat of summer, they met as in an earthly paradise, to exchange the products of either side of the Sierras, to engage in a grand hunt and festival offer up religious sacrifices, and awaken the echoes of the valley with their vociferous orations. Should their skill fail them in the chase, and the mountain or brook refuse their luscious offerings, they had a never-failing resource in the skill with which they could dispossess the native Californian, or the newly arrived immigrant of his much prized herds, and *translate* them to their mountain home. Nor was there need of herd-men to guard their fleecy flocks or

THE INDIAN BELLE.

roving herds, for the prancing horse or gentle kine, having once been slid over the slippery gateway, avoided the obstruction ever after; and remained contented in t h e i r fields of blue grass and clover.

But, when the influence of the "golden era" finally reached this once blissfully ig-

beaux had never known before, their imaginations excited by the superfluities of civilization, their natural cunning came at once to their aid, and lo! the "honest miner" or timid Chinaman contributed from their scanty stores and wardrobes, or the poorly sheltered goods of the mountain trader opened their canvas walls to the keen arguments of their flinty knives, and wants real or fancied were at once supplied.

What then was there lacking, to make the Yosemites a happy people, removed as they were from the bad influences of whiskey and the white man's injustice? Only this: "the whites would not let them alone." So Ten-ie-ya had said, as if aggrieved. Like all his race, and perhaps like all ignorant, passionate and willful persons, he appeared unconscious of his own wrong-doing, and of the inevitable fate that he was bringing upon himself and his people.

In his talk with Major Savage, he had spoken of the verdure clothing the valley, as sufficient for his wants, but at the time, knowing that acorns formed the staple of their food, and that clover, grass, sorrel and the inner bark of trees were used to guard against biliousness and eruptive diseases, little heed was given to his declaration. Now, however, that we saw the valley clothed with exquisite and useful verdure, for June was now at hand, Ten-ie-ya's remarks had a greater significance, and we could understand how large flocks and herds had been stolen, and fattened to supply their wants. The late claimants to this lovely locality, "this great moral show," have been relieved of their charge by act of Congress, and fifty thousand dollars given them for their claims. It will probably now remain forever free to visitors. The builders of the toll roads and trails should also receive fair compensation for their pioneer labors in building them, that they may also be free to all.

When this is done, this National Park will be esteemed entirely worthy of this great republic and of the great golden State that has accepted its guardianship.*

Perhaps no one can better than myself realize the value of the labors performed by the early pioneers, that has made it possible for tourists to visit in comfort some of the most prominent objects of interest; but " *a National Park* " should be entirely free. In suggesting a new name for the fall of Too-lool-lo-we-ack, or the absurd " Illilnette," I wish to honor Mr. Muir for his intelligent explorations and discoveries, and at the same time feel that the word glacier is the most appropriate. Of this, however, the residents of the valley will judge.

The names of the different objects and localities of especial interest have now become well established by use. It is not a matter of so much surprise that there is such a difference in the orthography of the names. I only wonder that they have been retained in a condition to be recognized. It is not altogether the fault of the interpreters that discrepancies exist in interpretation or pronunciation, although both are often undesignedly warped to conform to the ideality of the interpreter. Many of the names have been modernized and adorned with *transparencies* in order to illuminate the subject of which the parties were writing. Those who once inhabited this region, and gave distinctive appellations, have all disappeared. The names given by them can be but indifferently preserved or counterfeited by their camp followers, the " California Diggers; " but June is now with us, and we must hasten on to our work of following up the trail.

---

* All trails within the original grant have now been made free.

CHAPTER XIV.

A MOUNTAIN storm raged with such violence as to stampede the mules of the pack-train while the escort were encamped on the South Fork. The mules were not overtaken until they reached the foot-hills of the Fresno. In the meantime, while impatiently awaiting their return, our rations gave out. In order to somewhat appease our hunger, Dr. Black distributed his hospital stores among us. There were some canned fruits and meats, and several cans of oysters and clams. The southerners of the command waived their rights to the clams, but cast lots for the oysters. Thinking we had a prize in the clams, we brought to bear our early recollections of Eastern life, and compounded a most excellent and, what we supposed would be, a most nourishing soup. Our enjoyment, however, of this highly prized New England dish was of short duration; for from some cause, never satisfactorily explained by Dr. Black, *or other eminent counsel,* our Eastern mess, as if moved by one impulse of re-gurgitation, *gave up their clams.* Fortunately for us our supplies arrived the next morning; for the game procurable was not sufficient for the command.

Major Savage sent Cow-chitty, a brother of Pon-watch-ee, the chief of the Noot-choo band, whose village we surprised before we discovered the valley, as chief of scouts. He was accompanied by several young warriors, selected because they were all familiar with the Sierra Nevada trails and the territory of the Pai-utes, where it was thought probable the expedition would penetrate.

Captain Boling had in his report to Major Savage, complained of the incapacity of Sandino as guide, and expressed the opinion that he stood in awe of Ten-ie-ya. By letter, the Major replied, and particularly advised Captain Boling that implicit confidence could be placed in Cow-chitty and his scouts, as the sub-chief was an old enemy of Ten-ie-ya, and was esteemed for his sagacity and wood-craft, which was superior to that of any Indian in his tribe. Captain Boling had improved in health and strength, and concluded to venture on his contemplated expedition over the mountains. He at once ordered preparations to be made. A camp-guard was detailed, and a special supply train fitted out. All was ready for a start in the morning. During the evening Captain Boling consulted our new guide as to what trail would be best to follow to the Mono pass and over the mountains. Cow-chitty had already learned from our Po-ho-no scouts and those of his own tribe, the extent of our explorations, and had had a long talk with Sandino as well as with Ten-ie-ya. The mission Indian and the old chief tried to make the new guide believe that the Yosemites had gone over the mountains to the Monos. Indian-like, he had remained very grave and taciturn, while the preparations were going on for the expedition. Now, however, that he was consulted by Captain Boling, he was willing enough to give his advice, and in a very emphatic manner declared his belief to the Captain that Ten-ie-ya's people were not far off; that they were either hiding in some of the rocky cañons in the vicinity of the valley, or in those of the Tuolumne, and discouraged the idea of attempting the expedition with horses. Although this did not coincide with the views of our Captain, the earnestness of Cowchitty decided him to make another attempt in the near vicinity before crossing the mountains. The horses and supply-train were accordingly left in camp, and we started at daylight on foot, with three days' rations packed in our blankets. We left the valley this time by way of the Pywe-ack cañon, and ascended the north cliff trail, a short distance above "Mirror Lake." Soon after reaching the summit, Indian signs were discovered near the trail we were on. The old trail up the slope of the cañon, was here abandoned, and the fresh trail followed up to and along the ridges just below the snow line. These signs and the tortuous course pursued, were similar to the tracks followed on our trip up Indian Cañon, and were as easily traced until we reached an elevation almost entirely covered with snow from five to ten feet deep, except on exposed tops of ridges, where the snow had blown off to the north side or melted away.

I had accompanied our guide in advance of the command, but observing that our course was a zig-zag one, some times almost doubling on our trail, I stopped and told the guide to halt until the Captain came up. He had been following the ridges without a sign of a trail being visible, although he had sometimes pointed to small pieces of coarse granite on the rocky divides, which he said had been displaced by Ten-ie-ya's scouts. That in going out or returning from their camps, they had kept on the rocky ridges, and had avoided tracking the snow or soft ground, so as to prevent the Americans from following them. As we stopped, he called me a little out of hearing of those with me, and by pantomime and a few words indicated his belief in the near presence of Indians.

When the Captain came up he said: "The hiding-place of the Yosemites is not far off. If they had crossed the mountains their scouts would not be so careful to hide their trail. They would follow the old trail if they came to watch you, because it is direct, and would only hide their tracks when they were again far from the valley and near their rancheria." This was, in part, an answer to Captain Boling's inquiry as to why we had left the old trail, and gone so far out of our way. I explained to him what Cow-chitty had stated, and pointed out what the guide or scout said was a fresh trail. The Captain looked tired and dis-heartened, but with a grim smile said: "That may be a fresh Indian track, but I can't see it. If left to my own feelings and judgment, I should say we were on another wild-goose chase. If the guide can see tracks, and thinks he has got 'em this time, I reckon it is better to follow on; but if there is any short-cut tell him to give us some land-marks to go by; for I find I am not as strong as I thought. Let us take another look at this *fresh* trail, and then you may get Cow-chitty's idea as to the probable course this trail will take further on." As we moved up the trail a little farther, the expert scout pointed out more fresh signs, but Captain Boling failed to discern a trail, and gave up the examination, and as he seated himself for a momentary rest, said: "I reckon it is all right, Doc. The Major says in his letter that I can bet on Cow-chitty every time. But I can't see any more of a trail on this rocky ridge than I can see the trail of that wood-pecker as he flies through the air, but I have some faith in instinct, for I reckon that is what it is that enables him to follow a trail that he imagines should be there. We shall have to trust him to follow it, and let him have his own way as you would a fox-hound; if he don't, puppy-like, take the back track, or run wild with us over some of these ledges." Old Ten-ie-ya was now appealed to for information concerning the fresh signs, but he only reiterated his former statement that his people had gone over the mountains to the Monos, and the signs he said were those of Tuolumne Indians. Captain Boling had taken the old chief along with us on this trip, hoping to make him of some use, if not directly as guide, indirectly; it was thought he might betray his people's hiding-place. But the Captain was disappointed in this, for no finished gamester ever displayed a more immovable countenance than did Ten-ie-ya when questioned at any time during the expedition. A cord had again been placed around his waist to secure his allegiance, and as we were about to move ahead once more, he very gravely said that if we followed the signs, they would take us over to the Tuolumne.

Before this Sandino had professed to agree with Ten-ie-ya, but now he carefully withheld his own opinions, and as carefully rendered his interpretations. He feared Cow-chitty more than Ten-ie-ya; and he was frequently seen to cross himself while muttering his prayers. Spencer and myself re-assured the timid creature, and made him quite happy by telling him that we would guard him against the "Gentiles," as he called the natives.

I explained to Cow-chitty our inability to follow the tracks as he did over the bare granite. This flattered him, and he then pointed out his own method of doing so, which was simple enough with one of keen sight. It consisted entirely in discovering fragments of stone and moss that had been displaced, and broken off and scattered upon the ground. The upper surface of the broken fragments of stone were smooth and bleached, while the under surface was dark or colored. It was impossible to walk over these stony ridges without displacing some of the fragments, and these the quick eye of Cow-chitty was sure to discover. Cow-chitty was pleased when told of Captain

Boling's appreciation of his sagacity, and honored by the confidence the Captain began to show him. He expressed his gratification by being more communicative than he had been before. He said, "These signs tell me that the Yo-semite scouts have been watching all the movements of the Americans, and the trails that will take you to their camps. They will not look for you on this trail. They are watch-ing for you from the ridges nearer the valley. We will not have to go far to find their camps. This trail will lead us to the head of the Py-we-ack, where the Pai-ute or Mono trail crosses into the upper valley of the Tuolumne; and if we don't find them at the lake, we will soon know if they have crossed the mountains."

He then proposed that Captain Boling send out scouts to intercept and capture the Yosemite scouts, who might be below us watching the valley. This being interpreted to Captain Boling, he at once adopted the suggestion of the scout. He selected three of our best runners, and directed Cow-chitty to select three of his. These were sent out in pairs—an Indian and a white man. The scouts were placed under direction of the sub-chief, who followed the trail, and indicated to the Captain the most direct route for the main body to follow. In health Captain Boling was athletic and ambitious on the march. He had now, how-ever, over-estimated his strength, and suffered considera-bly from fatigue; but the halt afforded him a rest that very much refreshed him. I traveled with him during the re-mainder of the march, so as to be near him as interpretor, and took charge of Ten-ie-ya. The Captain, Ten-ie-ya, San-dino and myself traveled together. Our march was more leisurely than in the earlier part of the day. This allowed Captain Boling to somewhat recover from his fatigue.

On an ascending spur that ran down to the Py-we-ack, we found Cow-chitty quietly awaiting our approach. As we halted, he pointed out to Captain Boling a dim circle of blue smoke, that appeared to eddy under the lee of a large granite knob or peak, and said, "Rancheria." Old Ten-ie-ya was standing in front of me, but exhibited no interest in the discovery. As I lowered my line of vision to the base of the cliff, to trace the source of the smoke, there appeared the Indian village, resting in fancied security, upon the border of a most beautiful little lake, seemingly not more than a half mile away. To the lake I afterwards gave the name of Ten-ie-ya. The granite knob was so bare, smooth and glistening, that Captain Boling at once pointed it out, and selected it as a landmark. He designated it as a rallying point for his men, if scattered in pursuit, and said that we should probably camp near it for the night.

While the Captain was studying the nature of the ground before us, and making his arrangements to capture the village, our scouts were discovered in full chase of an Indian picket, who was running towards the village as if his life depended upon his efforts. In the excitement of the moment Captain Boling ordered us to double-quick and charge, thinking, as he afterwards said, that the huts could not be much more than half a mile away. Such a mistake could only originate in the transparent air of the mountains. The village was fully two miles or more away. We did, however, double-quick, and I kept a gait that soon carried Ten-ie-ya and Sandino, with myself, ahead of our scattering column. Finding the rope with which I held Ten-ie-ya an encumbrance in our rapid march, I wound it round his shoulder and kept him in front of me. While passing a steep slope of overlapping granite rock, the old chief made a sudden spring to the right, and attempted to escape down the ragged precipice. His age was against him, for I caught him just as he was about to let himself drop from the projecting ledge to the ground below; his feet were already over the brink.

I felt somewhat angered at the trick of the old fellow in attempting to relieve himself from my custody, and the delay it had occasioned me; for we had taken the most direct although not the smoothest course. I resumed our advance at a gait that hurried the old sachem forward, perhaps less carefully and more rapidly than comported with the dignity of his years and rank. I was amused at the proposition of one of the " boys " who had witnessed the transaction, to " shoot the old devil, and not be bothered with him any more." I of course declined this humane proposition to relieve me of further care, and at once became the chief's most devoted defender, which observing, he afterwards told Captain Boling that I was " very good." As we reached the more gently descending ground near the bottom of the slope, an Indian came running up the trail below us that led to the Rancheria. His course was at an acute angle to the one pursued by us toward the village, which was now but a few rods off. I ordered Sandino to cut him off and capture him before he should reach the camp. This was accomplished with great energy and a good degree of pride.

The Yosemites had already discovered our approach, but too late for any concerted resistance or for successful escape, for Lt. Crawford at the head of a portion of the command, dashed at once into the center of the encampment, and the terror-stricken Indians immediately threw up their bare hands in token of submission, and piteously cried out " pace! pace! " (peace, peace). As I halted to disarm the scout captured by Sandino, I was near enough to the camp to hear the expressions of submission. I was compelled to laugh at the absurd performances of Sandino, who to terrify his prisoner, was persistently holding in his face an old double-barreled pistol. I was aware the weapon was a harmless one, for one hammer was gone, and the other could not be made to explode a cap. I took the bow and arrows from the frightened savage, and as Captain Boling came up I reported the capture, telling him at the same time of the surrender of the village or Rancheria to Lt. Crawford. Seeing some of the Indians leaving the camp, and running down the lake to a trail crossing its outlet, the Captain and the men with him sprang forward through the grove of pines near the crossing, and drove them back. No show of resistance was offered, neither did any escape from us.

While Captain Boling was counting his prisoners and corralling them with a guard, I, by his previous order, restrained Ten-ie-ya from any communication with his people. The chief of this village was a young man of perhaps thirty years of age. When called upon by the Captain to state how many were under his command, he answered that those in the encampment were all that was left; the rest had scattered and returned to the tribes they sprung from. Ten-ie-ya seemed very anxious to answer the interrogations made to the young chief, but Captain Boling would not allow his farther interference, and jokingly told me to send him over among the women who were grouped a little aside, as he was now about as harmless. I acted upon the suggestion, and upon his being told that he had the liberty of the camp if he made no further attempts to escape, the old fellow stepped off briskly to meet his four squaws, who were with this band, and who seemed as pleased as himself at their re-union.

Captain Boling felt satisfied that the answer given by this half-starved chief, and the few braves of his wretched looking band, were as truthful as their condition would corroborate. Finding themselves so completely surprised, notwithstanding their extreme vigilance, and comparing the well kept appearance of their old chief with their own worn out, dilapidated condition, they with apparent anxiety expressed a willingness for the future to live in peace with the Americans. All hopes of avoiding a treaty, or of preventing their removal to the Reservation, appeared to have at once been abandoned; for when the young chief was asked if he and his band were willing to go to the Fresno, he replied with much emotion of gesture, and as rendered by Sandino to Spencer and myself: "Not only willing, but anxious;" for, said he: "Where can we now go that the Americans will not follow us?" As he said this, he stretched his arms out toward the East, and added: "Where can we make our homes, that you will not find us?" He then went on and stated that they had fled to the mountains without food or clothing; that they were worn out from watching our scouts, and building *signal-fires* to tire us out also.

They had been anxious to embroil us in trouble by drawing us into the cañons of the Tuolumne, where were some Pai-utes wintering in a valley like Ah-wah-ne. They had hoped to be secure in this retreat until the snow melted, so that they could go to the Mono tribe and make a home with them, but that now he was told the Americans would follow them even there, he was willing, with all his little band, to go to the plains with us." After the young chief had been allowed full liberty of speech, and had sat down, Ten-ie-ya again came forward, and would have doubtless made a *confession of faith*, but his speech was cut short by an order from Captain Boling to at once move camp to a beautiful pine grove on the north side of the outlet to the lake, which he had selected for our camping-place for the night. By this order he was able to have everything in readiness for an early start the next morning. There was an abundance of dry pine, convenient for our camp fires, and as the night was exceedingly cold, the glowing fires were a necessity to our comfort. The Indians were told to pack such movables as they desired to take with them, and move down at once to our camp-ground.

The scene was a busy one. The squaws and children exhibited their delight in the prospect of a change to a more genial locality, and where food would be plenty. While watching the preparations of the squaws for the transfer of their household treasures and scanty stores, my attention was directed to a dark object that appeared to be crawling up the base of the first granite peak above their camp. The polished surface of the gleaming rock made the object appear larger than the reality. We were unable to determine what kind of an animal it could be; but one of our scouts, to whom the name of "Big Drunk" had been given, pronounced it a papoose, although some had variously called it a bear, a fisher or a coon. "Big Drunk" started after it, and soon returned with a bright, active boy, entirely naked, which he coaxed from his slippery perch. Finding himself an object of curiosity his fright subsided, and he drew from its hiding-place, in the bushes near by, a garment that somewhat in shape, at least, resembled a man's shirt. "*The Glistening Rocks*" had rendered us all oblivious to the color, and that was left undetermined. This garment swept the ground after he had clothed himself with it. His ludicrous appearance excited our laughter, and as if pleased with the attentions paid to him, the little fellow joined heartily in the merriment he occasioned. It will not be out of place to here relate the sequel of this boy's history. Learning that he was an orphan and without relatives, Captain Boling adopted him, calling him "Reube," in honor of Lt. Reuben Chandler, who after Captain Boling was the most popular man in the battalion.

Some three or four years afterward, the boy, as if to illustrate the folly of the Captain in trying to civilize and educate him, ran away from his patron, taking with him two valuable, thorough-bred Tennessee horses, much prized by the Captain; besides money, clothing and arms belonging to the Captain's brother-in-law, Col. Lane, of Stockton, in whose charge Captain Boling had placed him, that he might have the advantages of a good school. After collecting together all the Indians found in this encampment; the total number was found to be but thirty-five, nearly all of whom were in some way a part of the family of the old patriarch, Ten-ie-ya. These were escorted to our camp, the men placed under guard, but the women and children were left free.

This was accomplished before sun down, and being relieved of duty, a few of us ran across the outlet of the lake, and climbing the divide on the south side of the lake, beheld a sunset view that will long be remembered. It was dark when we reached camp, and after a scanty repast, we spread our blankets, and soon were wrapped in slumber sweet.

We were awakened by the cold, which became more uncomfortable as night advanced, and finding it impossible to again compose ourselves to sleep, Captain Boling aroused the camp, and preparations were made by the light of the blazing camp-fires for an early start for the valley. Desiring some clean, fresh water, I went to the lake as the nearest point to obtain it, when, to my surprise, I found that the new ice formed during the night and connecting the old ice with the shore of the lake, was strong enough to bear me up. At a point where the old ice had drifted near, I went out some distance upon it, and it appeared strong enough to have borne up a horse. This was about the 5th of June, 1851. The change of temperature from summer in the valley to winter on the mountains, without shelter, was felt by us all. After a hasty breakfast, the word was passed to assemble, and we were soon all ready for the order to march. All at once there was turmoil and strife in camp, and what sounded to my ears very much like a Chinese concert. Captain Boling was always a man of gallantry, and in this instance would not allow the squaws to take the burden of the baggage. Hence the confusion and delay. He ordered the Indians to carry the packs—burdens they had imposed on their women. This order brought down upon him the vituperations of the squaws and sullen murmurs from the "noble red men;" as often happens in domestic interference, *the family was offended*. Ten-ie-ya rose to explain, and waxed eloquent in his protest against this innovation on their ancient customs.

As soon as the Captain was made aware of the old fellow's object in having "a talk," he cut short the debate by ordering one of the lieutenants to see that every Indian, as well as squaw, was properly loaded with a just proportion of their burdens. The real object of the Captain was to facilitate the return to the valley, by making it easy for the squaws and children to accompany us through without delays. One amusing feature in this arrangement was, that long after the men had been silenced, their squaws continued to murmur at the indignity practiced on their disgraced lords. I have my doubts, even to this day, whether the standard of women's rights was ever again *waved* among the mountain tribes after this "special order" was issued by our good-hearted Captain.

In order to take the most direct route to the valley, Captain Boling selected one of the young Yosemite Indians to lead the way with our regular guide. Being relieved of the charge of Ten-ie-ya, I took my usual place on the march with the guide. This position was preferred by me, because it afforded ample opportunity for observation and time for reflection; and beside, it was in my nature to be in advance. The trail followed, after leaving the lake, led us over bare granite slopes and hidden paths, but the distance was materially shortened. A short distance below the bottom land

of the lake, on the north side of the cañon and at the head
of the gorge, the smooth, sloping granite projects like a vast
roof over the abyss below. As we approached this, our
young guide pointed toward it.

By close observation I was able to discover that the trail
led up its sloping surface, and was assured by the guide
that the trail was a good one. I felt doubtful of the Captain's willingness to scale that rocky slope, and halted for
him to come up. The Captain followed the trail to its termination in the soil, and saw the cause of my having halted.
Upon the discoloration of the rock being pointed out as the
continuation of the trail, he glanced up the granite slope
and said, "Go on, but be watchful, for a slide into the
gorge would bring as certain death as a slide from that San
Joaquin trail, which I have not yet forgotten." Some of
the command did not fancy this any more than they did the
Ten-ie-ya trail down "Indian Cañon." We all pulled off
our boots and went up this slope bare-footed. Seeing there
was no real danger, the most timid soon moved up as fearless as the others. I, with the advance, soon reached the
soil above, and at the top halted until the Indians and our
straggling column closed up. As I looked about me, I discovered, unfolding to my sight, one of the most charming
views in this sublimest scenery of nature. During the day
before, we had looked with astonishment on the almost
boundless peaks, and snow-capped mountains, to be seen
from the Mt. Hoffman divide. But here some of the same
views appeared illuminated. In our ascent up the mountain, we had apparently met the rising sun. The scene was
one long to be remembered for its brilliancy, although not
describable.

Mr. Addison, in the *Spectator*, says: "Our imagination
loves to be filled with an object, or to grasp at anything
that is too big for its capacity. We are flung into a pleasing

astonishment at such unbounded views, and feel a delightful stillness and amazement in the soul." Mr. Addison has here expressed the feelings entertained by some of us, as the view met our gaze while looking out to the east, the south and the west. Although not sufficiently elevated to command a general outlook, the higher ridges framing some of the scenery to the north and eastward of us, the westerly view was boundless. The transparency of the atmosphere was here extreme, and as the sun illumined the snow-clad and ice-burnished peaks, the scene aroused the enthusiasm of the command to a shout of glad surprise.

The recollections of the discomforts of the night were banished by the glory of the morning as here displayed. Even the beauties of the Yosemite, of which I was so ardent an admirer, were for the moment eclipsed by this gorgeously grand and changing scene. The aurora that had preceded the rising sun was as many-hued, and if possible more glorious, than the most vivid borealis of the northern climes. But when the sun appeared, seemingly like a sudden flash, amidst the distant peaks, the climax was complete. My opportunities for examining the mountain scenery of the Sierra Nevada above the immediate vicinity of the Yosemite, were such as to only enable me to give a somewhat general description, but the views that I had during our explorations afforded me glimpses of the possibilities of sublime mountain scenery, such as I had never before comprehended, although familiar with the views afforded from some of the peaks of Mexico and of the Rocky Mountains. I doubt even if the Yellow Stone, supreme in some of its attractions, affords such varied and majestic beauty.

Looking back to the lovely little lake, where we had been encamped during the night, and watching Ten-ie-ya as he ascended to our group, I suggested to the Captain that we name the lake after the old chief, and call it "Lake Ten-

LAKE TEN-IE-YA, ONE OF THE YOSEMITE FOUNTAINS.

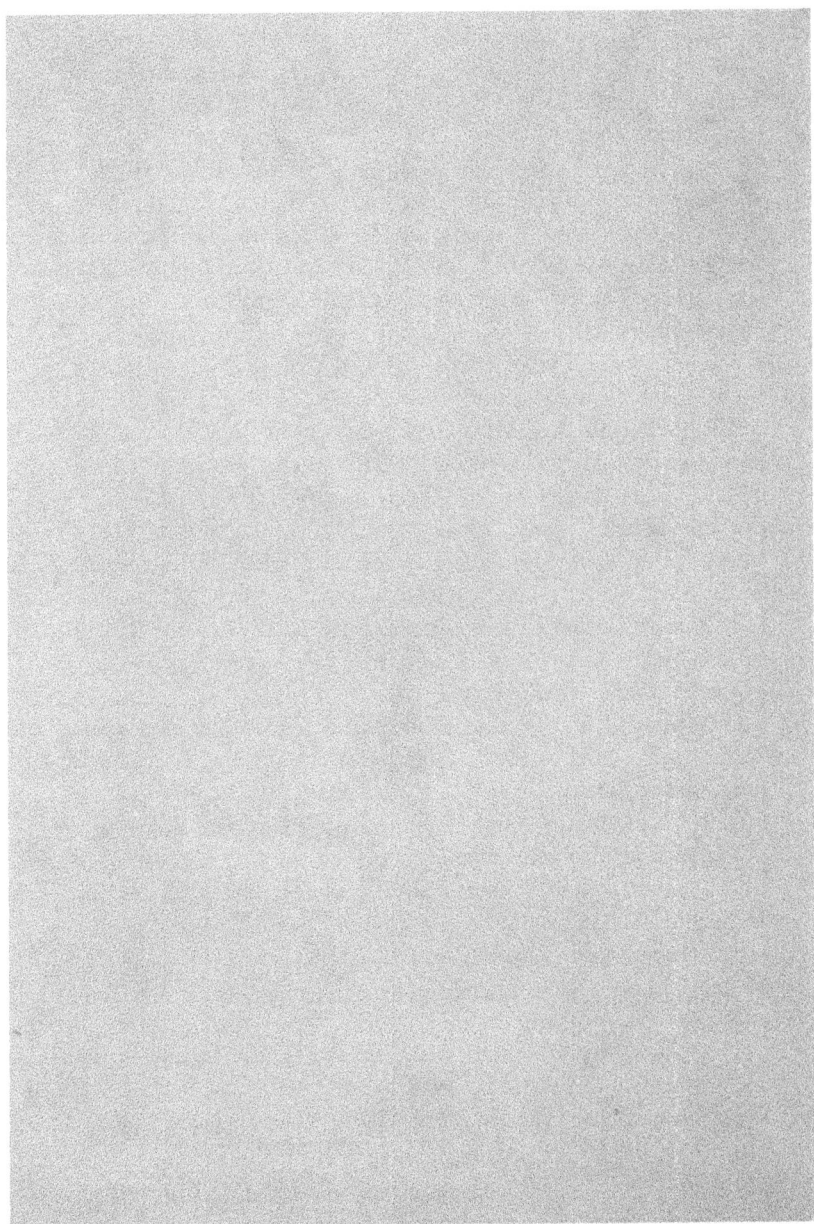

ie-ya." The Captain had fully recovered from his annoyance at the scene in camp, and readily consented to the name, but added that I had evidently mistaken my vocation.

Noticing my look of surprise, he jokingly said that if I had only studied divinity instead of medicine, I could have then fully gratified my passion for christening. This, of course, brought out a general guffaw, and thinking me annoyed, he said: "Gentlemen, I think the name an appropriate one, and shall use it in my report of the expedition. Beside this, it is rendering a kind of justice to perpetuate the name of the old chief."

When Ten-ie-ya reached the summit, he left his people and approached where the Captain and a few of us were halting. Although he had been snubbed by the Captain that morning, he now seemed to have forgotten it, and his rather rugged countenance glowed with healthful exercise in the sunlight. I had handled him rather roughly the day before, but as he now evidently wished to be friendly, I called him up to us, and told him that we had given his name to the lake and river. At first, he seemed unable to comprehend our purpose, and pointing to the group of Glistening peaks, near the head of the lake, said: "It already has a name; we call it Py-we-ack." Upon my telling him that we had named it Ten-ie-ya, because it was upon the shores of the lake that we had found his people, who would never return to it to live, his countenance fell and he at once left our group and joined his own family circle. His countenance as he left us indicated that he thought the naming of the lake no equivalent for the loss of his territory.

I never at any time had real personal dislike for the old sachem. He had always been an object of study, and I sometimes found in him profitable entertainment. As he moved off to hide his sorrow, I pitied him. As we resumed our march over the rough and billowy trail, I was more fully impressed with the appropriateness of the name for the beautiful lake. Here, probably, his people had built their last wigwams in their mountain home. From this lake we were leading the last remnant of his once dreaded tribe, to a territory from which it was designed they should never return as a people. My sympathies, confirmed in my own mind, a justness in thus perpetuating the name of Ten-ie-ya. The Indian name for this lake, branch and cañon, "Py-we-ack" is, although a most appropriate one, now displaced by that of the old chief Ten-ie-ya. Of the significations of the name Ten-ie-ya, I am uncertain; but as pronounced by himself, I have no doubt of its being pure Indian.

The whole mountain region of the water-sheds of the Merced and Tuolumne rivers afford the most delightful views to be seen anywhere of mountains, cliffs, cascades and waterfalls, grand forests and mountain meadows, and the Soda Springs are yet destined to become a favorite summer resort. Mr. Muir has well said that the "upper Tuolumne valley is the widest, smoothest, most serenely spacious, and in every way the most delightful summer pleasure park in all the High Sierras."

Now that it has become a part of the new National Park surrounding the old grant (see new map), and good trails reach it, wagon roads will soon be extended into the very "heart of the Sierras"

We reached our camp in the valley without accident. Captain Boling at once gave orders to make preparations for our return to the Fresno. The next day we broke camp and moved down to the lower end of the valley near where we camped on the first night of our discovery, near the little meadow at the foot of the Mariposa Trail.

At sunrise the next morning, or rather as the reflections on the cliffs indicated sunrise, we commenced our ascent of the steep trail. As I reached the height of land where the moving column would soon perhaps forever shut out from view the immortal "Rock Chief," my old sympathies returned, and leaving the command to pursue its heedless way, I climbed to my old perch where Savage had warned me of danger. As I looked back upon El Capitan, his bald forehead was cooling in the breeze that swept by me from the "*Summer land*" *below*, and his cheerful countenance reflected back the glory of the rising sun. Feeling my own inferiority while acknowledging the majesty of the scene, I looked back from Mt. Beatitude, and quoting from Byron, exclaimed:

Yosemite!
" Thy vale(s) of evergreen, thy hills of snow
Proclaim thee Nature's varied favorite now."

We reached the Fresno without the loss of a captive, and as we turned them over to the agent, we were formally commended for the success of the expedition.

CHAPTER XV.

A MARKED and peculiar feature observed in the landscape of the Merced River slopes, while going to the Yosemite, especially on the Coultersville route, is the dense growth of the chamiso and the manzanita. These shrubs are found most abundant below the altitude of the growth of sugar-pine, upon dry, slaty ground; though a larger variety of manzanita, distinguishable by its larger blossoms and fruit, and its love of shade and moist clay-slate soil, may be found growing even among the sugar-pine. A peculiarity of this shrub is, that like the Madroña and some trees in Australia, it sheds a portion of its outer bark annually, leaving its branches beautifully bright and clean. The manzanita, when in full bloom, is one of the most beautiful of shrubs; its delicately tinted and fragrant blossoms filling the air with the perfume of an apple-orchard, while its rich evergreen leaves are only shed as others put forth. The name, man-zanita, is Spanish, signifying little apple—the fruit in flavor, but more especially in smell, resembling the apple.

These chamiso and manzanita thickets are almost impenetrable to large animals, except the California lion and grizzly bear. At certain seasons of the year, during their trips to and from the High Sierras, when the berries are ripe, these coverts are the resort of such visitors. The grizzly comes to indulge his fondness for the little apples, and the lion (how hath the mighty fallen!) to feed upon the wood-rats, mice and rabbits that he surprises in these furzy thickets. Occasionally a deer, as he comes along unconscious of danger, but too near the feline lair, is pounced upon by the lion, or perhaps a stray horse or mule may fall a victim; but in no case dare the lion attack his savage associate the bear, or any of his progeny.

In going to the Yosemite by way of the Mariposa route, after reaching the summit of the gap or pass in the "Black Ridge" or Chow-chilla mountain, over which the Mariposa route passes, to the South Fork of the Merced River, the yellow pine, the sugar pine, the Douglass fir and two other species of fir, are seen in all their glory. Here, too, is to be found the variety of white or yellow cedar (*Libo cedrus decurrens*), growing to a size not seen at a less altitude, unless perhaps on the north side of some spur from these mountains. If the ridge be followed to the right as far as the Big Trees, instead of descending the road to the South Fork, some very large pine, cedar and fir trees will be seen, in addition to the great attraction, the Sequoia.

At the time I first passed over this route there was but a dim Indian trail; now, a very good stage or wagon-road occupies it. As the descent to the South Fork is commenced, dogwood will be observed growing at the head of a little mountain brook that has its source in the pass, together with willows and other small growths of trees and shrubs. The "bush-honeysuckle," when in bloom, is here especially beautiful; and several fragrant-blossomed shrubs will attract attention—the kalmia, especially. The forest on this route is equaled by few in California, and it extends to the Yosemite almost uninterrupted, except by the river and a few mountain meadows. The Coultersville route also affords like views of uninterrupted forest, even to the verge of the valley, but confined as the trail was when it was first made to the narrow divide, one could not so well appreciate the beauty of the trees while looking down upon their tops as he would while riding among them. A few sequoias can be seen on this route, near Hazel Green and near Crane Flat.

Mr. Greeley says: "The Sierra Nevadas lack the glorious glaciers, the frequent rains, the rich verdure, the abundant cataracts of the Alps, but they far surpass them; they surpass any other moun ains I ever saw, in wealth and grace of trees. Look down from almost any of their peaks, and your range of vision is filled, bounded, satisfied, by what might be termed a tempest-tossed sea of evergreens, filling every upland valley, covering every hillside, crowning every peak but the highest with their unfading luxuriance.

"That I saw, during this day's travel, many hundreds of pines eight feet in diameter, with cedars at least six feet, I am confident; and there were miles of such and smaller trees of like genus, standing as thick as they could grow. Steep mountain sides, allowing these giants, to grow rank above rank, without obstructing each other's sunshine, seem peculiarly favorable to the production of these serviceable giants. But the summit meadows are peculiar in their heavy fringe of balsam fir of all sizes, from those barely one foot high to those hardly less than two hundred; their branches surrounding them in collars, their extremities gracefully bent down by weight of winter snows, making them here, I am confident, the most beautiful trees on earth. The dry promontories which separate these meadows are also covered with a species of spruce, which is only less graceful than the firs aforesaid. I never before enjoyed such a tree-feast as on this wearying, difficult ride."

Had Mr. Greeley taken more time, it would not have been so wearying to himself or mule. He rode sixty miles, on one mule the day he went to the Yosemite, but his observations of what he saw are none the less just and valuable, though but few of the pine trees will measure eight feet in diameter. It is true, probably, that few forests in the United States are so dense and beautiful in variety as those seen on the old Mariposa route to the Yosemite by way of the meadows of the Pohono Summit. About these meadows the firs especially attract attention, from the uniform or geometrical regularity their branches assume. No landscape gardener could produce such effects as are here freely presented by the Great Architect of the universe for the admiration of his wayward children. Here in this region will also be found the California tamarack pine, and a variety of pine somewhat resembling the Norway pine, called Pinus Jeffreyi. There is still another pine, to be found only on the highest ridges and mountains, that may be said to mark the limit of arbol vegetation; this dwarf is known as *pinus albicaulis*, and could it but adapt itself to a lower altitude, and retain its dense and tangled appearance, it would make good hedge-rows.

Professor Whitney speaks of still another one of the pine family, growing about the head of King's and Kern Rivers, which he calls *pinus aristata*, and says it only grows on those highest peaks of the Sierras, although it is also found in the Rocky Mountains. Of the more noticeable undergrowth of these mountain forests and their borders, besides grasses, sedges, ferns, mosses, lichens, and various plants that require a better knowledge of botany than I possess to describe properly, may be mentioned the California lilac and dogwood, the latter of which is frequently seen growing along the mountain streams, and in the Yosemite. It grows in conjunction with alder, willow, poplar, or balm of Gilead, and a species of buckthorn. In isolated patches the Indian arrow-wood is found. This wood is almost without pith, and warps but little in drying. For these qualities and the uniformity of its growth, it was especially esteemed for arrow-shafts; although sprouts from other shrubs and trees were also used.

It will have been observed, while going to the Yosemite, that the chimaso, white-oak and digger-pine are upon the southern slopes, while the thickets of mountain-ash, shrub or Oregon maple, and shrub live-oak, chinquepin and trailing blue and white ceanothus and snow plant are found upon the north side of the ridges, except when found at a greater altitude than is usual for their growth. On descending into the Yosemite, the visitor will at once notice and welcome the variety of foliage.

Upon the highest lands grow pine, fir, cedar, spruce, oak and shrubs. In the meadows and upon open ground, according to the richness of the soil and moisture, will be seen flowers and flowering shrubs of great brilliancy and variety.

The whole valley had the appearance of park-like grounds, with trees, shrubbery, flowers and lawns. The larger trees, pines, firs, etc., are of smaller growth than are usually found on the mountain slopes and tables. Still, some are of fair dimensions, rising probably to the height of one hundred and fifty feet or more. One large pine, growing in an alcove upon the wall of Tote-ack-ah-noo-la,—apparently without soil—is quite remarkable. The balm of gilead, alder, dogwood, willow and buck-thorn, lend an agreeable variety to the scenery along the river. Their familiar appearance seem, like old friends, to welcome the eastern visitor to this strange and remarkable locality. The black-oak is quite abundant in the valley and upon the slopes below. It was the source of supply of acorns used by the Yosemites as food, and as an article of traffic with their less favored neighbors east of the Sierras.

Along the river banks and bordering the meadows are

found the wild rose, and where the soil is rich, dry and mellow, the wild sunflower grows luxuriantly. Of wild fruits, the red raspberry and strawberry are the only ones worthy of mention, and these are only found in limited quantities. A thornless red raspberry grows upon the mountains, but its blossoms are apt to be nipped by frosts and the plant is not a prolific bearer.

The meadows of the valley are generally moist, and in the springtime boggy. Later in the season they become firmer, and some parts of them where not in possession of sedges, afford an abundant growth of " wild Timothy;" blue joint, Canada red-top and clover. In addition to these nutritious meadow-grasses, there is growing on the coarse granite, sandy land, a hard, tough wire bunch grass unfit for grazing except when quite young. This grass is highly prized by the Indians for making baskets and small mats. Its black seeds were pulverized and used as food, by being converted into mush, or sometimes it was mixed with acorn meal and was then made into a kind of gruel. The common " brake " and many beautiful species of rock ferns and mosses are quite abundant in the shady parts of the valley, and in the cañons, and more especially are they found growing within the influence of the cool, moist air near the falls. Growing in the warm sunlight below El Capitan, may be seen plants common among the foot hills and slaty mountains. Of these plants, the manzanita, the bahia confertiflora and the California poppy are the most conspicuous.

The climatic and geologic or local influences upon vegetation in this part of California, is so remarkable as to continually claim the notice of the tourist, and induce the study of the botanist. So peculiar are the influences of elevation, moisture, temperature and soil, that if these be stated, the flora may be determined with almost unerring certainty, and *vice versa*, if the flora be designated, the rock's exposure and mineral character of the soil will be at once inferred. The extreme summer temperature of the valley rises but little over 80° Fahrenheit, during the day, while the nights are always cold enough to make sleeping comfortable under a pair of blankets.

Thus far in narrating the incidents connected with the discovery of the Yosemite, I have not been particularly definite in my descriptions of it. Unconsciously I have allowed myself to assume the position, that this remarkable locality was familiarly known to every one.

From the discovery of the valley to the present day, the wonders of this region of sublimity, have been a source of inspiration to visitors, but none have been able to describe it to the satisfaction of those who followed after them. The efforts that are still made to do so, are conclusive evidences that to the minds of visitors, their predecessors had failed to satisfactorily describe it to their comprehensions; and so it will probably continue, as long as time shall last, for where genius even, would be incompetent, egotism may still tread *unharmed*.

Realizing this, and feeling my own utter inability to convey to another mind any just conception of the impressions received upon first beholding the valley, I yet feel that a few details and figures should be given with this volume. Prof. J. D. Whitney in his " Yosemite Guide Book " says, in speaking of the history of the discovery and settlement of the Yosemite Valley: " The visit of the soldiers under Captain Boling led to no immediate results in this direction. Some stories told by them on their return, found their way into the newspapers; but it was not until four years later that so far as can be ascertained, any persons visited the valley for the purpose of examining its wonders, or as regular pleasure travelers. It is, indeed, surprising that so-remarkable a locality should not sooner have become known;

one would suppose that accounts of its cliffs and waterfalls would have spread at once all over the country. Probably they did circulate about California, and were not believed but set down as "travelers' stories." Yet these first visitors seem to have been very moderate in their statements, for they spoke of the Yosemite Fall as being "more than a thousand feet high," thus cutting it down to less than half its real altitude."

At the time of our discovery, and after the subsequent lengthy visit under Captain Boling, our descriptions of it were received with doubt by the newspaper world, and with comparative indifference by the excited and overwrought public of the golden era. The press usually more than keeps pace with public opinion. Although height and depth were invariably under-estimated by us, our statements were considered "too steep" even for the sensational correspondents, and were by them pronounced exaggerations. These autocrats of public opinion took the liberty to dwarf our estimates to dimensions more readily swallowed by their patrons.

I have made many visits to the Yosemite since "our" long sojourn in it in 1851, and have since that time furnished many items for the press descriptive of that vicinity. My recollections of some of these will be given in another chapter. Although many years have rolled off the calendar of time since the occurrences related in these chapters, no material change has affected that locality. Human agency can not alter the general appearance of these stupendous cliffs and waterfalls.

The picturesque wildness of the valley has since our first visits been to a certain degree toned down by the *improvements* of civilization. The regions among the foot-hills and mountains that serve as approaches to the valley, where we hunted for savages *to make peace with our National Gov-*

ernment, now boasts of its ranchos and other improvements. The obscure trails which we followed in our explorations, and on which we first entered, have long since been abandoned, or merged into roads or other trails used by the proprietors of the territory in the vicinity. The white man's civilized improvements have superseded them. Instead of the stormy bivouacs of our first visits, or the canvas of our longer stay, the visitor now has the accommodations of first-class hotels with modern improvements. The march of civilization has laid low many of the lofty pines and shady oak trees that once softened the rough grandeur and wildness of the scenery. Stumps, bridges and ladders now mark the progress of improvements. These, however, only affect the ornamental appendages of the scenery—the perishable portion of it alone. The massive granite walls are invulnerable to modern ingenuity of adornment. The trail over which we approached the valley on our first visit was below the more modern trails, and its general course has now been appropriated by the stage road over which the tourist visits the Yosemite. The rocky slabs and stretches down which we then slid and scrambled, have since been graded and improved, so that the descent is made without difficulty.

The "Mariposa Trail" first approached the verge of the cliffs forming the south side of the valley, near what is known as "Mount Beatitude," or, as the first full view above has been designated, "Inspiration Point"; which is about 3,000 feet above the level of the valley. In a direct line from the commencement of the first descent, to where the trail reaches the valley, the distance is probably less than a mile, but by the trail, it is nearly four miles in a circuitous zigzag westerly course. The vertical descent of the trail in that distance is 2,973 feet.*

I have adopted the statistics of measurements given by Prof. Whitney in his "Yosemite Guide Book" as my stand-

* A wagon road now enters upon a lower level.

ard, so as to be modernly correct. These statistics were from the State Geological Survey, and are scientifically reliable. From a point on this descending trail, my most impressive recollections of a general view were first obtained. My first sight of the Yosemite was suddenly and unexpectedly unfolded from its junction with the old Indian trail; the view was made complete by ascending to a granite table. The first object and the principal point of attraction to my astonished gaze was " El Capitan," although its immensity was far from comprehended, until I became familiar with the proportions of other prominent features of the valley. After passing it close to its base, on the next day, I made up my mind that it could not be less than 1,500 or 2,000 feet above the level of the valley.

Prof. Whitney in speaking of this object of grandeur and massiveness, says: " El Capitan is an immense block of granite, projecting squarely out into the valley, and presenting an almost vertical sharp edge, 3,300 feet in elevation. The sides or walls of the mass are bare, smooth, and entirely destitute of vegetation. It is almost impossible for the observer to comprehend the enormous dimensions of this rock, which in clear weather can be distinctly seen from the San Joaquin plains at a distance of fifty or sixty miles. Nothing, however, so helps to a realization of the magnitude of these masses about the Yosemite as climbing around and among them. Let the visitor begin to ascend the pile of *debris* which lies at the base of El Capitan, and he will soon find his ideas enlarged on the point in question. And yet these *debris* piles along the cliffs, and especially under El Capitan, are of insignificant size compared with the dimensions of the solid wall itself. They are hardly noticeable in taking a general view of the valley. El Capitan imposes on us by its stupendous bulk, which seems as if hewed from the mountain on purpose to stand as the type of eternal massiveness.

"It is doubtful if any where in the world there is presented so squarely cut, so lofty and so imposing a face of rock." The foregoing is the most concise and best description of El Capitan I have ever seen, and yet, it cannot impart the ecstacy of reverence for the sublime one feels in its presence.

Another peculiarity of El Capitan, is one that belongs to headlands that are designated points-no-point; that is the apparent difficulty of passing them. While passing at a distance, the convexity of the wall seems to remain immediately opposite the observer.

From the Mariposa trail as it descends, can be seen most of the prominent cliffs which form its massive side walls. This trail reaches the bottom of the valley near its lower extremity. Below this trail, it narrows to a rocky cañon, almost impassable except for the Merced river, which leaves the valley through this gorge. I shall again refer to this cañon in another chapter.

The valley is about six miles long and from half a mile to over a mile in width at the head of the valley proper. It is irregular in shape, but its general direction is nearly east towards its upper end. Its outlines will be better understood from a view of the accompanying map, which has been mostly copied from that of the State Geological Survey—Prof. Whitney's. The three cañons which open into the valley at its upper end, are so intimately connected with it that a general description will include them all, particularly the parts of them in close proximity to the valley. They will be specially described when reached.

The sides of the valley are walls of a grayish-white granite, which becomes a dazzling white in a clear sunlight. This intensity of reflection is, however, toned to a great extent by the varying haze which permeates the upper atmosphere of the valley for most of the time. This haze has sometimes the appearance of a light cloud of blue smoke, with its borders fringed with a silvery vapor. At other times—during August and September—the tint is enriched, and at sunrise and sunset for the valley the golden light seems to permeate the haze, and lend its charm to the gossamer film that shields the sight from the glare of the reflecting granite.

The walls on each side are in many places perpendicular. and are, from the level of the valley to the top of the cliffs, from 2,660 to 4,737 feet in height, or, as they are generally described, from half a mile to a mile in height. Prof. Whitney, however, says: "The valley is sunk almost a mile in perpendicular depth below the general level of the adjacent region." This is undoubtedly correct, for in his description, he says: "The Yosemite Valley is nearly in the center of the State, north and south, and just midway between the east and west bases of the Sierras; here a little over seventy miles wide."

Prof. Whitney's estimate of the depth of the valley must be literally correct, for the general slope of that region is toward the valley, except from the west, its lower end.

At the base of these cliffs is a comparatively small amount of *debris*, consisting of broken rocks which have fallen from above. A kind of soil has accumulated on this talus, which is generally covered with vegetation. Trees of considerable size—oaks, pines, firs, cedars, maples, bay and dwarf oak, and lesser shrubs, are frequent. Although this *debris* is scarcely observed in a general view, its height above the bottom of the valley is in many places from three hundred to five hundred feet next to the cliff, from which it slopes some distance into the valley. In a few places the bases of the cliffs appear as if exposed nearly to the level of the valley. The valley proper is generally level through its entire length. The actual slope given is "only thirty-five feet between the junctions of the Ten-ie-ya Fork and the Bridal Veil Creek with the main river, four miles and a half in a straight line." The elevation of the valley above the sea level is 3,950 feet. The Merced River, which is about seventy feet wide in an ordinary stage of water, courses down through the middle cañon, meanders through the valley, being restrained or confined to near the centre of it by the sloping talus at its sides—the sloping *debris* piles occupying nearly one-half of the bottom of the valley.

Although the soil is principally of a sandy character, the marshy land subject to overflow, and some of the dry bottom land, have a deep, rich alluvial soil.

The two beautiful little meadows in the lower section of the valley, afford forage for animals. On the slope above, not far from the Pohono Falls, the Yosemities built their huts, as if unconscious of "The Spirit of the Evil Wind," near their habitations.

Not far from the foot of the descent of the Mariposa trail, the original trail branched; one trail continuing on up the south side of the valley, the other crossing the Merced toward El Capitan. Another original trail came up on the north side from the gorge below. A small foot-trail entered this from the northern summit of the Coultersville trail, but it was purposely left so obscure by the Indians, as to lead to the belief that it was impassable for horses. This trail was modernized, and is now known as the "Coultersville Trail." On angle of El Capitan is "Ribbon Falls." The cliff over which the water pours is nearly 3,000 feet high, but the perpendicular height of the fall is but little over a thousand feet. This fall is "a beauty" while it lasts, but it is as ephemeral as a spring shower, and this fact must have been known to the sponsors at the baptism.

Just above El Capitan are the Three Brothers, the highest peak of these rocks is 3,830 feet.

Next above these is the Yosemite Fall. The verge of the cliff over which this fall begins its descent is 2,600 feet above the level of the valley. Prof. Whitney in describing this fall, says: "The fall is not in one perpendicular sheet. There is first a vertical descent of 1,500 feet, when the water strikes on what seems to be a projecting ledge; but which, in reality, is a shelf or recess, almost a third of a mile back from the front of the lower portion of the cliff. From here the water finds its way, in a series of cascades, down a descent equal to 626 feet perpendicular, and then gives one final plunge of about 400 feet on to a low *talus* of rocks at the base of the precipice." He also "estimates the size of the stream at the summit of the fall, at a medium stage of water, to be twenty feet in width and two feet in average depth." The upper portion of the full spread of its base is estimated to be a width of from one hundred to three hundred feet at high water. The wind gives this fall a vibratory motion; sometimes equal to the width of the column of water itself at the base of the perpendicular descent.

The ravine called Indian Cañon is less than a mile above the Yosemite Fall; between the two, is the rocky peak called the "Lost Arrow," which, although not perpendicular, runs up boldly to a height of 3,030 feet above the level of the Merced.

The Indian name for the ravine called Indian Cañon was Lehamite, and the cliff extending into the valley from the East side of the Cañon is known as the "Arrow-wood Rocks." This grand wall extends almost at a right angle towards the East, and continues up the Ten-ie-ya Cañon, forming the base of the North dome (To-co-ya) which rises to an elevation of 3,568 feet above the valley.

In the cliff which forms the base of this dome-shaped mass of rocks, are the "Royal Arches," an immense arched cavity evidently formed by portions of the cliff becoming detached from some cause, and falling out in sections to the depth of seventy-five or one hundred feet from the face of the cliff. The top of the arch appears to be 1,200 feet or more above the valley. The extreme width of the cavity is about the same, or perhaps a little more than the height. Adjoining the "Royal Arches" on the East, is what is called the "Washington Column." This projecting rounded mass of rock, may be said to mark the boundary of the valvey proper and the Ten-ie-ya Cañon, which here opens into the valley from a Northeasterly direction.

On the opposite side of Ten-ie-ya Cañon is the Half Dome (Tis-sa-ack) the loftiest peak of the granite cliffs that form a part of the walls of the Yosemite Valley. Its height above the valley is 4,737 feet. On the side next to Ten-ie-ya Cañon this cliff is perpendicular for more than 1,500 feet from its summit, and then, the solid granite slopes at about an angle of 60 degrees to its base. The top of this mass of rock has the appearance of having been at one time a dome-shaped peak, now however, but half remains, that portion split off has by some agency, been carried away. At its Northerly base is Mirror Lake, and farther up the Cañon is Mt. Watkins, Cloud's Rest, a cascade, and Lake Ten-ie-ya.

This brief outline of description includes the principal points of interest on the north side of the valley. From the lower part of the valley, the first prominent object reached on the south side, is the Bridal Veil Fall. The water of the "Po-ho-no" here falls over a cliff from a perpendicular height of 630 feet, onto a sloping pile of *debris*, about 300 feet above the level of the Merced, in reaching which it rushes down the slope among the rocks in cascades and branching outlets. The total height of the cliff over which the water falls is about 900 feet. The trees on the slope below conceal the lower part of the fall, so that at a distance it appears as if reaching to the bottom of the valley. Just above the Bridal Veil are what have been termed the "Three Graces," and not far above these, are the peculiar appearing pinnacles of rocks to which the names of Cathedral Rock and Cathedral Spires have been given. Cathedral Rock is 2,660 feet high. The spires just beyond are about the same height from the level of the valley. They are pointed columns of granite 500 feet high, attached at their base with the cliff forming the side of the valley. The next prominent object on the south side is Sentinel Rock, 3,043 feet high. This pinnacle of granite is on the extremity of a point of rocks extending into the valley. For a thousand feet or more, it has the form of an obelisk, below which it forms a part of the projecting rocks. The next object is the massive point projecting into the valley, and which here forms an angle towards the south; it is called Glacier Point. This has an elevation of 3,200 feet above the valley. From this point some of the finest views of the vicinity can be seen. Behind Glacier Point and Sentinel Rock, appearing as if these cliffs formed a part of its base, is the South Dome, known also as the Sentinal Dome. The name of "South Dome" was originally given to this dome-shaped mass of granite by our battalion. It is 4,150 feet above the valley. The South or Glacier Cañon is just above Glacier Point. At the head of this rocky impassable cañon, is the beautiful fall I have named "Glacier Fall." This fall is about 600 feet high. The middle cañon, Yanopah, opens from the east. The Merced river comes down this cañon into the valley.

In a distance of two miles, a descent from over 2,000 feet of perpendicular height is made. This includes the Vernal and Nevada Falls. The Vernal is about 350 feet high; the Nevada something over 600 feet. The rapids between the falls have a descent of adout 300 feet. The Vernal and Nevada are about one mile apart. On the north side of the middle cañon is the Cap of Liberty, rising to a height of 2,000 feet above its base near the foot of the Nevada Fall. This stupendous mass of rock stands nearly perpendicular on all sides but one. Farther up, on the south side of Ten-ie-ya Cañon, is Clouds Rest, which is 6,000 feet above the bottom of the Yosemite. Between Glacier Cañon and Yanopah is the Noble Starr King. The immense cliff forming the extreme westerly point of the divide between Ten-ie-ya Cañon and the Yanopah branch, has had various names affixed to it, none of which seems to have been satisfactory. It was between the lower face of this wall and Glacier Point that Capt. Boling laid off and had cleared for use his race-course; and hence, in speaking of the locality, it was some-times designated as Boling's Point, as the starting place for the race.

CHAPTER XVI.

A Trip to Los Angelos—Interview with Col. McKee—A Night at Col.
Fremont's Camp—Management of Cattle by the Colonel's Herdsmen—
Back to Los Angelos—Specimen Bricks of the Angel City—An Addi-
tion to our Party—Mules Versus Bears—Don Vincente—A Silver
Mine—Mosquitos—A Dry Bog—Return to Fresno—Muster out of Bat-
talion—A Proposition.

ON arriving at head-quarters on the Fresno, with the
remnant of the once numerous and defiant band of Yosemite Indians, whose thieving propensities and murderous
attacks had made them a dread to miners and "ranche"
men; we found a general feeling of confidence that the "Indian war" was ended. The commissioners, with a special
escort of U. S. soldiers which had accompanied them from
San Francisco, had gone to King's River to treat with the
bands collected for that purpose; and were then to visit the
region farther South on their way to Los Angelos, where
they expected to meet and co-operate with Gen. Bean, who
was stationed with his volunteer force at the Cahon Pass.
Major Savage had learned from his Indians, who once more
seemed to idolize him, that all the bands in the vicinity of
the Kings and Kah-we-ah rivers, had "made peace," and
that the commissioners had started for Te-jon Pass.

Considering the Indian outbreak as completely sup-
pressed, the major at once reported the condition of affairs
to the governor, and recommended that the "Mariposa Battalion" be mustered out and honorably discharged from

further service. He sent Captain Boling to report in person to the commissioners. I was detailed as one of the Captain's escort, and Mr. Winchester, a newspaper correspondent, accompanied us. Captain Boling expected to overtake the commissioners at Te-hon Pass.

This trip was in no way objectionable to me, for I was desirous to visit that part of the country with a view of selecting a location, if I found my plans to be practicable. Through the advice of Major Savage, I had in contemplation a design to establish a trading post in the vicinity of Te-hon Pass. In this project, I was assured of the Major's friendship and co-operation as soon as the battalion was mustered out. He designed to extend his trading operations, and thought that a post in the vicinity of the pass would control the trade destined to spring up on both sides of the mountains. I was provided with recommendations to the commissioners, to use in case I desired a trader's permit on one of the reservations. The commissioners were while *en route* prospecting for locations and selections of public lands for the Indians. The object of these selections, was to make the experiment of engaging them in agricultural pursuits under the management of the general government. I had but little confidence that the latter could be made self-supporting wards of the nation; but I was willing in political as in religious affairs, that each zealot should believe that he had discovered a sovereign balm for the wants of humanity. However, self-interest prompted me to be observant of passing events.

I was aware, even at that early day, that the California Indians had become objects of speculation to the "rings" that scented them as legitimate prey. The trip to the Tejon Pass was made without incident or accident to delay our movements, but on our arrival it was found that the Commissioners had been gone several days, and were probably then in Los Angelos. This we learned from an Indian styled by his "*christian name*" Don Vincente. This chief was a Mission Indian, and spoke some Spanish. His people, although in appearance hardly equal to the mountain tribes, provided themselves with fruit and vegetables of their own raising.

From "Senor Don Vincente" we obtained roasting ears of corn, melons, etc., which were an agreeable surprise. While on the trip we had found game in abundance, and, surfeited with fresh meat, the vegetables seemed better than any we had ever before eaten. Vincente's system of irrigation was very complete.

Captain Boling was not anxious to follow the trail of the Commissioners beyond this camp. I had already informed him of my desire to see the Commissioners and make some examination of that locality before our return. He therefore decided to retrace his own steps, but to send me on as a special messenger to the Commissioners.

He instructed me to make all possible despatch to deliver his report and messages, but on my return trip I had liberty to make such delays as suited my convenience. He also wished me to convey a verbal message from Major Savage to Colonel Fremont, to the effect that the Indians congregated at the Fresno were anxiously awaiting the arrival of some of his cattle. Col. Fremont had already made a large contract for supplying them with beef, and was supposed to be in Los Angelos or vicinity, buying up animals for the agencies. My arrangements for following the Commissioners were hardly commenced, before Col. William T. Henderson, a ranchman from near Quartzberg, rode up to our camp. He was an acquaintance, and was on his way to Los Angelos with a King's River Indian guide. I at once saddled my mule, and taking an extra animal furnished for the occasion, joined Henderson, making the trip a more agreeable and pleasant one than I had anticipated.

Col. Henderson afterwards became famous, at least among his friends, as chief instrument under Captain Harry Love, of causing the death of "Joaquin Muriata" and "Three fingered Jack," and in capturing two or three of Muriata's band of robbers. On entering the city of Los Angelos, I found Col. McKee at his hotel. Neither Col. Barbour nor Col. Fremont were in the city. Doctor Woozen-croft was in San Francisco. I was cordially received and hospitably entertained by Col. McKee while I made my report, and answered his questions. At his request, I stated a few facts relating to the Yosemite Valley, and he appeared an interested listener; but distinguishing a look of incredulity, when I gave him my estimates of heights, I made the interview as brief as possible. Ascertaining that Col. Fremont was only a few miles from the city, I rode out to his camp, delivered my message, and gave him a general view of the situation in Mariposa county, where his famous estate is situated. I staid over night with him and was hospitably provided for.

The Colonel's whole bearing was that of an accomplished man of the world, and I felt that I was in the presence of a gentleman of education and refinement. During the morning I watched his vaqueros or herdsman training the cattle preparatory to starting north for their destination. This breaking-in process was accomplished by driving them in a circle over the plain near the camp, and was done to familiarize them with each other, and with the commands of the herdsmen, before attempting to drive them from their native grazing grounds.

On my return to the city I again called on Colonel McKee to see if he had any return message to Major Savage. On my first visit the subject of reservations was not presented. Upon this occasion it was naturally brought up by an allusion to the Colonel's plan of " *christianizing the poor*

Indians. My doubt of the feasibility of this work was better concealed than were his doubts of my heights of the Yosemite, and with considerable fervor the good old gentle man unfolded his plans for the christianizing of the Indians. His estimate of the number in Mariposa county was simply fabulous, and when I quietly asked him if he supposed there were really so many, he, with some choler, answered, "Why, sir, these figures are official."

During this conversation, I was informed that the Fresno, King's River and Te-jon Pass selections would be recommended, although it appeared that the latter was claimed as an old and long disputed Spanish grant. On stating that I had had some idea of locating in the vicinity of the Tejon Pass as soon as that selection was decided upon, I was advised by Colonel McKee to be in no haste to do so, but was assured of his good will in any application I might make after their policy was established; for, added the Colonel, "Major Savage has already spoken of you as an energetic and efficient person, and one calculated to materially aid us in future work with these Indians."

Let it suffice here to say, that I never made application for a permit as a licensed trader on any Indian reservation; and I am not yet aware that any of these reservations have afforded the Indians means of self-support. I was somewhat familiar with the management of the Fresno agency, and do not hesitate to say that it was not wholly commendable. I was not personally familiar with that of the Te-jon Pass agricultural management. This was one of the most delightful regions of California; and the region covered by the Mexican or Spanish grant was, in my opinion, intrinsically more valuable than the whole of the celebrated Mariposa estate of Col. Fremont, which had "millions in it." After a vast amount of money had been expended on this reservation by the general government, I believe it was con-

firmed as a Spanish or Mexican grant, and finally passed into the possession of General Beal, who was for some years
Superintendent of Indian Affairs in Californi?. I never
saw General Beal, and therefore was only able to judge of
him or his management through his official reports and letters relating to the Indian Affairs of California. These will
receive some special notice further on.

My recollections of the interviews with Colonel McKee,
are of a most agreeable character. The sincerity with which
he advised me with regard to my individual affairs, and the
correctness of his representations of the prospective condition of the Tejon Pass, if it should prove a valid Mexican
grant, was serviceable to me, and subsequent events verified
his judgment. Colonel McKee was a high-minded christian
gentleman, but really unsuited to deal with the political
element then existing on the Pacific coast. The other
two commissioners, Colonel Barbour and Dr. Woozencroft,
I never became acquainted with, though upon one occasion
I met Colonel Barbour at head-quarters, and received a very
favorable impression of his character. In leaving Colonel
McKee after my second interview, I could not at once relin-
quish my design of ultimately establishing myself near the
Tejon. Having completed my business, I reported myself
to Henderson as ready, and found that he also had been able
to despatch his affairs, and had no business to detain him
longer. Together we took a stroll through the principal
street, and visited some popular resorts. However angelic
the unseen portion of this city—of then less than two thous-
and inhabitants—may have been, it appeared to us as a city
of fallen angels with their attendant satellites. Although
our observations were made in a dull portion of the day, we
witnessed on the street one pugilistic encounter, two shooting affrays, and a reckless disregard of life, and property
rights generally, never allowed in a civilized community.

We soon discovered that good arms and a firm demeanor were the only passports to respectful consideration.

The authorities seemed too indifferent or too timid to maintain order, or punish the offenders against law. Satisfied that the "City of Angels" could exhibit more unadulterated wickedness than any other town in the State at that time, we shook the dust from our feet, and in order to get an early start the next morning, rode out to the vicinity of Col. Fremont's camp. Our party was increased by the addition of two gentlemen, who joined us for protection and guidance. The name of one of them has escaped my memory; the other was Doctor Bigelow, of Detroit, Michigan, a geologist, who at one time was engaged in a geological survey of a portion of Lake Superior. We left our camp before sunrise, Henderson and myself riding in advance; our guests, Indian and pack-mule bringing up the rear. This order of traveling was maintained as a matter of convenience, for being well mounted, Henderson and myself were able to secure deer, antelope and a supply of smaller game, without hardly leaving the trail or delaying our progress.

Among the foot-hills of the mountain slopes we saw several black bears cross the trail ahead, but not being out of meat, we did not urgently solicit their company. We did, however, once have our appetite aroused for "bar meat," but failed to supply the material for the feast. Halting for a rest at the foot of a ravine, and being very thirsty, we followed the indications to water exhibited by our mules. These were secured while we explored the brushy ravine for the water-hole. As we reached the desired water, two fat cubs came waddling out of the pool, and ran into a clump of dwarf willow.

Congratulating each other on the prospect of roast cub for supper, we tried to get a shot with our revolvers, but a rousing demonstration from the parental bear, which suddenly appeared, alarmed our cautiousness, and we retreated hurriedly, but in good order, to the place where we had carelessly left our rifles. Hastily mounting, we returned the compliment by at once charging on the bear and her cubs, which were now endeavoring to escape.

As we approached near enough for the mules to see and scent the game, they halted, and commenced *marking time*. Neither spurs or the butts of our rifles could persuade them to make a forward movement. Thinking I might secure a cub that stood temporarily in sight, I raised my rifle, but in so doing slackened the reins, when with the ease and celerity of a well-drilled soldier, my mule came to an "*about face*," and instantly left that locality. Henderson's mule became unmanageable, and after a lusty "we-haw! we-haw!" followed me, while the affrighted bear family scrambled off in search of a place of security. Pulling up as soon as we could control our frightened animals, Henderson congratulated me on possessing one so active on a retreat, while I complimented the intelligence of his own, which would not voluntarily endanger his master.

After a hearty laugh at our comic illustration of a bear hunt, it was mutually agreed that a mule was not reliable in a charge upon bruin.

A mule may be the equal of a horse in intelligence, but his inferiority of spirit and courage in times of danger prevents his becoming a favorite, except as a beast for work or mountain travel.

On arriving at the rancheria of the chief Vincente, I induced Henderson to stop and explore the country. The luscious watermelons and abundant supplies of vegetables were strong arguments in favor of a few days' rest for our animals and recreation for ourselves. In the meantime Doctor Bigelow had told us of a traditional silver mine that he had been informed existed somewhere in the locality of the Tejon. I found the pompous old chief fond of displaying his knowledge of agriculture, which was really considerable, and I complimented him upon his success, as was deserved.

After paying him for the things liberally supplied our party, and which with a show of Spanish courtesy he intimated he had given us because he was "a good Christian"—though he frequently crossed himself while expressing his fear of "witches" or demons—I opened up the subject of the old silver mine. I designated it as some kind of a mine that had once been worked by an Englishman. We were told by "Don Vincente" that such a mine had been discovered many years before, by white men, who, after working it for awhile, had been driven off or killed; "but for the love of God" he could not tell which. We expressed a wish to visit the old mine, and asked permission of the chief. He told us it was not in the territory claimed by him, and he was thankful that it was not, as the location was haunted. When asked if he would furnish us a guide, who should be well paid for his service, he answered, "Go, and God go with you, but none of my people shall go, for it would bring upon us evil." We were shown the mouth of the ravine, after some persuasion, but no argument or inducement could procure a guide to the mine.

"Don Vincente," like all the Mission Indians of California, I found to be strongly imbued with the superstitions of the *wild tribes*, and a firm believer in the power of human departed spirits to harm the living. Many, like those of the east, believed that the wizards or sorcerers could put a spell upon a victim, that if not disenchanted would soon carry him to his grave.

Leaving our extra animals in the care of Vincente, we took our course towards the mouth of the ravine pointed out to us, southwest of the Tejon. After a tedious and difficult search, a discovery of some *float* mineral was made, and following up these indications, we found some very rude furnaces, and a long distance above discovered the mine, which had evidently been abandoned for years. We procured some of the best *specimens* of the ore, and being unable to determine its value, forwarded some to assayers in San Francisco. Doctor Bigelow pronounced the mineral to be that of antimony, but said that it might possibly contain some of the precious metals, but it was quite evident that he placed but little commercial value upon the mine. The reports finally received from the assayers were very unfavorable, and our visions of untold wealth vanished with the smoke of the assay.

On our return from the exploration of the "*Silver Mine,*" we carefully concealed our discovery from Vincente and his people, and avoided exciting their curiosity. Our animals were rested, and in an improved condition, for the grass was rich and abundant. Don Vincente was as much delighted with our presents of tobacco and trinkets, which we had carried with us for such occasions, as any of the "*Gentile*" nations would have been. We took our departure from the hospitalities of the Mission Chief without having had any occurrence to divert the mutually friendly feelings that had been fostered in our intercourse. We had designed, on starting from the rancheria of Don Vincente, to leave the direct trail to Mariposa, and explore the lake region of the Tulare valley. Unfortunately for the success of this undertaking, we made our first camp too near the marshy shore of Kern Lake. We had selected the camp ground for the convenience of water and fresh grass for our animals, but as night closed in, the mosquitoes swarmed from the surrounding territory, making such vigorous charges upon us and our animals, that we were forced to retreat from their persistent attacks, and take refuge on the high land away from the vicinity of the Tule or Bullrush marshes. Having no desire to continue the acquaintance of the inhabitants who had thronged to welcome our approach, our ambition for making further exploration was so much weakened, that we silently permitted our mules to take their course towards the direct trail. Col. Henderson declared that the mosquitoes on these lakes were larger, more numerous, and in greater variety, than in the swamps of Louisiana, and Doctor Bigelow said that hitherto he had rather prided himself, as a Michigander, on the *earnest* character of those of Michigan, but that in future, he should be willing to accept as a standard of all the possibilities of mosquito growth, those that had *reluctantly* parted with us at Kern Lake. Keeping the rich alluvial low lands on our left, we crossed a strip of alkali plain, through which our animals floundered as if in an ash heap. This Henderson designated as a "*dry bog.*" Deviating still farther to the right to avoid this, an old trail was struck, either Indian or animal, which led us into the main trail usually traveled up and down the valley. At the crossing of one of the numerous mountain streams, we found a good camping place on a beautiful table overlooking this rich territory, where we would be secure from the assaults of *enemies.*

After a refreshing bath in the cool waters of the stream, we slept the sleep of the blessed, and mosquitoes once more became to us unknown objects of torture. The next morning we found ourselves refreshed and buoyant.

Our animals, like ourselves, seemed to feel in elevated spirits, and as we vaulted into our saddles at an early hour, they moved rapidly along in the cool and bracing air. As we rode, drove after drove of antelope and elk were seen, and one small band of mustangs approached from the west, when, after vainly neighing to our mules, they turned and galloped back toward their favorite resort, the west side of the valley. Sometimes, with a halting look of scrutiny, a coyote would cross our trail, but their near vicinity was always recognized by our vigilant mules with a snort and pause in their gait, that was probably designed to intimate to us that it might be another bear. We beguiled the time in discussing the amazing fertility of the country we were traversing, and the probability of its future occupancy. At the present time, thriving cities and immense wheat fields occupy localities where in 1851 game and wild mustangs roamed almost undisturbed by the white man's tread, or the flash or gleam of his unerring rifle. There is still room for the enterprising settler, and the upper end of the San Joaquin Valley may yet be called the sportsman's paradise. The lakes and streams swarm with fish, and are the resort of water-fowl, and deer, elk and antelope are still plentiful in secluded localities.

We reached the Fresno in safety without interrupting incidents, and without further attempt at exploration. Colonel Henderson, Doctor Bigelow, and his companion *du voyage*, after a short halt passed on to Quartzberg, while I stopped over to make my report to the Major. To my extreme surprise, Major Savage questioned me as to the cause of my tardiness, saying he had been expecting me for two or three days past, and that the cattle were now within the valley and would in a short time be at the reservation. After sufficiently enjoying my astonishment at his knowledge of my movements and those of Fremont's herders, he informed me that his old power and influence over the Indians had been re-established, and that reports came to him from the different chiefs of all important events transpiring in their territory. He soon satisfied me that through a judicious distribution of presents to the runners, and the esteem in which he was held by the chiefs, he was able to watch the proceedings of strangers, for every movement of our party had been reported to him in detail. I was cordially received by the Major, as a guest in his new trading house, which he had erected during our absence. We discussed the probable future of the management of Indian affairs in California, and the incidents of my trip to Los Angelos. The Major informed me that the battalion had beed mustered out of service during my absence (on July 25th, 1851), but that my interests had been properly represented and cared for, as far as he had been able to act with out my presence. But in order to receive compensation as interpreter and for extra medical services, it was discovered that separate accounts and vouchers would be required, which he and Captain Boling would at any time certify. The major then informed me that he had made his arrangements to recommence his trading operations on as large a scale as might be required. That he could make more as a trader than as an employe of government, and at the same time be free from their cares and anxieties. He advised me to take a subordinate position until I should be able to decide upon a better location. He said he could make my position a profitable one if I desired to remain with him.

The major gave me a general insight into his future plans, and some of the sources of his expected profits. After this conversation, I gave up all idea of establishing at the Tejon or any where else as a government trader. Having been so long absent from my private business, which I had left under the management of a partner; I made this a sufficient excuse for my departure the next morning and for my inability to accept the major's kindly offer. As I was leaving, the major said: "I was in hopes to have secured your services, and still think you may change your mind. If you do, ride over at once and you will find a place open for you.

This confidence and friendship I felt demanded some return, and I frankly said; "Major Savage, you are surrounded by combinations that I don't like. Sharp men are endeavoring to use you as a tool to work their gold mine. Beside this, you have hangers-on here that are capable of cutting your throat." Contrary to my expectation the Major was not in the least offended at my frankness; on the contrary, he thanked me for my interest and said: "Doc, while you study books, I study men. I am not often very much deceived, and I perfectly understand the present situation, but let those laugh who win. If I can make good my losses *by* the Indians *out* of the Indians, I am going to do it. I was the best friend the Indians had, and they would have destroyed me. Now that they once more call me "Chief," they shall build me up. I will be just to them, as I have been merciful, for after all, they are but poor ignorant beings, but my losses must be made good." Bidding the Major good morning, I left him with many kindly feelings, and as I rode on my solitary way to Mariposa, I thought of his many noble qualities, his manly courage, his generous hospitality, his unyielding devotion to friends, and his kindness to immigrant strangers. These all passed in review before my mind, and then, I reversed the picture to see if anything was out of proportion, in the picture I had drawn of my hero. There were very serious defects, but such as would naturally result from a misdirected education, and a strong will, but they were capable of becoming virtues. As to the Major's kindly offer, although I appreciated his feeling's towards me, I could not accept it.

With many others, I had joined in the operations against the Indians from conscientious motives and in good faith to chastise them for the numerous murders and frequent robberies they were committing. Our object was to compel them to keep the peace, that we might be permitted to live undisturbed by their depredations. We had sufficient general intelligence and knowledge of their character to know that we were looked upon as trespassers on their territory, but were unwilling to abandon our search for gold, or submit to their frequent demands for an ever-increasing tribute. Beside other property, I had lost four valuable horses, which were taken to satisfy their appetites Neither Bonner's nor Vanderbilt's love for horses, was ever greater than was that of those mountain Indians. No horse was considered too valuable for them to eat. Notwithstanding all this sense of injury done to my personal interests, I could not justify myself in joining any scheme to wrong them, or rather, the government; and it was too plainly evident that no damages could be obtained for losses, except through the California Indian Ring that was now pretty well established. During the operations of the Battalion, the plans of the Ring were laid, and it was determined that when the war should be ended, "a vigorous peace policy" should be inaugurated. Estimates of the probable number of Indians that it would be necessary to provide for in Mariposa county alone, accidentally fell under my observation, and I at once saw that it was the design to deceive the government and the people in regard to the actual number, in order to obtain from Congress large appropriations. These estimates were cited as official by Col. McKee, and were ten times more than the truth would warrant. Major Savage justified his course in using the opportunity to make himself whole again, while acting as a trader, and in aiding others to secure "a good thing," by the sophism that he was not responsible for the action of the commissioners or of Congress.

CHAPTER XVII.

AFTER being mustered out, the members of the battalion at
once returned to their various avocations. I was fully occupied with mining and trading operations, and hence gave
little heed to affairs at the Fresno. Through Captain Boling, however, who was elected Sheriff of the county, and
whose business carried him to all parts of the country, I
learned of the appointment of Col. Thomas Henly as agent
for the tribes of Mariposa county, and as sub-agents M. B.
Lewis for the Fresno and Wm. J. Campbell for the King's
River Agencies. I afterwards met Col. Henly and Mr. Lewis
in Mariposa, and was much pleased with the Colonel. Both of
these gentlemen were kind and genial; but Mr. Lewis soon
tired of his office as unsuited to his taste, and accepted a
position in the State Government under Major Roman.
His successor, I believe, was Capt. Vincinthalor. Old
Ten-ie-ya, and his band, were never recipients of friendly
favors from Savage, nor was he in very good standing with
the agent. This was known to the other chiefs, and they

frequently taunted him with his downfall. The old chief chafed under the contemptuous treatment of those who had once feared him and applied to the sub-agent or farmer for permission to go back to his mountain home. He claimed that he could not endure the heat at the agency, and said he preferred acorns to the rations furnished him by the Government.

To rid itself of the consequences engendered by these petty squabbles with the old chief, the management at the Fresno consented to a short absence under restrictions. Ten-ie-ya promised to perform all requirements, and joyfully left the hot and dry reservation, and with his family, took the trail to the Yosemite once more. As far as is known, Ten-ie-ya kept faith and disturbed no one. Soon after his departure, however, a few of his old followers quietly left the Fresno as was supposed to join him, but as no complaints were made by their chiefs, it was understood that they were glad to be rid of them; therefore no effort was made to bring them back. During the winter of 1851–52 a considerable number of horses were stolen, but as some of them were found in the possession of Mexicans, who were promptly executed for the theft, no charge was preferred against the Yosemites.

Early in May, 1852, a small party of miners from Coarse Gold Gulch, started out on a prospecting tour with the intention of making a visit to the Yosemite Valley.

The curiosity of some of these men had been excited by descriptions of it, made by some of the ex-members of the Battalion who had gone to Coarse Gold Gulch, soon after their discharge. This party spent some little time prospecting on their way. Commencing on the south fork of the Merced, they tested the mineral resources of streams tributary to it; and then, passing over the divide on the old trail, camped for the purpose of testing the branches leading into the main Merced. While at this camp, they were visited by begging Indians; a frequent occurrence in the mining camps of some localities. The Indians appeared friendly, and gave no indications of hostile intentions. They gave the party to understand, however, that the territory they were then in, belonged to them, although no tribute was demanded. The miners comprehended their intimations, but paid no attention to their claim, being aware that this whole region had been ceded to the Government by treaty during the year before.

Having ascertained that they were a part of the Yosemite Band, the miners by signs, interrogated them as to the direction of the valley, but this they refused to answer or pretended not to understand. The valley however, was known to be near, and no difficulty was anticipated, when the party were ready to visit it, as an outline map, furnished them before starting, had thus far proved reliable. Unsuspicious of danger from an attack, they reached the valley, and while entering it on the old trail, were ambushed by the Indians from behind some rocks at or near the foot of the trail, and two of the party were instantly killed. Another was seriously wounded, but finally succeeded in making his escape. The names of the two men killed were Rose and Shurbon; the name of the wounded man was Tudor.

The reports of these murders, alarmed many of the citizens. They were fearful that the Indians would become excited and leave the reservations, in which case, it was thought, a general outbreak would result. The management of the Fresno agency was censured for allowing Ten-ie-ya to return to the valley, and for allowing so considerable a number of his followers to again assemble under his leadership. Among the miners, this alarm was soon forgotten, for it was found that instead of leaving the reservations, the Indians camped outside, fled to the agencies for protection, lest they should be picked off in revenge for the murders perpetrated by the Yo-sem-i-tes. The officer in command at Fort Miller, was notified of these murders, and a detachment of regular soldiers under Lt. Moore, U. S. A., was at once dispatched to capture or punish the red-skins. Beside the detachment of troops, scouts and guides, and a few of the friends of the murdered men accompanied the expedition. Among the volunteer scouts, was A. A. Gray, usualy called "Gus" Gray. He had been a member of Captain Boling's company and was with us, when the valley was discovered, as also on our second visit to the valley under Captain Boling. He had been a faithful explorer, and his knowledge of the valley and its vicinity, made his services valuable to Lt. Moore, as special guide and scout for that locality. The particulars of this expedition I obtained from Gray. He was afterward a Captain under Gen. Walker, of Nicaragua notoriety. Under the guidance of Gray, Lt. Moore entered the valley in the night, and was successful in surprising and capturing a party of five savages; but an alarm was given, and Ten-ie-ya and his people fled from their huts and escaped. On examination of the prisoners in the morning, it was discovered that each of them had some article of clothing that had belonged to the murdered men. The naked bodies of Rose and Shurbon were found and buried. Their graves were on the edge of the little meadow near the Bridal Vail Fall.

When the captives were accused of the murder of the two white men, they did not deny the charge; but tacitly admitted that they had done it to prevent white men from coming to their valley. They declared that it was their home, and that white men had no right to come there without their consent.

Lieutenant Moore told them, through his interpreter, that

they had sold their lands to the Government, that it belonged to the white men now; that the Indians had no right there. They had signed a treaty of peace with the whites, and had agreed to live on the reservations provided for them. To this they replied that Ten-ie-ya had never consented to the sale of their valley, and had never received pay for it. The other chiefs, they said, had no right to sell their territory, and no right to laugh at their misfortunes.

Lieutenant Moore became fully satisfied that he had captured the real murderers, and the abstract questions of title and jurisdiction, were not considered debatable in this case. He promptly pronounced judgment, and sentenced them to be shot. They were at once placed in line, and by his order, a volley of musketry from the soldiers announced that the spirits of five Indians were liberated to occupy ethereal space.

This may seem summary justice for a single individual, in a republic, to meet out to fellow beings on his own judgment; but a formal judicial killing of these Indians could not have awarded more summary justice. This prompt disposition of the captured murderers, was witnessed by a scout sent out by Ten-ie-ya to watch the movements of Lieutenant Moore and his command, and was immediately reported to the old chief, who with his people at once made a precipitate retreat from their hiding places, and crossed the mountains to their allies, the Pai-utes and Monos. Although this was in June, the snow, which was lighter than the year before at this time, was easily crossed by the Indians and their families. After a short search, in the vicinity of the valley, Lieutenant Moore struck their trail at Lake Ten-ie-ya, and followed them in close pursuit, with an expressed determination to render as impartial justice to the whole band as he had to the five in the valley. It was no disappointment to me to learn from Gray, that when once alarmed, old Ten-ie-ya was too much for Lieutenant Moore, as he had been for Major Savage and Captain Boling. Lieutenant Moore did not overtake the Indians he was pursuing, neither was he able to get any information from the Pai-utes, whom he encountered, while east of the Sierras. Lieutenant Moore crossed the Sierras over the Mono trail that leads by the Soda Springs through the Mono Pass. He made some fair discoveries of gold and gold-bearing quartz, obsidian and other minerals, while exploring the region north and south of Bloody Cañon and of Mono Lake. Finding no trace whatever of the cunning chief, he returned to the Soda Springs, and from there took his homeward journey to Fort Miller by way of the old trail that passed to the south of the Yosemite.

Lieutenant Moore did not discover the Soda Springs nor the Mono Lake country, but he brought into prominent notice the existence of the Yosemite, and of minerals in paying quantities upon the Eastern Slope. Mr. Moore made a brief descriptive report of his expedition, that found its way into the newspapers. At least, I was so informed at the time, though unable to procure it. I saw, however, some severe criticisms of his display of autocratic power in ordering the five Yosemites shot.

After the establishment of the "Mariposa Chronicle" by W. T. Witachre and A. S. Gould, the first number of which was dated January 20, 1854. Lieutenant Moore, to more fully justify himself or gratify public curiosity, published in the "Chronicle" a letter descriptiive of the expedition and its results. In this letter he dropped the terminal letter "y" in the name "Yosemity," as it had been written previously by myself and other members of the battalion, and substituted "e," as before stated. As Lieutenant Moore's article attracted a great deal of public attention at that time, the name, with its present orthography, was accepted. A copy of the paper containing Moore's letter was in my possession for many years, but, finally, to my extreme regret, it was lost or destroyed.

To Lieutenant Moore belongs the credit of being the first to attract the attention of the scientific and literary world, and "The Press" to the wonders of the Yosemite Valley. His position as an officer of the regular army, established a reputation for his article, that could not be expected by other correspondents. I was shown by Gray, who was exhibiting them in Mariposa, some very good specimens of gold quartz, that were found on the Moore expedition. Leroy Vining, and a few chosen companions, with one of Moore's scouts as guide, went over the Sierras to the place where the gold had been found, and established themselves on what has since been known as Vining's Gulch or Creek.

On the return of Lieutenant Moore to Fort Miller, the news of his capture of the Indians, and his prompt execution of them as the murderers of Rose and Shurbon, occasioned some alarm among the timid, which was encouraged and kept alive by unprincipled and designing politicians. All kinds of vague rumors were put in circulation. Many not in the secret supposed another Indian war would be inaugurated. Political factions and "Indian Rings" encouraged a belief in the most improbable rumors, hoping thereby to influence Congressional action, or operate upon the War Department to make large estimates for the California Indian Service.

This excitement did not extend beyond the locality of its origin, and the citizens were undisturbed in their industries by these rumors. During all this time no indications of hostilities were exhibited by any of the tribes or bands, although the abusive treatment they received at the hands of some, was enough to provoke contention. They quietly remained on the reservations. As far as I was able to learn at the time, a few persons envied them the possession of their King's river reservation, and determined to " *squat* " upon it, after they should have been driven off. This " border element " was made use of by an unprincipled schemer by the name of Harvey, whom it was understood was willing to accept office, when a division of Mariposa county should have been made, or when a vacancy of any kind should occur. But population was required, and the best lands had been reserved for the savages. A few hangers-on, at the agencies, that had been discharged for want of employment and other reasons, made claims upon the King's river reservation; the Indians came to warn them off, when they were at once fired upon, and it was reported that several were killed.

These agitations and murders were denounced by Major Savage in unsparing terms, and he claimed that Harvey was responsible for them. Although the citizens of Mariposa were at the time unable to learn the details of the affair at King's river, which was a distant settlement, the great mass of the people were satisfied that wrong had been done to the Indians. There had been a very decided opposition by the citizens generally to the establishment of two agencies in the county, and the selection of the best agricultural lands for reservations. Mariposa then included nearly the whole San Joaquin valley south of the Tuolumne.

The opponents to the recommendations of the commissioners claimed that " The government of the United States has no right to select the territory of a sovereign State to establish reservations for the Indians, nor for any other purpose, without the consent of the State." The State Legislature of 1851-52, instructed the Senators and Representatives in Congress to use their influence to have the Indians removed beyond the limits of the State. These views had been advocated by many of the citizens of Mariposa county in good faith; but it was observed that those who most actively annoyed and persecuted those located on King's river reservation were countenanced by those who professed to advocate opposite views. These men were often to be seen at the agency, apparently the welcome guests of the employes of government.

It soon became quite evident, that an effort was being made to influence public opinion, and create an impression that there was imminent danger; in order that the general government would thereby be more readily induced to continue large appropriations to keep in subjection the comparatively few savages in the country.

It was a well known fact that these people preferred horse-flesh and their acorn jelly to the rations of beef that were supposed to have been issued by the Government. During this time, Major Savage was successfully pursuing his trade with the miners of the Fresno and surrounding territory, and with the Indians at the agency. Frequently those from the King's River Agency, would come to Savage to trade, thereby exciting the jealous ire of the King's river traders. Self-interest as well as public good prompted Savage to use every means at his disposal to keep these people quiet, and he denounced Harvey and his associates as entitled to punishment under the laws of the Government. These denunciations, of course, reached Harvey and his friends. Harvey and a sub-agent by the name of Campbell, seemed most aggrieved at what Savage had said of the affray, and both appeared to make common cause in denouncing the Major in return. Harvey made accusations against the integrity of Savage, and boasted that Savage would not dare visit King's river while he, Harvey, was there. As soon as this reached the Major's ears, he mounted his horse and at once started for the King's River Agency.

Here, as expected, Harvey was found, in good fellowship

with Marvin, the quartermaster, and others connected with the agency. Walking up to Harvey, Major Savage demanded of him a retraction of his offens.ve remarks concerning himself. This Harvey refused to do, and said something to the effect that Savage had talked about Harvey. "Yes," replied Major Savage, "I have said that you are a murderer and a coward." Harvey retreated a pace or two and muttered that it was a lie. As quick as the word was uttered, Savage knocked Harvey down. Harvey appeared to play 'possum and made no resistance. As Savage stooped over the prostrate Harvey, a pistol fell from Savage's waist, seeing which, Marvin picked it up and held it in his hand as the Major walked off. Harvey rose to his feet at this moment, and seeing Marvin with the pistol in his hand exclaimed, "Judge, you have got my pistol!" Marvin replied, "No! I have not. This belongs to Major Savage." When, instantly, Harvey commenced firing at Major Savage, who, though mortally wounded by the first shot, and finding his pistol gone, strove hard to once more reach Harvey, whom he had scorned to further punish when prostrate before him.

This was in August, 1852. Harvey was arrested, or gave himself up, and after the farce of an examination, was discharged. The justice, before whom Harvey was examined, was a personal friend of the murderer, but had previously fed upon the bounty of Savage. Afterwards, he commenced a series of newspaper articles, assailing the Indian management of California, and these articles culminated in his receiving congenial employment at one of the agencies. Harvey, having killed his man, was now well calculated for a successful California politician of that period, and was triumphantly elected to office; but the ghost of Major Savage seemed to have haunted him, for ever after, he was nervous and irritable, and finally died of paralysis. The body of Major Savage was afterwards removed to the Fresno, near his old trading post. A monument was there erected to his memory by Dr. Leach, his successor in business.

I was in San Francisco at the time of these troubles at the agencies; but upon my return, obtained the main facts as here stated, from one of the actors in the tragedy.

At about this time, the management of California Indian affairs, became an important stake in the political circles of Mariposa. I took but little interest in the factions that were assaulting each other with charges of corruption. Notwithstanding my lack of personal interest, I was startled from my indifference by the report of the Superintendent dated February, 1853. His sweeping denunciations of the people of Mariposa county was a matter of surprise, as I knew it to be unjust. This report was considered in a general mass meeting of the best citizens of the county, and was very properly condemned as untrue. Among those who took an active part in this meeting were Sam Bell (once State Comptroller), Judge Bondurant, Senator James Wade, and other members of the State Legislature, and many influential citizens, who generally took but a minor interest in political affairs.

The records of the meeting, and the resolutions condemning the statements of the Superintendent of Indian Affairs, which were unanimously adopted, and were published in the "Mariposa Chronicle" after its establishment, I have preserved as a record of the times. The meeting expressed the general sentiment of the people, but it accomplished nothing in opposition to the Superintendent's policy, for the people soon discovered that the great "*Agitator*" at these meetings was a would-be rival of the Superintendent. We therefore bowed our heads and thought of the fox in the fable. I never chanced to meet the gentleman who was at that time Superintendent of Indian Affairs, and know nothing of him personally, but upon reading an official letter of his dated at Los Angeles, August 22nd, 1853, in which he speaks of "The establishment of an entire new system of government, which is to change the character and habits of a hundred thousand persons." And another letter dated San Francisco, September 30th, 1853, saying that his farm agent, Mr. Edwards, "Had with great tact and with the assistance of Mr. Alexander Gody, by traveling from tribe to tribe, and talking constantly with them, succeeded in preventing any outbreak or disturbance in the San Joaquin Valley." I came to the conclusion that the Superintendent of Indian Affairs was under astute management, or that he was one of the *shrewdest* of the many *shrewd operators* on the Pacific Coast. The schemes of the *Indian Ring* were not endorsed by Governor Weller, but were practically condemned in a public letter. The charges against the people of Mariposa by the Superintendent of Indian Affairs were absurd and grossly insulting to their intelligence. There had been no assault upon the Indians, except that at King's river, led by the hangers-on at one of his own agencies. These men continued to be honored guests at the tables of his employes, and one of his most vigorous assailants was given employment that silenced him.

The estimates made by him in his letters and report, were on an assumed probability of a renewal of Indian hostilities. It was true, murders were occasionally committed by them, but they were few as compared with those committed by the Mexicans and Americans among themselves. The estimate of a hundred thousand Indians in California, was known by every intelligent man who had given the subject any attention, to be fabulous. There was probably not a fifth of the number. But that was of no consequence, as the schemes of the "Ring" were successful. Large appropriations were made by Congress in accordance with stipulations of the treaty made between these ignorant tribes, and the Republic of the United States of America. The recommendations were generally carried out *in Washington*.

The making of a treaty of peace with Indian tribes, may be correctly defined as procuring a release of all claims of certain territory occupied by them. Congress may make appropriations to provide for the promises made, but it is a well known fact that these appropriations are largely absorbed by the agents of the government, without the provisions being fulfilled. The defrauded victims of the *treaty* are looked upon as pauper wards of a generous nationality; and the lavish expenditure of the Government, is mostly consumed by the harpies who hover around these objects of national charity. This farce of making treaties with every little tribe as a distinct nationality, is an absurdity which should long ago have been ended. With formal ceremony, a treaty of peace is made with people occupying territory under the jurisdiction of our national organization. A governmental power is recognized in the patriarchal or tribal representatives of these predatory bands, and all the forms of a legal and national obligation are entered into, only to be broken and rebroken, at the will of some succeeding administration.

An inherited possessive right of the Indians to certain territory required for their use, is acknowledged, and should be, by the Government, but to recognize this as a tribal or national right, is but to continue and foster their instinctive opposition to our Government, by concentrating and inflaming their native pride and arrogance.

The individual, and his responsibilities, become lost in that of his tribe, and until that power is broken, and the individual is made to assume the responsibilities of a man, there will be but little hope of improvement. The individual is now scarcely recognized by the people (except he be representative); he is but an integral number of a tribe. He has a nationality without a country, and feels that his people have no certain home. He knows that he has been pauperized by contact with the whites and the policy pursued by the Government towards him, and he scorns, while he accepts its bounty. These native-born residents of our common country, are not citizens; their inherent rights are not sufficiently protected, and, feeling this, they in turn, disregard the law or set it at defiance. The best part of my life has been spent upon the frontiers of civilization, where ample opportunities have been afforded me to observe our national injustice in assuming the guardianship and management of the Indian, without fulfilling the treaty stipulations that afford him the necessary protection. The policy of the Government has seemed to be to keep them under restraint as animals, rather than of protective improvement as rational human beings. What matters it, though the National Government, by solemn treaty, pledges its faith to their improvement, if its agents do not fulfill its obligations. I am no blind worshipper of the romantic Indian, nor admirer of the real one; but his degraded condition of pauperism, resulting from the mismanagement of our Indian affairs, has often aroused in me an earnest sympathy for the race. They are not deficient in brain-power, and they should rise from degradation and want, if properly managed. I am not classed as a radical reformer, but I would like to see a *ra lical* change in their management.

I would like to see the experiment tried by the Government and its agents of dealing justly with them, and strictly upon honor. I would like to see those who have the management of Indian affairs selected because of their fitness for their positions, without making political or religious considerations pre-requisite qualifications. Morality and strict integrity of character, should be indispensable requirements for official positions; but a division of patron-age, or of Indian *souls* among the various religious sects or churches, is contrary to the spirit, if not the letter, of our Federal Constitution, and the strife this policy has already engendered among the various sects, is not calculated to impress even the savage with a very high estimate of Christian forbearance and virtue. The cardinal principles of Christianity should be taught the children by *example*, while teaching them the necessity of obeying God's moral and physical laws. I would like to see the Indian individually held responsible for all his acts, and as soon as may be, all tribal relations and tribal accountability done away with, and ignored by the Government.

The question of a transfer of the Indian Bureau to the War Department, has been for some time agitated, but it seems to me that some facts bearing on the subject have not been sufficiently discussed or understood. These are that the various tribes are warlike in their habits and character, and have been engaged in wars of conquest among themselves ever since they first became known to the white settlers of the country. Their *immediate* right to the territory they now occupy is derived from the dispossession of some other tribe. They recognize the *lex talionis* as supreme, and their obedience to law and order among themselves is only in proportion to their respect for the chief, or power that controls them. Hence, for the Sioux and other unsubdued tribes, military control, in my opinion, would be best suited to their war-like natures and roving habits. The objection that their management by the War Department had proved a failure, is not a valid one, as when formerly the Bureau was under its nominal control, all appointments of agents were made from civil life, as political rewards from those in power. The political kites, scenting the fat things hidden away in the office of an agent, pounced down upon them, exclaiming: "To the victors belong the spoils." The title of "Major" given the agent was due to courtesy and the legitimate pay afforded, being that of a major in the army.

The duties of the office are anything but agreeable to an officer who has been educated for the profession of a soldier. Few are disposed to do the incessant drudgery required of an effective agent. As a rule, the permanency of office, the education and *amour propre* of military life, raises the army officer above the temptations of the ordinary politician; therefore, the *chances* of an honest administration of affairs are very much in favor of the War Department. To make that management more effective, reasonable pay should be given competent men, as the expenses of frontier life are usually considerable. Years are required to comprehend and order, a practical management of people who are, in one sense, but overgrown, vicious children. Such agents should be retained as long as they remain honest and effective, regardless of church or political creeds.

As the wild tribes recognize no authority but that of the *lex-taliones;* by this law they should be governed. *Any attempt to govern or civilize them without the power to compel obedience, will be looked upon by barbarians with derision,* and all idea of Christianizing *adult* Indians, while they realize the injustice done them by the whites, will prove impracticable. The children may be brought under some moderate system of compulsory education and labor, but the adults never can be. *Moral suasion* is not comprehended as a *power*, for the Indian's moral qualities seem not to have been unfolded.

The savage is naturally vain, cruel and arrogant. He boasts of his murders and robberies, and the tortures of his victims very much in the same manner that he recounts his deeds of valor in battle, his prowess in killing the grizzly, and his skill in entrapping the beaver. His treachery, is to him but cunning, his revenge a holy obligation, and his religion but a superstitious fear. The Indians that have resorted to labor as a means of future support, should be encouraged and continued under the care of civilians. Their religious instruction, like that of the whites, may safely be left to their own choice; but for the *wild* savage a just and humane control is necessary for their own well-being, as well as that of the white people; for even in this nineteenth century, life is sometimes sacrificed under some religious delusion.

The war between different tribes is a natural result of their efforts to maintain *independent* sovereignties. The motives that influence them are not very unlike those that operate upon the most highly favored *Christian nations*, except that religion, as a rule, has but little to answer for, as they are mostly of one religious faith. All believe in the influence of and communion with departed spirits. The limited support afforded by the game of a given territory, frequently compels encroachments that result in war. Ambition for fame and leadership prompts young aspirants for the honors awarded to successful warriors, and they bear an initiatory torture in order to prove their fortitude and bravery, that would almost seem beyond human endurance. After a reputation has been acquired as a successful leader, old feuds must be maintained and new wars originated to gratify and employ ambitious followers, or the glory and influence of the successful chieftain will soon depart or be given to some new aspirant for the leadership of the tribe. In their warlike movements, as in all their private affairs, their "medicine men" are important personages. They are supposed to have power to propitiate evil spirits or exorcise them. They assume the duties of physicians, orators and advisers in their councils, and perform the official duties of priests in their religious ceremonies. In my inquiries concerning their religious faith, I have sometimes been surprised, as well as amused, at the grotesque expressions used in explanations of their crude ideas of theology. With their mythology and traditions, would occasionally appear expressions evidently derived from the teachings of Christianity, the origin of which, no doubt, might have been traced to the old Missions. The fugitive converts from those Missions being the means of engrafting the Catholic element on to the original belief of the mountain tribes. Their recitations were a peculiar mixture, but they vehemently claimed them as original, and as revealed to them by the Great Spirit, through his mediums or prophets (their "medicine men"), in visions and trances. These "mediums," in their character of priests, are held in great veneration.

They are consulted upon all important occasions, let it be of war, of the chase, plunder or of marriage. They provide charms and amulets to protect the wearer from the evil influence of adverse spirits and the weapons of war, and receive for these mighty favors donations corresponding to the support afforded Christian priests and ministers. The sanctification of these relics is performed by an elaborate mysterious ceremony, the climax of which is performed in secret by the priestly magnate. The older the relic, the more sacred it becomes as an heirloom.

Marriage among the Indians is regarded from a business standpoint. The preliminaries are usually arranged with the parents, guardians and friends, by the patriarch of the family, or the chief of the tribe. When an offer of marriage is made, the priest is consulted, he generally designates the price to be paid for the *bride*. The squaws of these mountain tribes are not generally voluptuous or ardent, and notwithstanding their low and degraded condition, they were naturally more virtuous, than has been generally supposed.

Their government being largely patriarchal, the women are subjects of the will of the patriarch in all domestic relations. The result is, that they have become passively submissive creatures of men's will. Believing this to be the natural sphere of their existence, they hold in contempt one who performs menial labor, which they have been taught belongs to their sex alone.

The habits of these mountain tribes being simple; their animal passions not being stimulated by the condiments and artificial habits of civilized life; they, in their native condition, closely resembled the higher order of animals in pairing for offspring. The spring time is their season of love. When the young clover blooms and the wild anise throws its fragrance upon mountain and dell, then, in the seclusion of the forest are formed those unions which among the civilized races are sanctioned by the church and by the laws of the country.

LAKE STAR KING.

CHAPTER XVIII.

Murder of Starkey—Death of Ten-ie-ya and Extinction of his Band—A few Surviving Murderers—An Attempt at Reformation—A Failure and loss of a Mule—Murders of Robert D. Sevil and Robert Smith—Alarm of the People—A False Alarm.

DURING the winter of 1852-3, Jesse Starkey and Mr. Johnson, comrades of the Mariposa battalion and expert hunters, were engaged in supplying miners along the Mariposa Creek with venison and bear meat. They were encamped on the head waters of the Chow-chilla and fearing no danger, slept soundly in their encampment. They had met Indians from time to time, who seemed friendly enough, and even the few escaped Yosemites who recognized Starkey, showed no sign of dislike; and hence no proper precautions were taken against their treachery.

A few days only had passed in the occupation of hunting, when a night attack was made upon the hunters. Starkey was instantly killed, but Johnson, though wounded, escaped to Mariposa on one of their mules.

James M. Roan, Deputy Sheriff under Captain Boling, took direction of the wounded man, and with a posse of but 15 miners, went out to the Chow-chilla, where they found the naked and mutilated remains of poor Starkey, which they buried uncoffined at the camp.

After that sad duty was accomplished, the little party of brave men pursued the trail of the savages into the Snowy Mountains, where they were overtaken and given merited chastisement. Three Indians fell dead at the first fire, while others were wounded and died afterwards.

No united effort was made to repel the whites, and panic-stricken, the renegade robbers fled into their hidden recesses. Cossom, an Indian implicated, confessed, long afterwards, that their loss in the attack was at least a dozen killed and wounded, and that the robber murderers of Starkey were renegade Yosemite and other Indians who had refused to live at the reservation. It was several months after Mr. Roan's encounter with those Indians before I learned the full particulars, and when any of the remnants of the band of Yosemites appealed to me for aid, I still gave them relief.

DURING the summer of 1853, Mr. E. G. Barton and myself were engaged in trading and mining on the Merced. We had established a station on the north side of the river, several miles above the mouth of the North Fork. We here had the patronage of the miners on the river and its branches above, as well as in our own vicinity, and from the North Fork. From some of the miners who visited our store from the vicinity of the South Fork, I learned that a short time before, a small party of the Yosemities had come to their diggings and asked for food and protection from their enemies, who, they said, had killed their chief and most of their people, and were pursuing themselves. The affrighted and wounded wretches reported to them that they had been attacked while in their houses by a large party of Monos from the other side of the mountains, and that all of their band had been killed except those who had asked protection.

The miners had allowed the Indians to camp near by, but refused to give them any but a temporary supply of food.

Knowing that I was familiar with the Valley, and acquainted with the band, they asked my advice as to what they ought to do with their neighbors.

Feeling some sympathy for the people who had made their homes in the Yosemite, and thinking that I might aid and induce them to work as miners, I sent them word to come down to our store, as there were plenty of fish and acorns near by. A few came, when I told them that if in future they were *good Indians*, the whites would protect them from their enemies, and buy their gold. They expressed a willingness to work for food and clothing if they could find gold.

I furnished them some tools to prospect, and they came back sanguine of success. A Tu-ol-um-ne Indian named "Joe," and two or three families of Yosemities came down and camped on Bull Creek and commenced to gather acorns, while "Joe" as head miner, worked with the others in the gulches and on the North Fork. This experiment of working and reforming robbers soon proved a failure, for upon the death of one of them who had been injured, they could not be induced to remain or work any longer, and "Joe," and his new followers stampeded for the Hetch-Hetchy Valley.

From these Indians, and subsequently from others, I learned the following statements relative to the death of Old Ten-ie-ya. After the murder of the French miners from Coarse Gold Gulch, and his escape from Lieut. Moore, Ten-ie-ya, with the larger part of his band, fled to the east side of the Sierras. He and his people were kindly received by the Monos and secreted until Moore left that locality and returned to Fort Miller.

Ten-ie-ya was recognized, by the Mono tribe, as one of their number, as he was born and lived among them until his ambition made him a leader and founder of the Pai-Ute colony in Ah-wah-ne. His history and warlike exploits formed a part of the traditionary lore of the Monos. They were proud of his successes and boasted of his descent from their tribe, although Ten-ie-ya himself claimed that his father was the chief of an independent people, whose ancestors were of a different race. Ten-ie-ya had, by his cunning and sagacity in managing the deserters from other tribes, who had sought his protection, maintained a reputation as a chief whose leadership was never disputed by his followers, and who was the envy of the leaders of other tribes. After his subjugation by the whites, he was deserted by his followers, and his supremacy was no longer acknowledged by the neighboring tribes, who had feared rather than respected him or the people of his band. Ten-ie-ya and his refugee band were so hospitably received and entertained by the Monos that they seemed in no hurry to return to their valley.

According to custom with these mountaineers, a portion of territory was given to them for their occupancy by consent of the tribe; for individual right to territory is not claimed, nor would it be tolerated. Ten-ie-ya staid with the Monos until late in the summer or early autumn of 1853, when he and his people suddenly left the locality that had been assigned to them, and returned to their haunts in the Yosemite valley, with the intention of remaining there unless again driven out by the whites. Permanent wigwams were constructed by the squaws, near the head of the valley, among the rocks, not readily discernable to visitors. Not long after Ten-ie-ya had re-established himself in his old home, a party of his young men left on a secret foraging expedition for the camp of the Monos, which was then established at or near Mono Lake. According to the statement made to me, there had just been a successful raid and capture of horses by the Monos and Pai-Utes from some of the Southern California ranchos, and Ten-ie-ya's men concluded, rather than risk a raid on the white men, to steal from the Mono's, trusting to their cunning to escape detection.

Ten-ie-ya's party succeeded in *recapturing* a few of the stolen horses, and after a circuitous and baffling route through the pass at the head of the San Joaquin, finally reached the valley with their spoils.

After a few days' delay, and thinking themselves secure, they killed one or more of the horses, and were in the enjoyment of a grand feast in honor of their return, when the Mono's pounced down upon them. Their gluttony seemed to have rendered them oblivious of all danger to themselves, and of the ingratitude by which the feast had been supplied. Like sloths, they appear to have been asleep after having surfeited their appetites. They were surprised in their wig-wams by the wronged and vengeful Monos and before they could rally for the fight, the treacherous old chief was struck down by the hand of a powerful young Mono chief. Ten-ie-ya had been the principal object of attack at the commencement of the assault, but he had held the others at bay until discovered by the young chief, who having exhausted his supply of arrows, seized a fragment of rock and hurled it with such force as to crush the skull of "the old grizzly." As Ten-ie-ya fell, other stones were cast upon him by the attacking party, after the Pai-ute custom, until he was literally stoned to death. All but eight of Ten-ie-ya's young braves were killed; these escaped down the valley, and through the cañon below.

The old men and women, who survived the first assault, were permitted to escape from the valley. The young women and children were made captives and taken across the mountains to be held as slaves or drudges to their captors. I frequently entertained the visitors at our store on the Merced with descriptions of the valley. The curiosity of some of the miners was excited, and they proposed to make a visit as soon as it could be made with safety. I expressed the opinion that there would be but little danger from Indians, as the Mono's and Pai-utes only came for acorns, and that the Yo-sem-i-ties were so nearly destroyed, that at least, while they were mourning the loss of their chief, and their people, no fear need be entertained of them.

Three of these miners, from the North Fork of the Merced, visited the valley soon after this interview. These men were from Michigan. Their glowing descriptions on their return, induced five others from the North Fork to visit it also. On their return trip they missed the trail that would have taken them over the ridge to their own camp and kept cn down to the path which led to our establishment. While partaking of our hospitalities, they discussed the incidents of their excursion, and I was soon convinced that they had been to the Yosemite. They spoke of the *lower* and the *high* fall rather disparagingly, and expressed disappointment, when told of the existence of cascades and cataracts, that they had not known of or seen. I questioned them as to Indians, and learned that they had not seen any on the trip, but had seen deserted huts below the cañon.

I learned soon after, from some miners from the mouth of the " South Fork," that all of the Yosemites who had camped on the flats below the cañon, had left suddenly for the Tuolumne. These two parties were the first white men that visited the Yosemite Valley after the visit of Lieut. Moore, the year before (1852). The names of these miners have now passed from my memory, but I afterwards met one of these gentlemen at Mr. George W. Coulter's Hotel, in Coultersville, and another at Big Oak Flat, and both seemed well known to Lovely Rogers and other old residents. I was shown, by the first party, some good specimens of gold quartz that had been found on the north side of the Merced below the cañon. Late in the fall of this year (1853), three of the remnant of Ten-ie-ya's band came to our store. They did not offer to trade, and when questioned, told me that they had been camping on the Tuolumne, and had come down to the Merced to get some fish. I gave them some provisions, and they left, apparently satisfied if not thankful. A few nights afterwards, one of our best mules disappeared. This mule was a favorite mountain animal, sure footed and easy gaited under the saddle. In following up its tracks, I discovered that it had been stolen by Indians, and my suspicions were that my Yosemite friends were the culprits. I made every effort to recover the animal, but without success.

After the close of the mining season in the fall of 1853, we left our trading establishment and mining works in charge of two men in our employ, Robt. D. Sevil, of Smyrna, Delaware, and Robt. Smith, a Dane. The establishment was visited from time to time, by either Barton or myself during the winter of 1853–54, when upon one occasional visit, it was found by Mr. Barton to have been plundered. With Nat. Harbert, a brave Texan, I at once started for the establishment, only to find it a scene of desolation. I was informed by some miners who had been out prospecting, that the body of Smith had been found on a slaty point in the river below, but that nothing could be discovered of Sevil, or the murderers. We found the tracks of Indians and traced them to the mountains, but failed to find their hiding places. We lost their trail over the bare, slaty ground above the river. The tracks had indicated to us that Indians were the murderers, before we had learned from the miners the circumstances connected with the finding of Smith's body. It had been pierced by nine arrows, five of which were still found quivering in his flesh. Upon the discovery of the body by the miners, a burial party was led by Doctor Porter, from the North Fork, to the scene of the murders; and with the assistance of his associates, Mr. Long, and others, it was given proper burial. The body of

Sevil was not found until long afterwards. When discovered, it was undistinguishable, but from the location in the river, we had no doubt of its identity. I reported the murders and robbery to the authorities of Mariposa county. Captain Boling was sheriff; but having business that required his urgent attention, deputized me to act for him in the matter. He expressed a decided belief that the murders had been committed by the Yosemities. He recommended me to take a strong posse with me, and to be cautious and guarded against treachery; saying: "You know as well as I do, that all of the Yosemities are murderers and thieves." In reply, I informed him of the killing of Ten-ie-ya and nearly all of his band by the Monos; and told him that I had ridden alone through the country wherever business called me, and that whenever I had met any of the old band they seemed quite friendly. The Captain said he would not visit the valley without sufficient force to protect himself. Upon telling him of the encampment on the Tuolumne, Captain Boling said that was beyond his jurisdiction.

Mr. Harbert and myself concluded to make a thorough exploration for the murderers, and with this object in view, rode to Marble Springs, and commenced our search along the Tuolumne divide, hoping to find some place where the tracks would be found once more concentrated. After a tiresome search, without success or encouragement, we went down to the camp of the miners, on the North Fork, to consult with them. We found old acquaintances among these gentlemen, and Dr. Porter and Mr. Long were especially hospitable. It was the opinion of these intelligent gentlemen, that the murderers had gone to the Upper Tuolumne river and were banded with the renegades of the Tuolumne tribe that had once been under Ten-ie-ya. They expressed the belief that not less than twenty men should undertake an expedition against them. As the principal articles stolen from our store were clothing and blankets, it was supposed the murderers would probably be found near some of the acorn *caches* in the mountain cañons.

Feeling it would be useless to attempt anything further without an authorized expedition, we left the North Fork and our hospitable friends, and at once returned to Mariposa, where I reported to Sheriff Boling and Judge Bondurant the result of our trip. These officials decided that the territory which it would be necessary to explore, was not within their jurisdiction. That they had no authority to declare war against the Tuolumne Indians, but said that they would report the circumstances of the murders and robberies to the military authorities, to the Governor, and to the officials of Tuolumne county. Here the matter rested, and nothing more was ever done by public authority. I was afterwards advised to put in a claim on the two hundred and fifty thousand dollars voted by Congress for the Indians of California; but after some consideration of this advice, my conclusion was that the original claimants to this money would scarcely be willing to make any division of their legitimate spoils.

Although no action had been taken by the authorities, the murders of Sevil and Smith soon became generally known, and the inhabitants of Mariposa became alarmed from the rumors in circulation, of another general outbreak. I visited the Fresno Agency and found that the Indians there had heard of the raid on our establishment, and, on interrogating them, they expressed the opinion that the Yosemites were the ones who had murdered the men. Their theory of the attack was, that they had first killed the men for the sake of the clothing on their persons, and afterwards had robbed the store of the clothing and blankets, because they were cold in their mountain retreat, and yet dared not live among other people. Some of these, at the Fresno, said that if the whites would fit out an expedition, they would go and help *kill* the murderers; "for," said they, "those are bad Indians. They dare not visit the reservation, for we know that they would steal from us and the white people, and then we would all be made to suffer from their misconduct. We are now afraid to leave the reservation to hunt, lest we be mistaken and killed for what they have done."

I was convinced by my visit to the agency, that there was no grounds for fear of another outbreak among the Indians. I traveled about as I had usually done before. I was cautious in out-of-the-way places, but I cannot say that I hesitated at any time to prospect. When I heard people express an opinion that it would be dangerous to enter the Yosemite Valley without a strong escort, I refrained from expressing my convictions. I felt unwilling to publicly oppose the opinions of some of my late comrades, more especially after my recent experience with the Yosemites. During the summer of 1854 no visits were made to the valley, as far as I know, and if there had been, I was so situated as likely to have been acquainted with the fact. Many of my old companions in the battalion, never shared my admiration for the Yosemite. Their descriptions were so common-place as to lead the people of the village of Mariposa to suppose that, as a curiosity, the scenery would scarcely repay the risk and labor of a visit. The murders of Smith and Sevil deterred some who had designed to visit the valley that season. The nervous ones were still further alarmed by a general stampede of the miners on the South Fork of the Merced, which occurred in the summer of that year (1854). This was caused by a visit to their neighborhood of some Pai-Utes and Monos, from the east side of the Sierras, who came to examine the prospects for the acorn-harvest, and probably take back with them some they had *cached.*

This visit of strange Indians to some of the miners' camps, was not at first understood and a wild alarm was raised without a comprehension of the facts of the case. Captain Boling, as sheriff, summoned to his aid a number of the old members of his company. I was one of the number. We made a night ride to the place of alarm, and on arriving, found that we had been sold. We felt chagrined, although it was gratifying to learn that alarm had been made without a cause. An old '49er, that we found, apologized for the verdants. He said: "Probably, as long as men continue about as they now are, we must expect to find fools in all communities; but, if a premium for d—— fools should be offered by any responsible party, you will see a bigger stampede from these diggings than these Indians have made." The whiskey was ordered for the old stager, and the apology considered as acceptable. We returned to Mariposa wiser, if not *better* men.

CHAPTER XIX.

ALTHOUGH no visits were made during the year 1854 to the Yosemite Valley, it was at this time that the existence of such a locality began to be generally known outside of the limits of Mariposa county. Many of the inhabitants of that county, however, were still incredulous of its being any more remarkable than some other localities among the Sierras. As a matter of early history, I will give a few details of occurrences indirectly connected with the bringing of this valley to the attention of the public as a wonderful natural curiosity.

During the year 1854 an effort was made by a party of engineers from Tuolumne county, to explore a route by which water could be brought from the South Fork of the Merced river into the "dry diggings." After a reconnoissance, the route was pronounced too expensive to be profitable, as the supply of water would be insufficient, unless the ditch should be extended to the main river, which was not considered practicable.

Notwithstanding this adverse report, the Mariposa "Chronicle" continued to advocate the practicability of the proposed plan, and made some effort to induce capitalists to take an interest in the enterprise, claiming that like invest-

ments had proved profitable in the northern mines. To test
the feasibility of such a project, Colonel Caruthers and
Angevine Reynolds, then of Stockton, came up to explore and
run a line of levels over the route. They brought with them,
as engineer, Capt. Kiel, a practical surveyor, and a most accomplished mathematician. Captain Boling, having referred
these gentlemen to me as one most likely to aid in their
undertaking, and practically familiar with that part of the
country, I joined them in their enterprise. We started our
survey at the "Snow Creek" divide. Col. Caruthers was
enthusiastic over the prospect of success, as we advanced,
but after rounding the point at "Devil's Gulch," and while
Mr. Reynolds and myself were establishing a flag station
on the opposite side, the Colonel collapsed and ordered a
discontinuance of the survey.

Not feeling satisfied with this decision, Mr. Reynolds
and myself, mutually agreed to complete the survey. Reynolds was a man of energy and indomitable perseverance.
He was the first to establish an express to the Southern
mines, and afterwards was for fourteen years successively
elected to responsible offices in Mariposa county. I handled
the instrument, and Mr. Reynolds acted as rodman. We
continued the line up, passed all real obstacles, and then
Captain Kiel, who was quite an old gentleman, completed
the survey and mapped out the route. During this survey,
Mr. Reynolds and myself crossed the South Fork and explored along the divide. We were within six or seven miles
of the Yosemite, but did not go to it. *This was the only
year since its discovery, that it was not visited by white
men.* No Indians were seen by our party, during the time
of this survey.

The next season, 1855, the survey began by Caruthers,
Reynolds and myself, was pushed with vigor, and although
the subject matter of extending the ditch to the main

stream was freely discussed and advocated by the *Chronicle*, no action was taken. Up to this time, the Yosemite was scarcely thought of by the generality of gold hunters and denizens of Mariposa county ; that is, in connexion with its stupendous cliffs and wonderful scenery. The solemn grandeur of the locality, and the immensity of the rocks which formed the sides of its inclosing walls, as well as its lofty water-falls, were but barely noticed by Lt. Moore in his report, to which allusion has been made in a previous chapter.

Lt. Moore made no measurements, nor attempted to give any specific descriptions. He only stated unadorned facts and practical impressions. These, however, had in 1854 gone out into the world, and the wonders of the place were more generally known and appreciated by the literary and scientific, than by those in its more immediate vicinity. During the summer of 1855, Mr. J. M. Hutchings, editor and publisher of "Hutchings' California Magazine," conceived the idea of visiting the Calaveras "Big Trees" and the Yosemite Valley. As a literary man he was aware that these objects of wonder and curiosity would provide many interesting articles for his periodical. He engaged the services of a well-known artist of San Francisco, Mr. Thomas Ayres, to provide sketches for his descriptive articles. He first visited "The Big Trees" of Calaveras; at Coultersville and Horse Shoe Bend, Mr. Alex. Stair and Wesley Millard joined his party. Mr. Hutchings' announcement at Mariposa that he was on his way to visit "*their wonderful valley,*" was considered as an indifferent joke by some; others, who had heard of it in connection with the "Indian war," asked him if he was not afraid of the Indians; if it was worth the risk to go there. Mr. Hutchings failed to get much information from those of whom he made inquiries at Mariposa. He finally interviewed Captain Boling, who told him where he could procure a guide.

In anticipation of meeting with numerous difficulties on the way, or for other reasons, he hired two guides and started for the valley. The difficulties of the journey vanished as he approached. The excitement of the trip made the party forgetful of the fatigue and roughness of the mountain journey.

I met Stair and Millard,—who were especial friends of mine,—not long after their return from this trip. They were very enthusiastic on the subject of the Yosemite. The enthusiastic descriptions given by the Hutchings party, on its return, aroused the curiosity of the people, staggered the skeptics, and silenced the croakers. Not long afterwards, two parties visited it; one from Sherlocks and the other from Mariposa. With the party from Sherlocks, were the Mann brothers, who afterwards built a trail from Mariposa to the valley. They commenced it in the fall of that year, 1855. Mr. Hutchings' publications and lithographic illustration of the Yosemite, or highest fall, served to advertise the attractions. From this period may be dated the commencement of the visits of tourists. His influence has aided materially in affording improved facilities of access to it, and in providing for the comfort of visitors. The interest growing out of Mr. Hutchings' visit to the Yosemite, together with the rumored prospect that Fremont & Co. were about to do something with the "Mariposa Estate," aroused the energy of local capitalists, and encouraged the advent of settlers and miners. Another company was organized to bring water from the foot of the valley into the "dry diggings." The limited supply from the South Fork, it was thought, would be insufficient for the prospective demand. Sufficient inducements having been offered to warrant the undertaking, Mr. George K. Peterson, an engineer by profession, and myself, joined in making the necessary survey. We leveled two lines down through the cañon, below the Yosemite, on to the divide of the South Fork. To cross the South Fork without expending too much altitude, we found a long tunnel would be required, besides a suspension of over 800 feet.

This, for a time, discouraged a continuance of the survey. We returned to Mariposa and frankly reported the results of our work and explained the difficulties of the route to those who were most interested in the project. For certain reasons it was deemed advisable to complete the survey between the branches of the river; when it was thought that some equitable arrangement could be made with the South Fork Company for a union of interests in case of sale. The Yosemite Company proposed to convey water over or near the same route as the other, and also to supply water to the miners on the north side of the Merced. By this stroke of policy, it was supposed that a *legal* division of water could be obtained, that the New Yorkers (Fremont & Co.) would only be too glad to pay for. I did not feel sanguine in the success of this scheme, and so expressed myself. My experience in the cañon with Peterson taught me that an equivalent in cash, which was offered for my services (and which I accepted), was better than any speculative interest *in Spain*, or even New York. The survey was accordingly recommenced. Four of the company put up the body of a house in the valley. This was the first house ever erected there. It was of white cedar "*puncheons*," plank split out of logs. The builders of it supposed that a claim in the valley would doubly secure the water privileges. We made this building our headquarters; covering the roof with our tents. We continued work on this survey until late in November; and until the falling snow rendered the hillside work most difficult; we then returned to Mariposa.

During this survey, while exploring the dividing ridges of

the Merced river and the South Fork, our party ran on to an encampment of the wretched Yosemites ; mostly old men and women. They had gone out on the extreme south-western point of the divide on the slope of the South Fork.

As Peterson planted his instrument for an observation, the Indians cried out in alarm, thinking no doubt that he was aiming some infernal machine to destroy them. I approached to see if I could recognize any of them as those who had visited our store, before the murders of our men. I also scrutinized their clothing ; but their ragged garments would not admit of even a surmise as to their quality or pattern.

Although I failed to recognize our visitors among these miserable people; it was quite evident that I was known to them. I asked "who it was that had killed the men at our store?" They at first pretended not to understand me ; but seeing that they were not believed, one came forward, and in a mixture of Spanish and Indian informed me that it was the Tuolume Indians that were the criminals; while they themselves (if not the cleanest) were certainly the best Indians in the mountains. Upon being asked why they were camped in such a place—without water, they said they were at first afraid of our party and the glistening instrument that had been aimed at them; but, that when they saw we were measuring the ground, and marking the trees, they were no longer alarmed, but were afraid of the Monos, whom they said were still angry with them. I told them that it was because of their treachery and dishonesty that they had been made to suffer, and then left them in their wretchedness.

Quite early in the next year (1856), the survey for the water supply was recommenced under instructions from Colonel Fremont, and, under direction of his chief engineer, Mr. J. E. Clayton, Mr. Peterson was placed in charge of the field-work. This work was executed with great care, as on its accuracy the estimates depended. They were to be made by a very eminent engineer of the Erie Canal, upon whose report, it was supposed, Wall street would be governed. Peterson engaged me as his assistant in this survey. During this season the Mann Brothers finished their trail to the Yosemite, so that it was used by visitors. Hearing that they had felled some immense trees and bridged the South Fork, Mr. Peterson had hopes to reach the valley earlier in the season by crossing the river at that place.

On reaching the South Fork, where we supposed the bridge to be, we found that a large tree had been felled across the stream with the design of forming the foundation of a bridge, but it had fallen so low, or so near the water on the opposite side, that a flood would be likely to sweep it away, and it had, therefore, been abandoned. This was a great disappointment to Mr. Peterson. As we could not ford the stream, we would have to go into camp or wait for the water to fall or go back, for the snow-clad ridges were impassable. While Peterson was considering the matter, I took an axe and sloped and notched the butt of the tree so that I was able to get my horse, an intelligent animal, to clamber up on the prostrate trunk; when, without difficulty, I led him safely across and landed him on the other side of the stream. We had two mules, whose natural timidity caused them to hesitate before attempting to climb the log, but their attachment for the horse, which they had seen safely cross, with some *persuasion* effected with a stout cudgel counteracted their fears, and they too were safely led over.

The tree was about six feet in diameter. Its cork-like bark afforded sure footing for the animals. Peterson—very much pleased—pronounced this the most primitive bridge ever crossed by a pack-train, and declared that it should be recorded as an original engineering feat.

While we were re-loading our animals the Mann Brothers came down to us, as they said to learn how we had crossed the rushing torrent; and were surprised to hear that we had utilized the tree abandoned by them. They informed us that they were constructing a bridge further up the stream, which would be ready for crossing in a week or two. We found no further difficulty in reaching the valley. Not long after we had gone into camp, and commenced our survey again, visitors began to come into the valley. Several gentlemen from San Francisco visited our camp, one of whom I remember was the Rev. Doctor Spier, of the Chinese Mission, in San Francisco. Mr. Peterson had, upon my solicitation, "roded up" to the level of the Pohona Fall, and made as accurate an estimate of the probable height of El Capitan as could be done without the aid of his transit. Mr. Peterson was therefore able to enlighten some of the gentlemen from " the Bay," as to the approximate height of El Capitan and other prominent objects. Mr. Peterson afterwards made more accurate measurements of heights.

I have no doubt that the four gentlemen referred to as living in the valley, noticed in the note on page 18, in "Whitney's Yosemite Guide Book," were of our party, who had notified the public of their claim and intention to make that their residence. The house erected, however, was never honored with a roof, and the material of which it was composed, soon disappeared, after we ceased to occupy it. The difficulties developed by our survey, disheartened the claimants. The claim rights, as well as the claim shanty were alike abandoned.

The first white woman that ever visited the Yosemite was a Madame Gautier, the housekeeper at the Franklin House, Mariposa. A few days afterwards Mrs. Johnny Neil, of Mariposa, and Mrs. Thompson, of Sherlocks, came up. Their courage and endurance should certainly be made a matter of record. The next ladies to visit the place were of the party with Mr. Denman, of "Denman's High School," in San Francisco. After this it ceased to be a novelty to see ladies in the Yosemite. Mr. Denman published an account of his trip. His communication was a well written and instructive article. It was the *first* description that gave the public any definite idea of the magnitude of the scenery, or any accuracy of measurements of the heights of the cliffs and water-falls. I was present when Mr. Peterson gave to Mr. Denman the results of his observations, and consequent estimate of heights. I was amused at Mr. Denman's expressions of surprise, and his anxious but polite inquiries of Mr. Peterson if he was *sure* his angles had been correctly marked. Peterson colored slightly at the doubt implied of his professional skill, but with unusual politeness and apparent cheerfulness offered to make a re-survey of El Capitan or any other prominent cliff that Mr. Denman would select for measurement.

The offer was quickly accepted, and a new determination of several points of interest were made.

From the notes taken, each of the gentlemen computed the heights.

Mr. Peterson soon figured up the result of his work, and patiently awaited the result of Mr. Denman's, before he announced his own.

After figuring for sometime, Mr. Denman expressed a belief that he had made a grand mistake somewhere in his calculations, for he had made the result more than the previous estimates and above all seeming probabilities. They then compared figures and found but little difference in their heights. Mr. Denman again worked up the notes, and was convinced of their correctness and reported his conclusions in his descriptions. The first house erected in the valley for the accommodation of visitors was *commenced* in 1856, by Mr. Walworth and Mr. Hite. It was made of "boards" rived out of pine logs. The site was that of our old camp-ground of 1851, or a little above it, and nearly opposite the Yosemite Fall.

The next season a blue canvas-covered building was put up just above. In 1858, Mr. Beardsley joined with Mr. Hite, and erected a wooden house. This was afterwards kept by Mr. Peck, Mr. Longhurst, and after 1864, by Mr. Hutchings. Other accommodations for the public were also opened, a popular one of which was a house kept by G. F. Leidig, known to tourists as Leidig's Hotel." The first permanent resident, was J. C. Lamon, who made a claim in the upper part of the valley in 1860, and who occupied it both summer and winter for many years. The other residents in the valley only remaining during the season of tourists visits. Before hotel accommodations were provided for the public, visitors to the valley carried with them camp equipage and supplies according to the necessities and inclinations of the parties interested.

In order to dispense with a retinue of camp followers, and the expense of numerous employees, the duties of camp life were ordinarily divided among the party, without regard to wealth, rank, or station in life. It was usually made a point of honor, to at least try to share in the necessary laborious requirements of their associates; although the various duties were not always assigned to the capacity of the individual, or to his adaptation to the position. The blunders were as often sources of amusement, as serious inconveniences. As illustration, I will narrate an incident with a party of excursionists in those early days.

By invitation, I met and accompanied a party from San Francisco on a visit to the Yosemite. The gentlemen composing the party, were Mr. Thomas Ayers, Mr. Forbes, of the firm of Forbes & Babcock, agents of Pacific Mail S. S. Co.; Mr. Holladay, of same company; Mr. Easton, of San Francisco, and Col. Riply, of the Commodore Perry expedition, who, I believe, afterwards became General Riply, Chief of Ordinance, U. S. A. Mr. Ayers was the artist who accompanied Mr. Hutchings on his first visit to the valley. He was the first to sketch any of the scenery of the Yosemite. He was afterwards employed in sketching by the Harpers, of New York. While so employed, he was lost off the Farrilones Islands by the capsizing of the schooner "Laura Beven." Mr. Ayers was a gentleman in feeling and manners. His ingenuity and adaptability to circumstances, with his uniform kindness and good nature, made him the very soul of the party.

This party spent several days in the valley. On the last day, it was proposed to have a grand dinner. To make the event a memorable one, it was decided that each one should have a representative dish of his own individual preparation. We had a plentiful supply of canned meats, fruits, etc., but it was proposed that our bill of fare should consist of game and fish. Trout, grouse and quail, were then tolerably abundant. To guard against a possibility of failure to supply a full variety, Colonel Riply volunteered to provide a dish of beans of his own cooking, which he thought he was prepared to furnish. The cooking of beans was theoretically familiar to him, the Colonel said, from having frequently observed the process among his soldiers. He admitted that, practically, he had never tested the theory, but he felt confident that he would not disgrace his position as a soldier in the cooking of such a prominent army dish. From my knowledge of their haunts, it was assigned to me to provide the game, while Messrs. Easton, Ayers and Holladay, engaged to supply the spread with trout. Mr. Forbes engaged to perform the duty of supplying wood and water,

—a very important office, he claimed, the very foundation of all our endeavors. I left the Colonel busy on his part of the programme, and soon acquired a liberal supply of grouse and quail.

As I came into camp from my hunt, my nostrils were saluted with the smell of burnt beans. Mr. Forbes had supplied the fire most liberally, and was resting from his labors to the *windward*. I removed the kettle and inquired for the Colonel. Mr. Forbes replied that "Col. Riply went down where the fishermen are engaged, and has been gone an hour or more; no doubt he has forgotten his beans." I hastened to repair damages as far as I was able by removing those not scorched from off the burnt ones. After scouring the kettle with sand, I succeeded in getting them over a slow fire before Col. Riply returned. He soon came hurriedly into camp, and after taking a look at his cookery, pronounced them all right, but said he had *almost* forgotten that he was on duty as cook.

Observing that he was about to charge the kettle with an undue proportion of salt pork, I again saved the beans, this time from petrifaction, by remarking that their *delicacy* would be enhanced by parboiling the pork.

With my guardianship, the Colonel's dish was brought on to the board in a very good condition for eating, and all united in bestowing upon him unstinted praise for providing so palatable an addition to our feast. Col. Riply regretted that he had not provided *more*, but explained by saying that he had supposed *they would swell more while cooking*.

The secret of the *burnt beans*, was known to all the others, but was kept inviolate from the Colonel. He was unconscious of the joke, and bestowed more attention on this standard New England dish than he did upon the delicious trout and game. Our dinner was finished in bumpers to Colonel Riply as *chef de cuisine*.

During the survey of the year, in addition to measurements, we gave some attention to the geological features of the country we were passing over. We found that the cañon below the Yosemite is about six miles long, and so filled with vast granite bowlders and talus, that it is impossible for any but the agile and sure-footed to pass safely through. The river has to be crossed and recrossed so many times, by jumping from bowlder to bowlder, where the water goes whirling and dashing between—that if the rocks be moss-grown or slimy, as they may be outside of continuous current—one's life is endangered. During our survey through this cañon, in the month of November, 1855, we failed to get through in one day on our preliminary survey, and were compelled to camp without food or blankets, only sheltered from a storm—half snow, half rain—by an overhanging rock. The pelting mountain storm put out our fires, as it swept down the cañon, and baffled all our attempts to kindle a new flame.

The fall through the cañon is so great, that none but the largest bowlders remain in the current. Some of these immense rocks are so piled, one upon another, as to make falls of nearly one hundred feet. The fall for the entire distance is about fifteen hundred feet. Notwithstanding the fall is so great in so short a distance, advantage may be taken of the configuration of the walls on either side to construct a railroad up through the cañon into the valley, upon a grade and trestle, that may be made practicable. This will, of course, cost money, but it will probably be done. By tunneling the divide and spanning the South Fork with a bridge, a narrow-gauge road could very readily be built that would avoid the necessity of going *entirely* through the cañon. This could be accomplished most economically by trestling over the talus—at a favorable point—high enough to obtain and preserve a suitable grade, until the

be run without difficulty to the most favorable point of crossing the divide and the South Fork.

The obstructions from snow, encountered in a winter trip to the valley, would by this route, be entirely avoided. Beside, the distance would be somewhat lessened. By rail and stage it is now about 225 miles from San Francisco.

After emerging from the cañon, with its precipitous granite cliffs and water falls, the entire character of the river's bed and banks are changed. The cliffs have now all disappeared with the granite, and although the steep high mountain divides encroach hard upon the river; high bars or low flats continue on down to the mouth of the South Fork on one side or the other, and then the flats rise higher to the plains.

The fall of the Merced river from the foot of the cañon to the valley of the San Joaquin, averages about thirty-five feet to the mile as estimated by Mr. Peterson.

The outcroppings from the rocky divides below the cañon, are porphyritic, metamorphic, and trappean rocks, silicious limestone, gneiss, green stone, quartz and several varieties of slate. At a point on the left bank of the Merced, near the plain, there is an outcropping of very good limestone, and it is also found, at one point in the Yosemite.

The quartz lodes drained by the Merced river, especially those of Marble Springs, Gentry's gulch and Maxwells creek, bore a good reputation in early days; and as the drainage may be made complete, no difficulty in working them need be encountered. In some cases, the more prominent lodes, maintain their general direction and thickness (seldom richness) on both sides of the Merced; as, for instance, the celebrated Carson vein. This vein outcrops at the Peña Blanca, near Coultersville, and again south of the Merced river, on a spur running down from Mount Bullion. Here the vein is known as the Johnson Lode, and is divided into the Pine Tree and Josephine sections. These were made famous as the subject of a legal dispute, and were occupied by opposing and armed forces in the interest of "The Merced Mining Company," on the one side, and Col. Fremont and his associates on the other.

This lode was discovered in the winter of 1850–'51, by a progressive Virginia liberal, named B. F. Johnson, familiarly known as "Quartz Johnson."

His discoveries led to the investment of millions of capital in mining enterprises, and if the share-holders of Mariposa Stock have not yet realized upon their investments, it cannot be for want of material; but, I must return to my subject. After having completed the survey of this year, 1856, and having interests at Marble Springs, I joined with George W. Coulter, of Coultersville, and other citizens in constructing what became known as "*The Coultersville Free Trail.*" We thought the scheme advisable, but the "*general public*" thought the trail a little too progressive for the wants of Coultersville, and the burden of construction was left to be borne by a few. I never realized any return from this investment. This trail was well located, and considering the amount expended, a comparatively easy one, for the trip to and from the valley was made with comfortable ease.

The trail completed this year by the Mann brothers required greater labor, and was not as good a route, but the views of the Yosemite from their trail, were the best. The Mann brothers did not find theirs a paying investment. They never realized their expenditures, and eventually sold the trail at a loss.

In locating the Coultersville trail, little or no aid was afforded me by the Indian trails that existed at that time; for horses had not seemingly been taken into the valley on the north side, and the foot trails used by the Indians left no traces in the loose granite soil of the higher ridges, but what were soon obliterated by the wash from the melting snow. Where trails were found, they had been purposely run over ground impassable to horses, and they were, consequently, unavailable for our use. Through liberal aid from the "Empire State Mining Company," located at their quartz lode near the Marble Springs, Mr. Barton and myself had built a wagon road from Coultersville to Bull Creek. This road afforded a good commencement for the Yosemite trail.

The first encampment reached after leaving Bull creek, was "Deer Flat," so named by us from having startled a small drove, as we went into camp here. One of the deer was shot, and afforded an addition to our camp supplies.

The next camp named was "Hazel Green," from the number of hazel bushes growing near a beautiful little meadow.

Our next move was to "Crane Flat." This name was suggested by the shrill and startling cry of some sand-hill cranes we surprised as they were resting on this elevated table. Going from this camp, we came to what I finally called "Tamarack Flat," although the appealing looks of the grizzlies we met on their way through this pass to the Tuolumne, caused me to hesitate before deciding upon the final baptism; the Grizzlies did not stay to urge any claim, and being *affectionately* drawn to the trees, we named the camp "Tamarack Flat." From this flat I blazed out two trails, the lower one for early, the upper for later use; as from this point the snow remains upon the upper trail until quite late; and although much nearer, the snow renders it difficult to travel in the early part of the season. From "Tamarack Flat" to the edge of the valley is but little more than three miles. The whole distance from Coultersville being 41½ miles as stated by Prof. Whitney.

With but little fatigue to one accustomed to the saddle, the trip *down* to Coultersville or to Mariposa was made in a day.

The wagon roads now opened, are calculated to avoid the deep snow that delays the use of higher trails, or roads, until later in the season; but one traveling by these routes, loses some of the grandest views to be had of the High Sierras and western ranges of hills and mountains; on the old Coultersville Trail, or by way of the old Mariposa Trail. In winter or early spring, in order to avoid the snow, visitors are compelled to take the route of the lowest altitude. The route by Hite's cove is called but thirty-two miles from Mariposa to the valley; while that by Clark's, on the South Fork, has been usually rated at about forty-two miles. Where the time can be spared, I would suggest that what is called "the round trip" be made; that is, go by one route and return by another; and a "*Grand Round*" trip will include a visit to the "High Sierra:" going by one *divide* and returning by another.

As to guides and accommodating hosts, there will always be found a sufficient number to meet the increasing wants of the public, and the enterprise of these gentlemen will suggest a ready means of becoming acquainted with their visitors. Soon, no doubt, a railroad will be laid into the valley, and when the "*iron horse*" shall have ridden over all present obstacles, a new starting point for summer tourists will be built up in the Yosemite; that the robust lovers of nature may view the divine creations that will have been lost to view in a Pullman. The exercise incident to a summer *lounge* in the "High Sierras," will restore one's vigor, and present new views to the eyes of the curious; while those with less time or strength at their disposal, will content themselves with the beauties and pleasures of the valley.

The passes and peaks named in Prof. Whitney's guidebook are only the more prominent ones; for turn the eyes along the course of the Sierra Nevada in a northerly or southerly direction at the head of Tuolumne, Merced, San Joaquin, King's, Kah-we-ah or Kern rivers, and almost countless peaks will be seen, little inferior in altitude to those noted in his table.

The highest of these peaks, Mount Whitney, is, according to Prof. Whitney, at least 200 feet higher than any measured in the Rocky Mountains by the topographers of the Hayden survey. A writer in the Virginia (Nevada) *Enterprise* says: " Whitney stands a lordly creation amid a rugged and grand company of companion peaks, for his nearest neighbor, Mount Tyndall, rises 14,386 feet, and Mount Kah-we-ah, but a few miles off, is 14,000 feet." Whitney affords " the widest horizon in America; a dome of blue, immeasurable, vast sweeps of desert lowlands, range on range of mighty mountains, grand and eloquent; grace, strength, expansion, depth, breadth, height, all blended in one grand and awful picture. And as the eye takes in these features, a sense of soaring fills the mind, and one seems a part of the very heavens whose lofty places he pierces. The breadth and compass of the world grows upon the mind as the mighty distances flow in upon the view like waves of the sea. * * * * The best that can be said or written but suggests; the eye alone can lead the mind up to a true conception of so mighty and marvelous a group of wonders."

It is true that one standing upon the dividing ridges of the Rio Grande, Arkansas, Colorado or Platte, is charmed by the views presented of far reaching plains and noble mountains, but it is doubtful if any one view can be found in North America so grand and thrillingly sublime as may be seen in the Sierra Nevadas. The scenery of the Yellow Stone and of the Colorado canyon have characteristic wonders that are *sui generis;* but those localities are not desirable for continuous occupation.

CHAPTER XX.

Golden Theories and Glaciers.

The many inquiries that the author has received concerning his views upon the gold deposits of California, has induced him to add this chapter to his work.

It has been said by an earnest and astute observer, that "The cooled earth permits us no longer to comprehend the phenomena of the primitive creation, because the fire which pervaded it is extinguished," and again that "There is no great foundation (of truth), which does not repose upon a legend." There has been a tradition among the California Indians, that the Golden Gate was opened by an earthquake, and that the waters that once covered the great plain of the Sacramento and San Joaquin basins were thus emptied into the ocean. This legendary geology of the Indians is about as good and instructive as some that has been taught by professors of the science, and as scarcely any two professors of geology agree in their theories of the origin and distribution of the gold in California, I have thought it probable that a few *unscientific* views upon the subject will interest my readers.

The origin of the gold found in California seems to me to have been clearly volcanic. The varying conditions under which it is found may be accounted for by the varying heat and force of the upheaval, the different qualities of the matrix or quartz that carried the gold and filled the fissures of the veins or lodes, the influence that resistance of the inclosing walls may have exerted when it was slight or very great, and finally the disintegrating influences of air, water, frost and attrition of the glaciers, and the deposition in water.

The theories of aqueous deposit (in the lodes) and of electrical action, do not satisfy my understanding, and I go back in thought to the ten years of observation and practical experience in the gold mines, and to the problems that were then but partially solved. Looking at California as it is to-day, it will be conceded that its territory has been subjected to distinct geological periods, and those periods greatly varying in their force in different parts of the State. Within the principal gold-bearing region of California, and especially along the line of or near the Carson vein or lode, coarse gold has been found, and in such large masses, free of quartz, as to force the conviction upon the mind that the gold so found had been thrown out *through* and *beyond* its matrix into a bed of volcanic ashes, very nearly assuming the appearance that lead might assume when melted and thrown in bulk upon an ash heap. Where the resistance was great, as when thrown through wall rocks of gneiss, or green stone, the liquefaction of the quartz seems to have been more complete, and the specific gravity of the gold being so much greater than that of the quartz, its momentum, when in large quantities, carried it out beyond its matrix, leaving the more diffused particles to be held suspended in the fast cooling quartz, or to settle into "pockets," or small fissures.

Prof. Le Conte says: "The invariable association of metaliferous veins with metamorphism demonstrates the agency of heat." Experiments of Daubre and others prove that water at 750° Fahr. reduces to a pasty condition nearly all rocks. Deposits of silica in a gelatinous form, that hardens on cooling, may be seen at some of the geysers of the Yellowstone; the heat, no doubt, being at a great depth. Quartz, like glass and lava, cools rapidly *externally* when exposed to air, or a cool surface, and would very readily hold suspended any substance *volatilized*, or crudely mixed into its substance. Its difficult *secondary* fusion is no obstacle to a belief in the capacity of heat under great pressure, to account for the phenomena that may be observed in the gold mines. Ashes derived from lavas have been found rich in crystalline substances. Crystals and microliths, and pyrites in cubes are, no doubt, of volcanic origin. The eruptions of moderate character seem to be the result of igneous fusion, while those of an explosive type are probably aquæ-igneous.

It is altogether probable from experiments tried by Stanislas Muenier and others, that the sudden removal of pressure is a sufficient cause of superheated water and mineral substances flashing into steam and lava. The geysers are evidently formed by varying temperature and interruption of flow by removal of pressure. Mr. Fanques, in an article in the *Popular Science Monthly* for August, 1880, says: "Discovery of microliths enclosed in volcanic rocks is a proof of immediate formation of crystals."

The phenomena attending the recent eruptions in Java demonstrate the incredible force and chemical effects of superheated steam. Modern researches and experiments in mechanical and chemical forces have greatly modified the views once entertained by geologists, and I think that it will now be conceded that repeated volcanic disturbances, taken in connection with the action of glaciers, will account for most, if not all, the phenomena discoverable in the gold fields and mountains of California. As a rule, gold-bearing veins in clay or talcose slates have the gold more evenly diffused than those found in the harder rocks, where pockets of crystals, pyrites and gold will most likely be found. If gold is found in seams or masses it will be very free from impurities, and the quartz itself will be most likely white and vitreous. When gold is found in or near to a lode that has been decomposed, it will be found porous and ragged, but if it has been deposited some distance from its source it will be more or less rounded and swedged by contact with the stones and gravel that were carried with it by the stream of water or ice that conveyed it to its placer. In the beds of the ancient and more modern rivers the gold is much more worn than that found in the ravines or gulches, and the coarser gold will be found at the bottom, the scale gold in the gravel above, and the fine or flour gold in the mixture of clay, gravel and sand nearer the surface. The scale gold, no doubt, has been beaten by repeated blows of stones brought in contact with it while moving in the bed of the stream, and the flour gold is that reduced by the continual attrition of the moving mass upon the gold.

Prof. Le Conte says: "There are in many parts of California two systems of river beds—an old and a new. * * The old, or dead, river system runs across the present drainage system in a direction far more southerly; this is especially true of northern members of the system. Farther south the two systems are more nearly parallel, showing less movement in that region. These old river beds are filled with drift gravel, and often covered with lava." The lava referred to is relatively of modern origin, and the molten streams have in many instances covered the ancient streams, and in others cut them in twain. The "Blue Lead" is a very old river bed that has been the principal source of supply of the placer gold of the northern mines, and it must have existed as a river long anterior to the more modern upheavals that disturbed its course by forming mountain torrents to rend its barriers and cut across its channel. That channel crosses some of the present tributaries of the Sacramento and San Joaquin and contains fossil remains of trees, plants and fruits not now indigenous to California.

The well rounded boulders and pebbles found in the beds of these ancient rivers render it probable that they were of considerable length, and that they may have been the channels of very ancient glaciers. It is also probable that the region covered by glaciers at different epochs is much more extensive than has been generally supposed. To me it appears probable, that during some of the eras of formation, they may have stretched across the entire continent. I have not space to give in detail the evidences of glacial action, but will simply state that *remains* of glaciers may be seen by an observing eye at intervals from the Atlantic to the Pacific; in Minnesota and in the Rocky Mountains, they are especially abundant. Prof. Le Conte says: "The region now occupied by the Sierra range was a marginal sea bottom, receiving abundant sediments from a continent to the east. At the end of the Jurassic, this line of enormously thick off-shore deposits yielded to horizontal thrust, was crushed together and swollen up into the Sierra range. All the ridges, peaks and canyons, all that constitutes the grand scenery of these mountains are the result of an almost inconceivable subsequent erosion."

I have no doubt of the truth of this theory of formation as it relates to the Sierra Nevada ranges as they exist to-day, for the intrusion of the granite into the slate formations suggests a force far greater than can be ascribed to volcanic action alone. The *previous* condition of the "continental mass" can not be so well imagined; yet reasoning from what we know of the present condition of the Sierras we may with propriety assume that great changes had occurred in the territory embracing the Sierras Nevada long prior to their upheaval. The changes that have occurred since are too abundant and enduring to require more than a reference to the localities. The "glacier pavements" of the Sierras are so conspicuous that, as Mr. John Muir says: "Even dogs and horses gaze wonderingly at the strange brightness of the ground, and smell it, and place their feet cautiously upon it, as if afraid of falling or sinking." These glacier-smoothed rocks "are simply flat or gently undulating areas of solid granite which present the unchanged surface upon which the ancient glaciers flowed, and are found in the most perfect condition in the sub-alpine region, at an elevation of from 8,000 to 9,000 feet. Some are miles in extent, only interrupted by spots that have given way to the weather, while the best preserved portions are bright and stainless as the sky, reflecting the sunbeams like glass, and shining as if polished every day, notwithstanding they have been exposed to corroding rains, dew, frost and snow for thousands of years."

This statement of Mr. Muir will especially apply to the "glistening rocks" at the sources of the Merced and Tuolumne rivers, in view on this trail through the Mono Pass. The evidences of past glacial action in polishing the domes, mountains and valleys *above* the Yosemite valley, are too undeniable for controversy, but how much of the Yosemite itself may have been produced by glacial action will probably always remain a theme for discussion among geologists.

Prof. Samuel Kneeland, the well known author of "Wonders of the Yosemite," in a letter to me upon the subject, says: "I think there can be no doubt that the valley was filled, and 1,000 feet above, by ice—that while the *mass above*, moved, that in the valley, conforming to its configuration, was comparatively stationary, lasting much longer than the first, gradually melting to a lake, now represented by the Merced river.

"I agree with Prof. Whitney that the valley was the result of a subsidence, long anterior to the glacial epoch, and that the valley itself, except upon its edges and upper sides, has not been materially modified by the glacier movement." Prof. J. D. Whitney, in his geological report says: "The Yosemite valley is a unique and wonderful locality; it is an exceptional creation; * * * cliffs absolutely vertical, like the upper portions of the Half Dome and El Capitan, and of such immense height as these, are, so far as we know, to be seen nowhere else. * * How has this unique valley been formed, and what are the geological causes which have produced its wonderful cliffs, and all the other features which combine to make this locality so remarkable? These questions we will endeavor to answer, as well as our ability to pry into what went on in the deep-seated regions of the earth in former geological ages will permit." Mr. Whitney explicitly states his belief that most of the great canyons and valleys have resulted from aqueous denudation and erosion and cites the cutting through the lava of Table Mountain at Abbey's Ferry on the Stanislaus river as proof, and, continuing, to the exception, says: "It is sufficient to look for a moment at the vertical faces of El Capitan and the Bridal Veil Rock turned down the valley, or away from the direction in which the eroding forces must have acted, to be able to say that aqueous erosion could not have been the agent employed to do any such work. * * Much less can it be supposed that the peculiar form of the Yosemite is due to the erosive action of ice. * * Besides, there is no reason to suppose, or at least no proof, that glaciers have ever occupied the valley, or any portion of it. * * So that this theory, based on entire ignorance of the whole subject, may be dropped without wasting any more time upon it.

"The theory of erosion not being admissible to account for the formation of the Yosemite valley, we have to fall back on some one of those movements of the earth's crust to which the primal forms of mountain valleys are due. The forces which have acted to produce valleys are complex in their nature, and it is not easy to classify the forms, which have resulted from them, in a satisfactory manner." After describing the generally received theories of mountain and valley formations, Mr. Whitney says: "We conceive that, during the process of upheaval of the Sierra, or possibly at some time after that had taken place, there was at the Yosemite a subsidence of a limited area, marked by lines of 'fault' or fissure crossing each other somewhat nearly at right angles. In other and more simple language, the bottom of the valley sank down to an unknown depth, owing to its support being withdrawn from underneath, during some of those convulsive movements which must have attended the upheaval of so extensive and elevated a chain, no matter how slow we may imagine the process to have been. Subsidence over extensive areas of portions of the earth's crust is not at all a new idea in geology, and there is nothing in this peculiar application of it which need excite surprise. It is the great amount of vertical displacement for the small area implicated which makes this a peculiar case; but it would not be easy to give any good reason why such an exceptionable result should not be brought about amid the complicated play of forces which the elevation of a great mountain chain must set in motion. By the adoption of the subsidence theory for the formation of the Yosemite, we are able to get over one difficulty which appears insurmountable to any other. This is the very small amount of debris at the base of the cliffs, and, even at a few points, its entire absence." In the space allotted to this chapter, I am able only to quote a few passages from Prof.

Whitney, but refer the curious to his recent work, "Climatic Changes of Later Geological Times."

In contrast to the conclusions arrived at by Prof. Whitney, I extract from Prof. Le Conte's Elements of Geology, pages 526 and 527, the following: "1st. During the epoch spoken of (the glacial) a great glacier, receiving its tributaries from Mount Hoffman, Cathedral Peaks, Mount Lyell and Mount Clark groups, filled Yosemite valley, and passed down Merced canyon. The evidences are clear everywhere, but especially in the upper valleys, where the ice action lingered longest. 2nd. At the same time tributaries from Mount Dana, Mono Pass, and Mount Lyell met at the Tuolumne meadows to form an immense glacier which, overflowing its bounds a little below Soda springs, sent a branch down the Ten-ie-ya canyon to join the Yosemite glacier, while the main current flowed down the Tuolumne canyon and through the Hetch-Hetchy valley. Knobs of granite 500 to 800 feet high, standing in its pathway, were enveloped and swept over, and are now left round and polished and scored in the most perfect manner. This glacier was at least 40 miles long and 1,000 feet thick, for its stranded lateral-moraines may be traced so high along the slopes of the bounding mountains." In an article by John Muir, published in the New York *Tribune*, and kindly furnished me by Prof. Kneeland, will be seen views differing from those of Prof. Whitney, but Mr. Muir has spent long years of study upon the glacial summits of the Sierras, and if an enthusiast, is certainly a close student of nature. The paper was written to his friend Prof. Kunkle, of Boston, who had views similar to his own. Mr. Muir says: "I have been over my glacial territory, and am surprised to find it so small and fragmentary. The work of ancient ice which you and I explored, and which we were going to christen 'Glacial System of the Merced'

glacial forest.

"All of the magnificent mountain truths that we read together last Autumn are only beginning sentences in the grand Sierra Nevada volume. The Merced ice basin was bounded by the summits of the main range and by the spurs which once reached to the summits, viz.: the Hoffman and Obelisk ranges. In this basin not one island existed; all of its highest peaks were washed and overflowed by the ice—Starr King, South Dome and all. Vast ice currents broke over into the Merced basin, and most of the Tuolumne ice had to cross the great Tuolumne canyon.

"It is only the vastness of the glacial pathways of this region that prevents their being seen and comprehended at once. A scholar might be puzzled with the English alphabet if it was written large enough, and, if each letter was made up of many smaller ones. The beds of those vast ice rivers are veiled with forests and a network of tiny water channels. You will see by the above sketch that Yosemite was completely overwhelmed with glaciers, and they did not come squeezing, groping down to the main valley by the narrow, angular, tortuous canyons of the Ten-ie-ya, Nevada or South canyons, but they flowed grandly and directly above all of its highest domes, like a steady wind, while their lower currents went mazing and swedging down in the crooking and dome-blocked channels of canyons.

"Glaciers have made every mountain form of this whole region; even the summit mountains are only fragments of their pre-glacial selves.

"Every summit wherein are laid the wombs of glaciers is steeper on its north than its south side, because of the depth and duration of sheltered glaciers, above those exposed to the sun, and this steepness between the north and south sides of summits is greater in the lower summits, as those of the Obelisk group. This tells us a word of glacial climate. Such mountains as Starr King, Cloud's Rest, and Cathedral Peak do not come under this general law because their contours were determined by the ice which flowed about and above them, but even among these inter-basin heights we frequently find marked difference of steepness between their north and south sides, because many of the higher of these mountains and crests extending east and west, continued to shelter and nourish fragmentary glacierets long after the death of the main trunk to which they belonged.

"In ascending any of the principal streams of this region, lakes in all stages of decay are found in great abundance, gradually becoming younger until we reach the almost countless gems of the summits with basins bright as their crystal waters. Upon the Nevada and its branches, there are not fewer than a hundred of these lakes, from a mile to a hundred yards in diameter, with countless glistening pondlets about the size of moons. Both the Yosemite and the Hetch-Hetchy valleys are lake basins filled with sand and the matter of morains easily and rapidly supplied by their swift descending rivers from upper morains. The mountains above Yosemite have scarce been touched by any other denudation but that of ice. Perhaps all of the post glacial denudation of every kind would not average an inch in depth for the whole region.

"I am surprised to find that water has had so little to do with the mountain structure of this region. None of the upper Merced streams give record of floods greater than those of to-day. The small water channel, with perpendicular walls, is about two feet in depth a few miles above the Little Yosemite. The Nevada here, even in flood, never was more than four or five feet in depth. Glacial striæ and glacial drift, undisturbed on banks of streams but little

proof."

The views entertained by Mr. Muir are, for the most part, in consonance with my own. That the valley was originally formed as supposed by Prof. Whitney I do not doubt, but to suppose that the vast bodies of ice, stated by Mr. Whitney to have existed at the sources of the Merced river, could have halted in their glacial flow down the steep declivities of its canyons, seems as absurd as to suppose one entertaining opposite views "ignorant of the whole subject." As a matter susceptible of eternal proof, I will state that in the canyon below the Yosemite there are existing to-day, large, well rounded bowlders that I think a geologist would say had been brought from above the valley; and if so, water alone could scarcely have brought them over the sunken bed of the valley, or if filled to its present level of about thirty-five feet descent to the mile, the laws that govern aqueous deposits would have left those huge masses of rock far above their present location in the canyon. Some of the bowlders referred to will weigh twenty tons or more, and, in connection with flat or partially rounded rocks fallen, probably, from the adjacent cliff, form waterfalls in the middle of the canyon, of from fifty to one hundred feet of perpendicular height. The fall through the canyon averages over two hundred feet to the mile. Well rounded bowlders of granite and other hard stones may be seen for long distances below the Yosemite, on hillsides and flats far above the present bed of the river, and, in some instances, deposited with those bowlders, have been found well rounded and swedged masses of gold. The experiments and observations of Agassiz, Forbes and others, render it probable that the valley of the Yosemite was filled with ice, but that the upper surface moved more rapidly, carrying down most of the material brought from mountains above the valley. The observations of Prof. Tyndall render it almost certain that a glacier does *not* move as a rigid mass or on its bed, but as a plastic substance, as asphalt for instance.

Partial liquefaction by pressure would enable a glacier in the Yosemite to conform to the inequalities of its configuration, and regelation would perhaps retard its flow sufficiently to enable the more rapid moving surface and center of the glacier to carry its burden on from above without marking the lower portion of the inclosing walls, as for instance, may be seen at Glacier Point. It has been suggested that "the immense weight of ice that once filled the Yosemite had an important part in the formation of it." This idea is untenable, because the valley must have already been formed, in order for space to have exist d for "the immense weight of ice;" and unless the earth's crust under the valley was previously broken as suggested in the able theory of Prof. Whitney, no possible weight of any kind could exert a depressing influence upon the surface.

If it were possible, for the reconciliation of geologists, to believe that the subsidence in the valley occurred at about the close of the glacial flow, thereby changing the appearace of the inclosing walls, yet still leaving material to fill the chasm, a great part of the mystery that will always remain as one of the "Wonders of the Yosemite," would then disappear. As it is, we are compelled to believe, not in miracles, but that the glacier that flowed over the Yosemite was so great in depth as to leave, like some deep sea or ocean, its bottom undisturbed by the tumultuous aeriel strife upon its surface.

Now, those glacial heights have, at times, a solitude unutterly profound! Not a bird or beast to break the stillness, nor disturb the solemn charm. Nor does the Indian, even, loiter on his way, but hastens on down to his mount-

ain meadows or wooded valleys. There, if anywhere, the
poet's idea can be realized, that:

"Silence is the heart of all things; sound the fluttering of its pulse,
  Which the fever and the spasm of the universe convulse.
  Every sound that breaks the silence only makes it more profound,
  Like a crash of deafening thunder in the sweet, blue stillness drowned
  Let thy soul walk softly in thee, as a saint in heaven unshod,
  For to be alone with silence, is to be alone with God."

BIG TREE
(Height, 325 feet; circumference, 100 feet.

CHAPTER XXI.

IN speaking of the discovery of the "*Big Trees*" of Calavaras, Mr. Hutchings, in his "Scenes of Wonder and Curiosity," says that: "In the spring of 1852 Mr. A. T. Doud, a hunter, was employed by the Union Water Company of Murphy's camp, Calavaras county, to supply the workmen with fresh meat from the large quantity of game running wild on the upper portion of their works. Having wounded a bear, and while industriously following in pursuit, he suddenly came upon one of those immense trees that have since become so justly celebrated throughout the civilized world.

"So incredulous were Doud's employers and companions, when told of his discovery, that a ruse had to be resorted to, to get men to go and view the trees."

Big trees in Mariposa county, were *first* discovered by Maj. Burney, of North Carolina, first sheriff of Mariposa county (after its organization), John Macauly of Defiance, Ohio, and two others, whose names I have now forgotten. The discovery was made in the latter part of October, 1849, while in pursuit of some animals stolen by the Indians.

The trees seen and described by Major Burney and his party, were only a few scattering ones on the Fresno and South Fork divide. The major spoke of the trees as a new variety of cedar, and when he gave the measurements that he claimed the party had made with their picket-ropes tied together, his auditors thought he was endeavoring to match some "big yarns" told around our camp fire at the mouth of the Merced river. Afterwards, while sheriff, the Major indicated the locality and size of the trees, in reply to some one's description of the big yellow pine that lay prostrate on what became the Yosemite trail, and when rallied a little for his extravagance of statement, declared that though true, he should not speak of the big trees again, for it was unpleasant to be considered an habitual *joker,* or something worse.

I asked the major, seriously, about the trees he had described, and he as seriously replied that he measured the trees as stated, but did not regard them as very remarkable, for he had seen accounts of even taller ones, if not larger, that were growing in Oregon.* In referring to these large trees, they were spoken of as being on the ridge known to us afterwards as the Black Ridge. The big trees of the Kah-we-ah and Tu-le river regions, were first noticed by a party of miners returning from the " *White River* " excitement of 1854, but as these men were uncultured, and the Calavaras grove was already known, no notice was taken by "*The Press*" of the reports of these miners, who were regarded by their friends as entirely truthful.

It has been thought strange that no member of the " Mariposa battalion" should have discovered any of the big trees, but they did not.

Among forests of such very large pines, cedar and fir trees, as grow adjacent to and among the sequoia, an unusually large tree would not probably have attracted much attention. Had a grove of them, however, been discovered, the fact would have been spoken of in the battalion. As the species was not known to any of us at the time, even had any been

---

* See Gen. John Bidwell's account in *Century* magazine for Nov. 1890.

seen, and even the pendant character of their branches noticed, doubtless they would have been classed and spoken of as "*cedar.*" I do not believe, however, that any of the battalion ever *noticed* these trees, for the reason that strict orders were given against straggling, and our explorations were, for the most part, in the mountains *above* the line of growth of the sequoia. While hunting for game, during our first expeditions, the depth of snow forced the hunt below.

A few of the Mariposa big trees were first brought into notice by the discoveries of Mr. Hogg in the summer of 1855. The year previous, Mr. Hogg was in the employ of Reynolds, Caruthers and myself, and proving an able assistant and expert hunter, he was employed by our successors, the "South Fork Ditch Company," to supply them with game. During one of his hunting expeditions, Mr. Hogg discovered some sequoia on a branch of "Big Creek," and relating his discoveries to Mr. Galen Clark, Mr. Mann and others, the exact locality was indicated, and became known. During the autumn of this year (1855), other trees were discovered by Mr. J. E. Clayton, while exploring and testing, by barometrical measurements, the practicability of bringing water from the branches of the San Joaquin to increase the supply from the South Fork of the Merced. Upon Mr. Clayton's second visit, a few days later, I accompanied him, and was shown his discoveries.

About the first of June, 1856, Galen Clark and Milton Mann discovered what has now become famous as the "Mariposa Grove." The next season Mr. Clark came upon two smaller groves of sequoia in the near vicinity of the big grove. Not long after, he discovered quite a large collection at the head of the Fresno. This grove was visited two days after its discovery by L. A. Holmes, of the "Mariposa Gazette," and Judge Fitzhugh, while hunting; and after-

wards by Mr. Hutchings in 1859, accompanied by the discoverer, Mr. Clark.

The groves of big trees on the North and South Tule
rivers, said to contain thousands, were discovered in 1867,
by Mr. D'Henreuse, of the State Geological Survey. From
the foregoing statement concerning the *Sequoia*, or Big
Trees, and the well known fact of their easy propagation
and distribution over the whole civilized world, it is no
longer feared that the species is in any *immediate* danger
of becoming extinct.

Upon the tributaries of the Kah-we-ah river, these trees
are converted by the mills into lumber, which is sold about
as cheap as pine. The lumber is much like the famous
red-wood of California, and is equally durable, though perhaps not so easily worked. Although of the same genus as
the red-wood, the *species* is distinct, the " Big Trees " being
known as the Sequoia Gigantea, while the California red-
wood is known as the Sequoia Sempervirens. This statement may seem unnecessary to the botanist, but the two
species are so frequently confounded in respectable eastern
periodicals, that the statement here is deemed proper. Besides this, absurd fears have been expressed by those unin-
formed of the facility with which these trees have been cul-
tivated in Europe and in this country, that the species will
soon become extinct.* Professor Whitney says: " It is astonishing how little that is really reliable is to be found in
all that has been published about big trees. No correct
statement of their distribution or dimensions has appeared
in print; and if their age has been correctly stated in one
or two scientific journals, no such information ever finds its
way into the popular descriptions of this tree, which are
repeated over and over again in contributions to newspapers
and in books of travel. * * * * * No other plant
ever attracted so much attention or attained such a celebrity

---

* Most o. the Big Trees of Tulare County are within the new "Sequoia Park."

within so short a period. * * * * * Seed were first sent to Europe and to the Eastern States in 1853, and since that time immense numbers have found their way to market. They germinate readily, and it is probable that hundreds of thousands of the trees (millions it is said) are growing in different parts of the world from seed planted. They flourish with peculiar luxuriance in Great Britain, and grow with extraordinary rapidity. * * * * * The genus were named in honor of Sequoia or Sequoyah, a Cherokee Indian of mixed blood, better known as George Guess, who is supposed to have been born about 1770, and who lived in Wills Valley, in the extreme northeastern part of Alabama, among the Cherokees. He became known to the world by his invention of an alphabet and written language for his tribe. * * * * *

The big tree is extremely limited in its range, even more so than its twin brother, the red-wood. The latter is strictly a coast-range or sea-board tree; the other, inland or exclusively limited to the Sierra. Both trees are also peculiarly Calfornian. A very few of the red-wood may be found just across the border in Oregon, but the big tree has never been found outside of California, and probably never will be." In a note Prof. Whitney says:

"There are several *fossil* species of the *genus sequoia.*" Also, "that the Calavaras Grove contains, as will be seen in the table on page 125 (Whitney's Yosemite Guide Book), four trees over 300 feet high, the highest one measured in the Mariposa Grove being 272 feet. The published statements of the heights of these trees are considerably exaggerated, as will be noticed, but our measurements can be relied on as being correct. The Keystone State has the honor of standing at the head, with 325 feet as its elevation, and this is the tallest tree yet measured on this continent, so far as our information goes."

"When we observe how regularly and gradually the trees diminish in size from the highest down, it will be evident that the stories told of trees having once stood in this grove over 400 feet in height, are not entitled to credence. It is not at all likely that any one tree should have overtopped all the others by seventy-five feet or more. The same condition of general average elevation and absence of trees very much taller than any of the rest in the grove will be noticed among the trees on the Mariposa grant, where, however, there is no one as high as 300 feet."

The average height of the Mariposa trees is less than that of the Calavaras Grove, while the circumference of the largest is greater. Prof. Whitney measured the annual growths of one of the largest of the Calavaras group that had been felled, which he made out to be only about 1,300 years old. The Professor says:

"The age of the big trees is not so great as that assigned by the highest authorities to some of the English yews. Neither is its height as great, by far, as that of an Australian species, the *eucalyptus amygdalina*, many of which have, on the authority of Dr. Müller, the eminent government botanist, been found to measure over 400 feet; one, indeed, reaches the enormous elevation of 480 feet, thus overtopping the tallest sequoia by 155 feet.

"There are also trees which exceed the big trees in diameter, as, for instance, the baobab (adansonia digitata), but this species is always comparatively low, not exceeding sixty or seventy feet in height, and much swollen at the base."

Mr. Whitney concludes his chapter on the sequoia by saying:

"On the whole, it may be stated, that there is no known tree which approaches the sequoia in grandeur; thickness and height being both taken into consideration, unless it be

RIDING THROUGH THE TREE TRUNK.

the *eucalyptus.* The largest Australian tree yet reported, is said to be eighty-one feet in circumference at four feet from the ground. This is nearly, but not quite, as large as some of the largest of the big trees of California."

Prof. Whitney gives the measurement of the largest tree in the Mariposa Grove as ninety-three feet seven inches, at the ground, and sixty-four feet three inches at eleven feet above. This tree is known as the "Grizzly Giant;" its two diameters were, at the base, as near as could be measured, thirty and thirty-one feet. This tree has been very much injured by fire, no allowance for which was made. It is probable that could the tree—and others like it—have escaped the fires set by the Indians, to facilitate the gathering of their annual supplies and the pursuit of game, exact measurements would show a circumference of over 100 feet. But, even as large as it is, its size does not at once impress itself upon the understanding.

There are nine or ten separate groves of "Big Trees," in California, and all lie upon the western slopes of the Sierra Nevada at an altitude of from five to seven thousand feet above the sea. Mr. A. B. Whitehall has given a very interesting account of these in the Chicago *Tribune*, from which I extract such portions as will best serve to interest my readers.

"The wood is soft, light, elastic, straight grained, and looks like cedar. The bark is deeply corrugated, longitudinally, and so spongy as to be used for pin cushions. The branches seldom appear below 100 feet from the ground, and shoot out in every direction from the trunk. The leaves are of two kinds—those of the younger trees and the lower branches of the larger set in pairs opposite each other on little stems, and those growing on branches which have flowered, triangular in shape, and lying close down to the stem. The cones are remarkable for their diminutive size,

much smaller conifers are larger than pine-apples. The seeds are short and thin as paper. * * * The magnificent proportions of the trees and the awful solitude of the forest gives an almost sublime grandeur to this part of the Sierra. The Tuolumne grove is situated almost due north of the Merced, and is on the Big Oak Flat trail to the Yosemite. There are about thirty trees in the group, and they are excellent representatives of the sequoia family. The Siamese Twins, growing from the same root and uniting a few feet above the base, are thirty-eight feet in diameter and 114 feet in circumference at the base. A unique piece of road making is here seen. In the construction of the highway for coaches and wagons to the Yosemite, the engineers suddenly found themselves face to face with one of these monster trees, and not choosing to build around it, they cut through it, thus forming a tunnel, the like of which can only be found in the Mariposa grove. The diameter of the tree being over thirty feet, there remained an abundance of material on each side of the cut to retain the tree in a standing position, and the hole ten feet high and twelve feet wide is sufficiently large to allow the passage of any coach or team."

"In the South Park and Calaveras groves there are some remarkable trees. One tree in the South Park grove will hold forty persons in the hollow of its trunk; another has sheltered sixteen horses. The four highest trees in the Calaveras grove, are the Keystone State, 325 feet high, Gen. Jackson, 319 feet, Mother of the Forest, 315 feet, and the Daniel Webster of 307 feet high. The Husband and Wife are a pair of trees gracefully leaning against each other, 250 feet high, and each sixty feet in circumference. The Hermit is a solitary specimen of great proportions; the Old Maid, a disconsolate looking spinster, fifty-nine

THE TUNNELLED TREE.

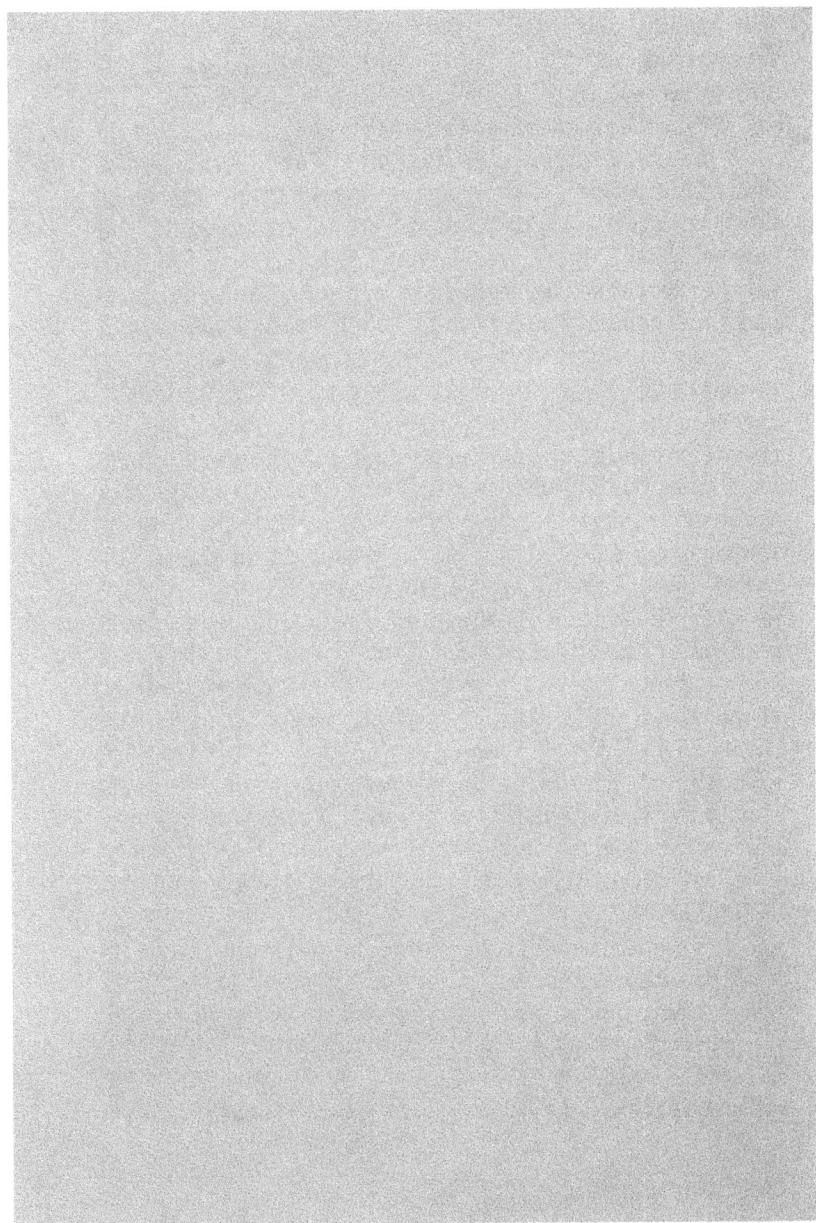

feet around, and the Old Bachelor, a rough, unkempt old fellow nearly 300 feet in height. The Father of the Forest is prostrate, hollow, limbless and without bark; yet across the roots the distance is twenty-eight feet. * * Into the tree a tourist can ride ninety feet on horseback. One of the largest trees of the Calaveras grove was bored down with pump augurs, and the stump smoothed off and converted into a floor of a dancing hall. Thirty-two persons, or four quadrille sets, have ample room to dance at one time, and yet leave room for musicians and spectators."

I can give my readers no better idea of the solemn immensity of the trees, than by again quoting Mr. Whitehall. He says in conclusion: "Although it was then June, yet the eternal snows of the mountains were everywhere around us, and, as the huge banks and drifts stretched away off in the distance, the melting power of heat and the elements was on every side defied. Not a weed or blade of grass relieved the monotony of the view; not the chirping of an insect or the twittering of a bird was heard. The solemn stillness of the night added a weird grandeur to the scene. Now and then a breath of wind stirred the topmost branches of the pines and cedars, and as they swayed to and fro in the air the music was like that of Ossian, 'pleasant but mournful to the soul.' There were sequoias on every side almost twice as high as the falls of Niagara; there were pines rivaling the dome of the capitol at Washington in grandeur; there were cedars to whose tops the monument of Bunker Hill would not have reached. There were trees which were in the full vigor of manhood before America itself was discovered; there were others which were yet old before Charlemagne was born; there were others still growing when the Savior himself was on the earth. There were trees which had witnessed the winds and storms of twenty centuries; there were others which would endure long after countless generations of the future would be numbered with the past. There were trees crooked and short and massive; there were others straight and tall and slender. There were pines whose limbs were as evenly proportioned as those of the Apollo Belvedere; there were cedars whose beauty was not surpassed in their counterparts in Lebanon; there were firs whose graceful foliage was like the fabled locks of the gods of ancient story. It was a picture in nature which captivated the sense at once by its grandeur and extent; and, as we drove back to Clark's through six miles of this forest luxuriance, with the darkness falling about us like a black curtain from the heavens, and the mighty canyons of the Sierra sinking away from our pathway like the openings to another world, then it was not power, but majesty, not beauty but sublimity, not the natural but the supernatural, which seemed above us and before us."

CHAPTER XXII.

Statistics—Roads and Accommodations—Chapel and Sunday School—
Big Farms and Great Resources—A Variety of Products—Long Hoped
for Results

Records of the number of visitors to the Yosemite down
to and inclusive of 1875, show that in 1852 Rose and Shur-
ban were murdered by the savages, while their companion,
Tudor, though wounded, escaped. The next year, 1853,
eight men from the North Fork of the Merced, visited the
valley, returning unharmed. Owing to murders of Starkey,
Sevil and Smith, in the winter of 1853-'4, as it was believed,
by the Yosemites, no visitors entered the valley during the
summer of 1854. In 1855 Messrs. Hutchings, Ayers, Stair
and Milliard, visited it without being disturbed by the sight
of any of the original proprietors, either Indians or grizzlies.
Mr. Hutchings, on his return to San Francisco, began to
draw the attention of the public to the Yosemite, through
his magazine and otherwise. Notwithstanding the ample
means afforded by his magazine, and his facilities as a
writer, Mr. Hutchings found it difficult to bring the valley
into prominent and profitable notice, and few Californians

could be induced to make it a visit. A peculiarity of those days was a doubt of the marvelous, and a fear of being "*sold.*" Any statements of travelers or of the press, that appeared exaggerated, were received by the public with extreme caution. Not more than twenty-five or thirty entered during that year, though Mr. Hutchings' efforts were seconded by reports of other visitors.

The following season, 1856, it was visited by ladies from Mariposa and San Francisco, who safely enjoyed the pleasures and *inconveniences* of the trip; aroused and excited to the venture, no doubt, by their traditional curiosity. The fact being published that ladies could safely enter the valley, lessened the dread of Indians and grizzlies, and after a few *brave reports* had been published, this fear seemed to die away completely.

From this time on to 1864, a few entered every season; but during these times California had a *wonder* and interest in its population and their enterprises, greater than in any of its remarkable scenery. Everything was at high pressure, and the affairs of business and the war for the Union were all that could excite the common interest. In 1864, there were only 147 visitors, including men, women and children. The action of Congress this year, in setting the Yosemite and big trees apart from the public domain as national parks, attracted attention to them. The publicity given to the valley by this act, was world-wide, and since 1864 the number visiting it has steadily increased.

According to the *Mariposa Gazette*, an authentic record shows that in the season of 1865 the number was 276, in 1866, 382, in 1867, 435, in 1868, 627, and increasing rapidly; in 1875 the number for that year had reached about 3,000. The figures are deemed reliable, as they were obtained from the records of toll-roads and hotels. They are believed to be very nearly correct.

The *Gazette* " estimates the proportion of eastern and European in the total number to be at least nine-tenths," and says: " It is safe to place the Atlantic and European visitors for the next ten years at 2,000 per annum."

I have no doubt the number has been greater even than was estimated, for improved facilities for entering the valley have since been established. Seven principal *routes* have been opened, and a post office, telegraph and express offices located. A large hotel has been built by the State, the trails have been purchased and made free, and the management is now said by travelers to be quite good. There is no reason why still further improvements should not be made. A branch railroad from the San Joaquin Valley could enter the Yosemite by way of the South Fork, or by the Valley of the Merced river. Mineral ores and valuable lumber outside and below the valley and grant, would pay the cost of construction, and no defacement of the grand old park or its additions would be required, nor should be allowed.

With cars entering the valley, thousands of tourists of moderate wealth would visit it; and then on foot, from the hotels, be able to see most of the sublime scenery of the mountains.

If horses or carriages should be desired, for the more distant points of interest, they may readily be obtained in the valley at reasonable rates. At present, the expense of travel by stage, carriage and horseback, is considerable, and many visiting California, do not feel able to incur the extra expense of a visit to the Yosemite.

Visitors intending to see both the big trees and the Yosemite Valley, should visit the trees first, as otherwise the forest monarchs will have lost a large share of their interest and novelty

The hotel charges are not much higher than elsewhere in the State, and the fare is as good as the average in cities. If extras are required, payment will be expected as in all localities. There is more water falling in the spring months, but the water-falls are but fractions of the interest that att ches to the region. Yosemite is always grandly beautiful; even in winter it has attractions for the robust, but invalids had better visit it only after the snow has disappeared from the lower levels, generally, from about the first of May to the middle of June.

From that date on to about the first of November, the valley will be found a most delightful summer resort, with abundant fruits and vegetables of perfect growth and richest flavor.

All modern conveniences and many luxuries of enlightened people are now to be found, gathered in full view of the great fall and its supporting scenery. The hotels, telegraph, express and post offices are there, and a Union Chapel dedicated at a grand gathering of the National Sunday School Union, held during the summer of 1879, is regularly used for religious services. Those who may wish to commune with Nature's God alone while in the Yosemite, will be in the very innermost sanctuary of all that is Divine in material creation for the va.ley is a holy Temple, and if their hearts are attuned to the harmony surrounding them, "the testimony of the Rocks" will bring conviction to their souls.

The unique character of Mirror Lake will leave its indelible impressions upon the tourist's mind, and residents of the Yosemite will gladly inform him of the varying proper time in the morning when its calm stillness will enable one to witness its greatest charm, the "*Double Sunrise.*" That phenomena may be ascribed to the lake's

sheltered closeness to the perpendicular wall of the Half
Dome (nearly 5,000 feet high), and the window-like spaces
between the peaks East and South, looked through by the
sun in his upward, westward flight.

As a matter of fact, differing according to the seasons of
the year, "sunrise on the lake" may be seen in its reflections
two or more times in the same morning, and, if the visitor be at the lake when the breeze first comes up on its
daily appearance from the plains, shattering the lake mirror into fragments, innumerable suns will appear to dazzle
and bewilder the beholder.

The wonderful scenery and resources of California are
becoming known and appreciated. A large addition has
been made to, and surrounding the Yosemite and Big
Tree Parks, which in time may become one (see map);
and another very large National Park has been established in Tulare County, to be known as the
Sequoia Park, which includes most of the Big Trees
of that entire region; but it is not so generally
known in the Eastern States that there are such vast landed
estates, such princely realms of unbroken virgin soil
awaiting the developments of industry. Official reports of
the California State Board of Equalization show that there
are 122 farms of 20,000 acres each and over. Of these there
are 67 averaging 70,000 acres each, and several exceed
100,000 acres.

These figures are published as official, and were well calculated to make the small farmers of the east open their
eyes; they will yet open the eyes of the land owners themselves to the importance of bringing their estates under
successful and remunerative cultivation. This will have to
be done in order that these acres may be made to pay a just
taxation. Thousands of acres that are of little use to the
owners or the public—of no value to the state—can, by the

judicious introduction of water, be made to pay well for the investment. Irrigating ditches or canals from the Merced, one on the north side and the other on the south, a short distance above Snelling, in Merced county, were located by the writer, and soon after completion, the arid and dusty land was transformed into blooming gardens and fertile vineyards. These were the first irrigating ditches of any considerable magnitude, constructed in Mariposa or Merced counties, though irrigation was common enough in other parts of the state. The advance that has since been made in California agriculture is wonderful. New methods adapted to the peculiarities of soil and climate have been introduced, and new machinery invented and applied that cheapen the cost of production and lessen manual labor to a surprising degree: for instance, machinery that threshes and cleans ready for the market, over 5,000 bushels of wheat to the machine per day. Capital is still being largely invested in railroads, and in reclaiming the Tule (Bull Rush) lands.

These lands are among the richest in the world. They grow cotton, tobacco, rice and other southern staples, equal to the best of the Southern States, with much less danger from malaria. The valleys of the San Joaquin and Sacramento, which are simply *local* divisions of the same great valley, produce according to altitude, moisture and location, all the cereals, fruits and vegetables of a temperate clime, as well as those of semi-tropical character; even the poorest hill-side lands grow the richest wine and raisin grapes. The yield is so astonishing, as to appear incredible.

The raisins grown and cured in California are said to be equal to the best Malaga; while the oranges, lemons, olives, figs, almonds, filberts and English walnuts, command the highest prices in the market. Peaches, pears, grapes and honey, are already large items in her trade; and her wheat crops now reach a bulk that is simply enormous.

The grade of horses, cattle, swine, sheep and wool, are being brought to a high degree of perfection; for the climate is most salubrious and invigorating. Her gifts of nature are most bountiful and perfect. No wonder, then, that the Californian is enthusiastic when speaking of his sublime scenery, salubrious climate and surprising products.

But I must no longer dwell upon my theme, nor tell of the fruitful Fresno lands, redeemed from savage barbarity. Those scenes of beauteous enchantment I leave to those who may remain to enjoy them. And yet—

> El Capitan, I turn to gaze upon thy lofty brow,
> With reverent yearnings to thy Maker be.
> But now farewell, Yosemite;
> If thou appearest not again in sight,
> Thou'lt come, I know, in life's extremity.
> While passing into realms of light.

THE END.

www.ingramcontent.com/pod-product-compliance
Lightning Source LLC
Chambersburg PA
CBHW062358090426
42740CB00010B/1325